AMERICAN FURNITURE
ANATOMY

KERRY PIERCE

A Guide to Forms and Features

SCHIFFER
PUBLISHING

4880 Lower Valley Road • Atglen, PA 19310

Other Schiffer Books by the Author:

Hand Planes in the Modern Shop, ISBN 978-0-7643-3558-7

Other Schiffer Books on Related Subjects:

The Shaker Furniture Handbook, Timothy D. Rieman and Jean M. Burks, ISBN 978-0-7643-2001-9

Designed by Molly Shields
Type set in Advent Pro/Cambria

ISBN: 978-0-7643-6184-5
Printed in China

Published by Schiffer Publishing, Ltd.
4880 Lower Valley Road
Atglen, PA 19310
Phone: (610) 593-1777; Fax: (610) 593-2002
E-mail: Info@schifferbooks.com
Web: www.schifferbooks.com

For our complete selection of fine books on this and related subjects, please visit our website at www.schifferbooks.com. You may also write for a free catalog.

Schiffer Publishing's titles are available at special discounts for bulk purchases for sales promotions or premiums. Special editions, including personalized covers, corporate imprints, and excerpts, can be created in large quantities for special needs. For more information, contact the publisher.

We are always looking for people to write books on new and related subjects. If you have an idea for a book, please contact us at proposals@schifferbooks.com.

Back cover left: Michael Gloor window chair. *Photo courtesy of Michael Gloor*

Back cover center: Roux sideboard. *Courtesy of the Metropolitan Museum of Art*

Back cover right: Edwards clock. *Photo by David Harrison, courtesy of W. Patrick Edwards*

For the people at the Metropolitan Museum of Art, the Art Institute of Chicago, the Yale University Art Gallery, the Los Angeles County Museum of Art, and the Indianapolis Museum of Art who made my life easier by placing photos of some of the work in their collections in the public domain.

For Susan at Winterthur Museum.

For Megan Fitzpatrick, the former editor of *Popular Woodworking*, who first thought of me in connection with this title.

For the good people at Schiffer Publishing who rescued me when *Popular Woodworking* bailed.

For Andrew Zoellner, who located and sent to me images from the files of *Popular Woodworking* so that I might include them in this book.

For Rick, who is a valued friend despite his problematic affection for opera (I mean really, Rick: Opera? How is that even possible?).

For Verne, a good friend of many years.

For my father, Jim, who first put a plane in my hands.

For my mother, Sally, who first put a book in my hands.

And as always for Elaine, who has spent the better part of fifty years swatting my knuckles with a ruler in the forlorn hope that I might someday grow up.

And for Emily and Brian, for Brandon and Olivia, for Andy and Richelle, and then, of course, for Mason, the newest and most precious member of our tribe.

And one more—for Gray Cat, the 25-pounder, who sat in my lap correcting grammar and mechanics as I wrote this book.

CONTENTS

Neo-classical secretary. This secretary is one of the boldest existing statements of American neo-classical furniture, featuring a number of classical elements: the oversized animal feet, the acanthus leaves, the columns with gilded capitals, and its overall architectural stance. It is also a functional secretary. The molded center section pulls out to reveal a writing surface below an arrangement of cubbyholes and drawers. It is loosely attributed to Robert Fisher, who was active in New York City from 1824 to 1837. The materials are ebonized mahogany, mahogany, pine, poplar, cherry, brass, bronze, glass, and fabric. *Courtesy of the Metropolitan Museum of Art*

PREFACE

I began the writing of this book thinking it would be little more than a recitation of facts based on research: in other words, the cold, hard truths of furniture design and execution.

But of course, I was wrong. I'd forgotten the first principle of writing. I'd forgotten that everything anyone writes is infected with the biases of the writer, no matter how hard the writer works to assume a neutral pose.

Now, with the book complete, now that I can look back over the two years of research and writing and drawing it required, I'm struck by the fact that not only were my prewriting biases apparent going in, but also that those biases were reshaped by the book-making process.

When I began, I believed the finest furniture ever made in this country was made by craftsmen in Boston, Newport, New York, and Philadelphia between 1730 and 1830. I knew there were outliers in both time and geography who, nevertheless, produced work of singular quality, but the overwhelming majority of the work that I and my biases saw as truly great originated in those four cities during that one century.

This wasn't something I shouted from a sidewalk soapbox. It wasn't even something I openly expressed to friends. It was simply a belief I privately clutched to my furniture-making heart.

It wasn't until a friend reviewed an early draft of this book that I saw how deeply that bias had penetrated into this simple "recitation of facts." I discovered, for instance, that in that first draft, I had completely left out the wonderful work done by the craftsmen Peter and John Hall for the design firm of Charles and Henry Greene. In fact, I had made no mention whatsoever of Greene-and-Greene furniture, and I had made no mention of the anatomical features common in their work: the cloud lifts, the *tsuba*, the ebony plugs.

I made the necessary additions and thought about what else I may have missed. I read a couple of books on midcentury modern furniture and one on contemporary American furniture, two genres in which I had previously had only a passing interest. I reviewed the catalogs of several Arts and Crafts makers. I paged through a mountain of back issues of the *Magazine Antiques*. I studied catalogs both for Sotheby's and Christie's auction houses. I read everything I could find about the decorative arts during the Gilded Age. And I took one more trip through all the publications listed in my bibliography. The result was that the book grew another 50,000 words.

Well, that was one result. Another result—and to me on a personal level, more important—was a shift in the furniture-making biases with which I'd begun the book. While I still believe that *some* of the greatest furniture ever made in this country was made in Boston, Newport, New York, and Philadelphia between 1730 and 1830, I eventually came to realize that there was a good deal of really terrific stuff made before and after that time period and outside the limits of those cities, ranging from the fiercely imaginative work of Gilded Age designers such as the Herter Brothers and Robert Smith (I had never heard of Robert Smith until I did the research for this book) to the sleek simplicities of midcentury modern designers such as Sam Maloof and Art Carpenter, and on to contemporary designer/makers such as Michael Gloor, Jeff Lynn, Gregg Lipton, and Patrick Edwards.

There is still a large part of me that remains bedazzled by the technical virtuosity and the classical forms of eighteenth-century makers such as the Goddard/Townsend families of cabinetmakers from Newport, Rhode Island; the father and son Seymours of the Federal era; and Duncan Phyfe's encyclopedic mastery of all things wood. But I am now also deeply impressed by the wide-ranging excellence of American furniture making as it has been practiced beyond the limits of eastern urban areas and outside the artificial time boundaries I had previously seen as almost impenetrable.

INTRODUCTION

A FURNITURE LOVER'S GUIDE TO AMERICAN FURNITURE FORMS AND THEIR ANATOMICAL FEATURES

We furniture designer/makers have a specialized language with which we identify furniture forms and their constituent parts. This nomenclature is essential to our discussion of the work we perform, but it can be intimidating for the uninitiated and even for those—like me—who should be thoroughly initiated. After more than half a century of making things from wood, I had never encountered the term "Campeche chair" until I started work on this book. (A Thomas Jefferson favorite, the Campeche is a sling chair with the seat and back made up of one continuous length of fabric.)

But that kind of ignorance wasn't my biggest problem. The biggest problem was the fact that the very same furniture form or anatomical feature could have one name in one region of the country and a completely different name in a different region.

Plus, those names sometimes changed over time.

Take the word "chifforobe." This is a term I had never encountered in my Ohio childhood. When I was growing up there, we had "chests of drawers" and "wardrobes" and occasionally "bureaus" but no "chifforobes." However, I encountered "chifforobe" a half-dozen times as I browsed magazines and books for the terms I would need to define for this book, but when I looked up "chifforobe," nearly everything I found led me in a different direction. Both Wikipedia and Dictionary.com agree that the term is probably a combination of "chiffonier" and "wardrobe" dating to the first decade of the twentieth century, but its use is not widespread geographically. It turns out there's a reason why I had never encountered it in Ohio: According to Wikipedia,

the word "chifforobe" is primarily a southern US expression.

Then I ran into another problem. Also according to Wikipedia, in Georgia (the South) and in Vermont (definitely not the South), the term "chifforobe" has also been used to identify a "water closet" or "potty."

Really? "Chifforobe"? How does that make sense?

And, of course, "chifforobe" wasn't the only term I encountered with a slippery definition.

"Lowboy," for instance. At some point in my furniture-making youth, I learned to call those low chests of drawers standing on relatively tall turned or cabriole legs "lowboys," as opposed to their bigger brothers, the "highboys." Since then, however, I have learned that often, in period household inventories, those pieces were referred to as "dressing tables," a term I used to designate later low chests to which mirrors had been attached. And then, of course, there is the term "vanity," which some sources suggested as a synonym for "lowboy." But in my personal lexicon, "vanity" was used to identify only modern low chests with mirrors or those simple bathroom cupboards into which sinks are fit.

To explain what I did next, I need to confess that I am such a word nerd that I collect old dictionaries.

The 1971 edition of *The Oxford English Dictionary*—the source usually seen as the ultimate authority on words in the English language—assigns two meanings to the term "lowboy." First, in England, the term is defined as follows: "One who supports the 'low' party in matters of church polity." But in the United States, according to the *OED*, the term is defined as "A low chest of drawers." Well, okay.

That second definition is pretty much what I've always thought.

But in an 1899 edition of the *Universal Dictionary of the English Language*, a multivolume guide to *American* English words as used in 1899, there is no mention of the term "lowboy," which—together with the use of "dressing table" in period inventories—suggests that "lowboy" is a relatively modern American construction attached to a 250-year-old form. Further, in that same dictionary the term "dressing table" is assigned this definition: "A toilet table." Hmmm. Finally, I turned in that 1899 dictionary to the term "vanity" and could find no entry whatsoever.

Very curious.

Very confusing.

I mention all this to explain why the definitions I composed for this book—often after much gnashing of teeth—may not agree with what you expected to find based on the region of the country in which you live and the specific books that informed your furniture-making youth.

In other words, if you don't see what you expect to see, I apologize. I did the best I could.

A word about the photos: you will notice that the work of seventeenth-, eighteenth-, and nineteenth-century makers is disproportionately represented on these pages. There are two reasons for this. First, most of the museum-owned, public-domain sources in which I foraged for pictures don't contain imagery of twentieth- or twenty-first-century work. That work is, by and large, protected by copyright. But there is also the matter of my personal preference. I just love the old stuff, the handbuilt stuff. That's where my heart is.

Lowboy. The renowned antique dealer Albert Sack (1915–2011) called this Queen Anne lowboy—by an unknown maker in the Salem, Massachusetts, area—a masterpiece. In his book *The New Fine Points of Furniture*, he said: "If one casepiece were chosen to represent the creative genius of American Queen Anne design, this could well be the one." I couldn't agree more. First, there are the sensuous outside curves of the legs, curves that run from the top of the knees all the way to the tips of the platformed spoon feet in one continuous arcing line. Second, there is the vibrant and powerful scroll-sawn apron. And finally there is a smattering of seductive detail: the tiny diamond cutout just below the ring of the drop pull, and the smallest possible volutes terminating the knee blocks. The material is mahogany and white pine. The lowboy is dated 1750–1770. *Courtesy of the Art Institute of Chicago*

PART 1

FURNITURE PERIODS FROM 1620 TO THE PRESENT

In order for readers to better understand the definitions offered in this book, I thought it might be useful to share the furniture periods in which I saw individual forms or anatomical features evolving or becoming ascendant. The following list of American furniture periods and their dates is the one I constructed to guide me through the writing. I recognize that not every reader will agree with my classification of important American furniture periods, particularly since two of the periods on my list are not stylistic periods at all: they're historical eras. I'm talking here about the Federal era and the Victorian era. Nevertheless, I believe there's enough stylistic glue to solidify these historical eras as furniture periods. In the Federal era, whether the furniture originated in the design book of George Hepplewhite (1727–1786) or the design book of Thomas Sheraton (1751–1806), furniture shifted from work decorated with carving to work decorated with veneering and inlay work. And in the Victorian era, regardless of the stylistic influences at work on a particular piece of furniture, work shifted from the lightness and delicacy of Federal-era forms to pieces that wouldn't be out of place in a house on the English moors; that is, furniture that's heavy, dark, and just a little scary.

So I agree: my list is arbitrary and reflects my personal biases, but it is the framework on which I hung the many furniture forms and anatomical features discussed here.

PILGRIM

From 1620 to 1700. The term "Pilgrim furniture" as I use it here denotes that furniture made by the first European immigrants to New England, who contributed—among other forms— the Carver and Brewster chairs to the American lexicon. Casework from this era tends to be both heavy and heavily ornamented. It was usually made of oak, but sometimes maple and pine found their way into Pilgrim cabinet shops. Bible boxes, Wainscot chairs, and Hadley chests often sported the low-relief carving for which Pilgrim cabinetmakers are known.

Detail of Pilgrim chest carving. *Courtesy of the Metropolitan Museum of Art*

Carved Pilgrim chest. This red and white oak chest with its vigorously carved surfaces was likely the work of William Searle (d. 1667) or Thomas Dennis (1638–1706). Both worked in Ipswich, Massachusetts, and both came from Devonshire, England, which had a long history of this style of carving. The chest is dated 1663–1690. *Courtesy of the Metropolitan Museum of Art*

WILLIAM AND MARY

From 1700 to 1730. The first grand American style. Named for two English monarchs, the William and Mary period gave birth to several important forms, among them the highboy, which—in the William and Mary period—rises on six boldly turned legs, and its companion piece, the lowboy or dressing table, which stands on four similarly bold legs, as well as the chest of drawers and the drop-leaf desk with bun feet. Whereas the cabriole leg is the signature feature of the Queen Anne period, bold turnings on legs as well as flat bandsawn stretchers are the most distinctive cabinet motifs of the William and Mary period.

William and Mary highboy. The highboy or high chest of drawers was developed during the William and Mary period, and this piece is a superlative example of the form. It features a lively undercarriage of boldly turned legs and curved stretchers, and the surfaces of the drawers are nicely modulated with walnut veneer panels framed in herringbone veneer. The Boston maker is unknown. This black walnut, maple, poplar, hickory, and white pine construction is dated 1700–1730. *Courtesy of the Metropolitan Museum of Art*

Late-seventeenth-century interior of Wentworth House. The Metropolitan Museum of Art purchased the entire home of John Wentworth (1671–1730), a merchant and sea captain living in Portsmouth, New Hampshire, with the intention of displaying the home fitted with period-appropriate furnishings. Only two rooms from that home remain in the Met's collection today: the main staircase and this room from the second floor of the Wentworth home. Notice the early Queen Anne wing chair in the right foreground. The remaining furniture—the gateleg dining table, the six-legged highboy, and the six cane-back chairs with boldly carved crest rails—more properly fits in the William and Mary period. *Courtesy of the Metropolitan Museum of Art*

QUEEN ANNE

From 1730 to 1775. Named for the seventeenth- and eighteenth-century English queen, the furniture of this period is based on simplicity of form and the grace of the cyma curve as it is expressed in the cabriole leg and ogee scroll-work and moldings. Carving—particularly as it exists in the execution of scallop shells and sunbursts—replaced bold turning as the principal means of enhancing basic forms. During this era, the shops of Boston; Newport, Rhode Island; Hartford, Connecticut; and Philadelphia produced some of the most magnificent work in the history of American cabinetmaking.

This handsome Queen Anne lowboy stands on four nicely articulated Spanish feet at the bottom of four perfectly curved cabriole legs. Although the pattern of the scroll-saw work in the apron might be too geometrical for modern tastes, it was right in line with tastes of the period. The material is black walnut and yellow pine. The piece is dated 1740–1760. *Courtesy of the Yale University Art Gallery*

Queen Anne side chair. This early and spectacular Queen Anne side chair features a crotch-grain splat, a shell carving on the crest rail, powerful ball-and-claw feet, and a complex geometry of curves on the back's stiles. The chair was built for Charles Apthorp (1698–1758) of New York by an unknown maker. The material is walnut, maple, and white pine. The chair is dated 1730–1750. *Courtesy of the Metropolitan Museum of Art*

CHIPPENDALE

From 1750 to 1790. Originating in the seminal design book of Thomas Chippendale (1718–1779), *The Gentleman and Cabinet Maker's Director*, this style introduced rococo ornamentation to American makers and consumers. It saw the evolution of the ball-and-claw foot, which had first appeared on a few Queen Anne forms. And it introduced acanthus leaves draping over the knees of cabriole legs, powerful pediments with elaborately carved cartouches, and a blizzard of low-relief carving on the drawers, aprons, and tympanums of Philadelphia highboys. Whereas restrained ornamentation typified the finest Queen Anne work, the finest Chippendale work—such as that produced in the Philadelphia shops of William Savery (1721–1787) and Thomas Affleck (1745–1795)—was an exuberant expression of the rococo spirit.

Chippendale secretary drawing. This ink drawing by the English designer/craftsman Thomas Chippendale (1718–1779) shows one of the forms appearing in his influential book *The Gentleman and Cabinet-Maker's Director*. This form was one of the progenitors of the American rococo secretary. *Courtesy of the Metropolitan Museum of Art*

Chippendale side chair. This superb example of Boston rococo chair making has a back based on a design in Robert Manwaring's 1765 design book *The Cabinet and Chair-Maker's Real Friend and Companion*. (Manwaring was an approximate contemporary of Thomas Chippendale [1718–1779], although Manwaring's birth and death dates are unknown.) However, the Manwaring design featured plain, straight legs, for which the Boston maker swapped bold cabriole legs terminating in sharply carved ball-and-claw feet. *Courtesy of the Metropolitan Museum of Art*

Philadelphia highboy. This masterpiece of Philadelphia design and craftsmanship by an unknown maker dates to 1762–1765. The scroll pediment, the bust, and the cornice moldings originated in the 1762 edition of the famed *The Gentleman and Cabinet-Maker's Director* by Thomas Chippendale (1718–1779). The primary woods are mahogany and mahogany veneer, with tulip poplar, white pine, and white cedar used as secondary woods. *Courtesy of the Metropolitan Museum of Art*

FEDERAL

From 1790 to 1830. The Federal era was less a design period than a historical period, one denoting those decades following the birth of the United States. To celebrate this achievement, American furniture makers often incorporated patriotic motifs into their work, in particular images of the eagle. Furniture making of that era was energized by the design books of the English writers George Hepplewhite (1727–1786) and Thomas Sheraton (1751–1806), who —along with Thomas Chippendale—were the most-influential furniture designers of the eighteenth and early nineteenth centuries. Hepplewhite's book *The Cabinet-Maker and Upholsterer's Guide* was published in 1788 after his death, while Sheraton serially published his book *The Cabinet Maker and Upholsterers' Drawing Book* beginning in 1791. Hepplewhite work was usually characterized by tapered legs, rectangular or square in cross section, while Sheraton work featured slender turned legs tapering as they descended to the floor. Both styles became immensely important to American turn-of-the-century furniture, and both were indebted to the earlier work of Robert Adam (1728–1792), who—with his brother James (1732–1794)—had advocated for a classical style of architecture and home furnishings inspired by ancient Greece and Rome.

Federal sideboard. The sideboard form debuted in the Federal era, and this particular example by an unknown maker from Charleston, South Carolina, offers everything you might want in a dining room accessory: lots of storage and display space with a nicely modulated facade of inlay and veneer work. According to the Yale University Art Gallery website, this is the only known Federal-era sideboard to survive with its gallery intact. The materials are mahogany, inlay of various species, gum, tulip poplar, yellow pine, cedar, and pine. The piece is dated 1790–1810. *Courtesy of the Yale University Art Gallery*

Hepplewhite-style shield-back side chair. Samuel McIntire (1757–1811) of Salem, Massachusetts, was a gifted architect and carver, and there are many Federal-era chairs attributed to his hand, among them this handsome example. The materials are mahogany, ash, birch, and white pine. The chair is dated 1794–1799. *Courtesy of the Metropolitan Museum of Art*

EMPIRE

From 1800 to 1840. The Empire style, named for the First French Empire under Napoleon, was triggered by neo-classicism as it was expressed in French neo-classical furniture of the time and the continuing influence of the work of the English architects James and Robert Adam. It featured animal paw feet, elaborately ornamented columns, ormolu castors, gilding, and exotic veneers. Among its leading American exponents were the supremely gifted New York makers Duncan Phyfe (1768–1854), Charles-Honoré Lannuier (1779–1819), and Michael Allison (1773–1855).

Empire sideboard. This sideboard by an unknown New York maker has little in the way of storage capacity for dining-room necessaries, but—at least visually—it makes up for that shortcoming with its striking appearance. Its animal-paw feet, the use of classical columns, and the stately neo-classical stance places it firmly within the Empire style. The materials are mahogany, marble, gilded bronze, white pine, and poplar. The piece is dated 1815–1820. *Courtesy of the Metropolitan Museum of Art*

Lannuier card table. The French immigrant Charles-Honoré Lannuier (1779–1819) was one of the guiding lights of early-nineteenth-century New York City furniture making. This magnificent card table is one of a pair in the collection of the Metropolitan Museum of Art in New York. The surviving invoice for these tables shows that they were purchased for $250, a breathtaking amount for the period and a testament to the high regard his contemporaries had for the work of Charles-Honoré Lannuier. *Courtesy of the Metropolitan Museum of Art*

VICTORIAN

From 1840 to 1900. Yet another American furniture era named for an English monarch, the term "Victorian" is really a catchall encompassing a wide variety of furniture styles. During this era, American shops continued to produce Empire furniture, as well as furniture inspired by the Gothic Revival movement, the Elizabethan Revival movement, the Rococo Revival movement, the Renaissance Revival movement, and the Aesthetic movement, as well as furniture influenced by the European Biedermeier style. The Victorian era also included the furniture that Gilded Age makers produced for their robber baron clients. Probably the most important individual maker of the era was John Henry Belter (1804–1863), whose shop produced furniture so heavily ornamented that, to some modern viewers, it might look overcooked. Somehow these very different styles coexisted during the second half of the nineteenth century. In fact, according to Oscar P. Fitzgerald, author of *Three Centuries of American Furniture*, several of these styles could often be found in the same home: "It was an era of specialization—the Rococo Revival in the parlor, Renaissance in the dining room, and Gothic in the den, library or hall." To further confuse the issue of classification, elements of two or more styles might appear on the same piece of furniture.

1866 New York City interior. In this genre painting by Seymour Joseph Guy (1824–1910), we see a room outfitted with all manner of era-appropriate furnishings, from the étagère-style Renaissance Revival sideboard on the right to the Wardian case standing in the window on the left. *Courtesy of the Metropolitan Museum of Art*

Neo-Grec cabinet. The Victorian era in American furniture making was awash in short-lived styles. The Gothic Revival period was followed by the Elizabethan, the Renaissance, and the Rococo Revival periods, which was followed by Neo-Grec, and the New York maker of this masterfully wrought cabinet, Alexander Roux (1813–1886), worked in each one. This piece is constructed of rosewood, tulipwood, cherry, poplar, and pine, and it combines motifs of the Antiquity, Renaissance, and late Louis XVI periods. The piece is dated circa 1866. *Courtesy of the Metropolitan Museum of Art*

Belter sofa. John Henry Belter (1804–1863) of New York was the leading exponent of the American Rococo Revival style, and this sofa from the 1850s is a masterpiece of Rococo Revival ornamentation. The crest rail features energetically carved griffins, cornucopias, floral garlands, urns, and dolphins—in short, just about every rococo motif known to man. The primary wood is rosewood. *Courtesy of the Metropolitan Museum of Art*

Sewing table. This late Biedermeyer sewing table is attributed to the shop of Johann Michael Jahn (1816–1883) of New Braunfels, Texas. The Biedermeyer style will forever be associated with Europe's rising middle class in the mid-nineteenth century and later the rising middle class in the United States. It is descended from the Empire style, but it lacks the degree of ornamentation found on high-style Empire work. There is no ormolu, little if any carving, little if any marquetry. It was designed to evoke the spirit of the time without being so expensive that it put itself beyond the means of the middle class. The material is walnut and yellow pine. The table is dated 1870–1880. *Courtesy of the Yale University Art Gallery*

Gothic Revival armchair. Gothic Revival furniture of the mid-nineteenth century drew heavily from Gothic architecture, and it takes little imagination to see Gothic church windows in the back and stretcher of this magnificent walnut chair. The chair was originally in the Belvoir estate in Yonkers, New York, and a photo taken in the library at Belvoir shows other furniture that is similar to known Gustav Herter (1830–1898) work. The assumption, therefore, is that this chair was likely the work of Herter as well. The chair is made of walnut and dates to 1855. *Courtesy of the Metropolitan Museum of Art*

SHAKER

From 1800 to 1920. Shaker furniture was very similar to the furniture being made in country shops in the areas surrounding Shaker communities; that is, it typically offered muted representations of the high-style period work being done in the urban centers of the day. This is because the original craftsmen working in Shaker shops had been working in the World before signing the Covenant, and they brought their skills and their design preferences with them to the Shaker communities they joined. However, in the various editions of the Millennial Laws, Shaker leaders attempted to codify the teachings of their founder, Mother Ann Lee, as they related to matters of daily life, including the making of furniture. The thrust of her teachings was simplicity above all else. As a result, it's possible to find Shaker tripod tables with cabriole legs, but not with hairy paw feet.

Shaker chair. This diminutive side chair was probably made in the New Lebanon, New York, Shaker community in the mid-nineteenth century. Lowbacks like this were often used in Shaker dining rooms because they could be pushed under the table to facilitate sweeping. The material is maple. The woven seat is replacement Shaker tape. *Courtesy of the Metropolitan Museum of Art*

Shaker chair-making shop. In this view of the Shaker chair-making shop at Hancock Village in Massachusetts, you can see the fixtures of a seat-weaving room. First, in the foreground, there is a weaving needle pushed into the warp (the warp consists of the strands of material wrapped around the front and back rungs) of a half-woven chair seat. Second, in the middle ground, you can see stacks of coiled Shaker tape (cotton listing). Then, in the background, there are a number of Shaker chairs hanging upside down from Shaker pegs, awaiting the attention of the seat weaver. *Courtesy of Getty Images*

Furniture and accessories from the North Family Dwelling Retiring Room at New Lebanon, New York. Reconstructed in the Metropolitan Museum of Art, this Shaker retiring room is outfitted with all manner of goods that would have been found in such a room in the first half of the nineteenth century: *from the left*, a dry sink, a revolving chair, a trundle bed, a candlestand, and a rocking chair, as well as sewing steps to raise a Shaker sister's knee to a more convenient working height, and on the left wall, a Shaker favorite: the sconce, which hangs from a peg rail. But this room is more than the sum of its individual parts. In its clean, plain simplicities, this room is the physical embodiment of the Shaker ideals. *Courtesy of the Metropolitan Museum of Art*

ARTS AND CRAFTS (AMERICAN CRAFTSMAN/MISSION)

From 1880 to 1920. The Arts and Crafts movement was a reaction against the industrialization of the Victorian world, articulated first in the social criticism of the Englishman John Ruskin (1819–1900) and later by another Englishman, William Morris (1834–1896), who advocated, in every practice of human making, a return to traditional craftsmanship and—in the specific world of furniture making—a return to medieval forms and materials. In response, the American leaders of this movement—men such as Gustav Stickley (1858–1942)—created lines of furniture made from solid woods (in particular, oak), wrought iron, copper, and leaded glass that could be produced on a scale small enough to allow for an intelligent mix of hand and machine processes.

The furniture designed by Henry (1870–1954) and Charles Greene (1868–1957)—sometimes classified as Arts and Crafts work—was initially influential primarily in those California cities where the homes they designed were located. It wasn't until much later that Greene and Greene became anything like a national force.

1904 Arts and Crafts library table. The opening decade of the twentieth century saw the birth—and usually quick demise—of a number of cabinetmaking shops working in the Arts and Crafts style. The Rose Valley Shops, where this was made, was one such venture, opening its doors in 1901, then shuttering them just five years later. The table was built under the direction of the founder of the Rose Valley Shops: William Lightfoot Price (1861–1916). The material is stained white oak. *Courtesy of the Metropolitan Museum of Art*

Roycroft Arts and Crafts Morris chair, *tabouret*, and accessories. This setting is from the Roycroft Desktop Exhibit at the Muckenthaler Cultural Center in Fullerton, California. Notice the hinged shelf on the chair's right arm. *Photo by Kari Rene Hall / Los Angeles via Getty Images*

Charles Rohlfs's chair. Charles Rohlfs (1853–1936) was an outlier of the Arts and Crafts movement. Historically, he paralleled leaders of the movement such as Gustav Stickley (1858–1942), and he worked primarily in their wood of choice: honest oak. But Rohlfs's designs lacked the blocky stiffness of so much Arts and Crafts work, and more to the point, Rohlfs delighted in adding eccentric detail to his compositions, such as the little doodads at the top of this chair's back posts. *Courtesy of the Art Institute of Chicago*

ART NOUVEAU

From 1890 to 1910. An offshoot of the Arts and Crafts movement featuring organic shapes. Art Nouveau furniture also celebrated handwork, but it was handwork with a difference. As opposed to the rectilinear—some might say blocky—Arts and Crafts furniture of the day, the Art Nouveau style celebrated free-flowing curvilinear forms, often biomorphic in origin.

Wall of built-ins from the Blacker House. Charles Sumner Greene (1868–1957) and his brother Henry Greene (1870–1954) have proven to be two of the most influential designers of the late Arts and Crafts / Art Nouveau eras. Like Frank Lloyd Wright, they designed furnishings for the homes they'd designed. This wall of built-ins from the Blacker House built in 1907 in Pasadena, California, represents just a smattering of the wood interiors the Greene brothers designed for the home. Their Arts and Crafts ties can be seen in the solid-wood frame-and-panel doors, in the dovetailed cases, and in such handmade details as the solid-wood pulls on the doors and drawers. And their connection to the Art Nouveau tradition is visible in the free-flowing vines, leaves, and flowers of the windows. And if you look closely at the radiussed edges of every wood detail, you can see why many point to Greene and Greene as the progenitors of the California round-over style. *Courtesy of Getty Images*

EARLY TWENTIETH CENTURY

An era in which a number of sometimes contradictory forces were active in American furniture design. In some parts of the country, the Arts and Crafts movement and its subsidiaries, such as the Mission style of the Southwest and Greene and Greene of Southern California, lumbered along through the teens. This was then followed by the sleekness of the Art Deco movement and the subsequent Streamline Moderne, probably best represented by the work of Donald Deskey (1894–1989), who became a furniture (and interiors) designer to the cosmopolitan rich and famous. Then the de Stijl designers offered their brightly colored and severely rectilinear forms, many of which echoed the paintings of Piet Mondrian (1872–1944). Finally the Bauhaus/Scandinavian movement gave birth to mid-century modern.

Deskey-designed suite at Radio City Music Hall, New York. Donald Deskey (1894–1989) designed this Art Deco suite in the 1930s for impresario S. L. Rothafel (1882–1936). *Photo by Angelo Hornack / Corbis, courtesy of Getty Images*

MID-CENTURY MODERN, MANUFACTURED

From 1940 to 1970. Makers of manufactured mid-century modern furniture sought to provide people with furniture that was simple in design and inexpensive to manufacture, and that embraced nontraditional furniture-making materials. More specifically, it is furniture that is clean in line and unornamented and was often made of glass, metal, and plastics. At its worst, it's the cheap and poorly made furniture that— those of us old enough to have lived through the 1950s— recall from our childhoods. It's the ovoid coffee table with the screw-in cone legs and the rock-hard Cubist couch and matching chairs, but I have to admit that in the hands of designers such as Charles (1907–1978) and Ray (1912–1988) Eames and Isamu Noguchi (1904–1988), the style did bring something new to American furniture design. But I just can't wrap my arms around this work. I find it cold and uninviting, furniture reduced to mere functionality with little or no aesthetic presence. Just look at the famed Eames chairs that are now beginning to show up on *Antiques Roadshow*. They're nothing but plastic shells perched on four wire legs. When I look at a chair, I want to see something more than a parking space for my butt.

Mid-century modern chair. The Heywood-Wakefield Company (1897–1979) manufactured furniture for almost a century, including a line of mid-century modern forms such as this sleek 1950s maple dining chair. Although the Heywood-Wakefield pieces were constructed in large numbers in a factory, they have nonetheless become of interest to antique collectors. *Courtesy of Getty Images*

Noguchi table. Isamu Noguchi (1904–1988) was one of the most important figures in mid-century modern design. This laminated plywood, maple, and steel wire table reflects his interest in abstract art, as opposed to the focus on natural forms found in so much traditional furniture. The table was manufactured by Knoll, Inc. The design is dated circa 1956. *Courtesy of the Yale University Art Gallery*

individuals—produced bodies of very appealing work, work with edges that were often not simply rounded but were instead sculpted. Sam Maloof, the best known of these designer/makers, created a line of justifiably famous rockers with sweeping angle-ground curves. This *is* work I can put my arms around. This is work in which I'd be pleased to park my butt. Unfortunately, in the mid-century modern universe, the work of these men constitutes only a pebble thrown into a vast ocean.

CONTEMPORARY

From 1970 to the present. Some contemporary makers continue the experimentation with nontraditional materials begun in the mid-century modern period, often working with molded laminates, steel, anodized aluminum, and cardboard, as opposed to the solid or veneered wood that has characterized American furniture making throughout most of its history. Some contemporary forms tend toward the severe geometries of cubes and bent steel. It is often furniture with a brash, hey-look-at-me sensibility. In the realm of manufactured contemporary furniture, the mid-century

MID-CENTURY MODERN, HANDBUILT (CALIFORNIA ROUNDOVER)

Running parallel to the manufactured mid-century modern furniture was another strain, often identified as California Roundover. This is furniture made of actual wood by actual craftsmen. It is named for the roundover router bit, a bit that turns square corners into radiussed corners. It is often traced to the design work of Henry (1870–1954) and Charles Greene (1868–1957), the now-famous Southern California architects and interior designers. The primary exponents of handbuilt mid-century modern furniture were Arthur Espenet Carpenter (1920–2006), Sam Maloof (1916–2009), and John Nyquist (1936–2018), who—as

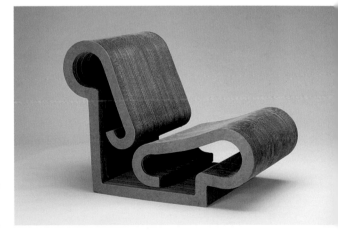

Gehry corrugated-cardboard chair. Frank Gehry (b. 1929) was designing paper chairs for window displays when someone from Bloomingdale's suggested he more fully develop his designs. This chair is one of the results of that encouragement. The materials are corrugated cardboard, particle board, and beech. The chair was designed in 1970, then manufactured by Chiru Enterprises, Inc., in 1982. *Courtesy of the Yale University Art Gallery*

modern / Scandinavian ethos continues to rear its ugly head, with marketing literature extolling the virtues of plainness, simplicity, and minimalism—in other words, furniture bearing no evidence of the makers' hands. But fortunately for traditionalists like myself, it coexists with the work of other contemporary makers such as Andy Rae, David Kiernan, Tom Owens, Jamie Robertson, Seth Janovsky, Michael Cullen, et al., who are breathing new life into traditional forms while working with that most traditional of furniture-making materials: real wood.

Lipton Keystone Sideboard. This dramatic sideboard features Swiss pearwood and quilted maple doors and drawer fronts, as well as etched glass panels on the top. It is the work of current maker Gregg Lipton (b. 1957) of Cumberland, Maine. *Photo by Paul Avis, courtesy of Gregg Lipton*

WHAT KIND OF CHAIR IS THAT?

The business of furniture classification can be pretty confusing.

Since furniture periods don't begin and end on identifiable dates, you can't say that a piece made in 1815 must be Federal. It might be. A lot of 1815 work fits into the Federal category, but it might also be an early Empire piece, and in rural areas there was plenty of 1815 work still done in the Chippendale style.

Unfortunately, even specific stylistic details can't always be used to say that a particular piece fits into a particular stylistic period. The ball-and-claw foot is a widely accepted identifier of work from the Chippendale period, but the ball-and-claw foot is also found on some work that is clearly Queen Anne.

In addition, we don't classify work solely based on stylistic period. For instance, the chair in the photo is based on a particular design in a book by George Hepplewhite (1727–1786), *The Cabinet-Maker and Upholsterer's Guide*, so it is a Hepplewhite chair. Second, it is a shield-back chair because of the shield contour of the back. It can also be called an urn-back because of the urn, which appears as a splat, and it could be called a swag-back chair because of the carved drapery that connects the back's outer stiles with the splat. And because it was made in the Federal era and is based on a design by George Hepplewhite, one of the two most important design sources for American

Federal furniture, it is most definitely a Federal chair. In addition, because the maker of the chair was probably Samuel McIntire (1757–1811) of Salem, Massachusetts, it wouldn't be inappropriate to identify this as a McIntire chair. And finally, in terms of its generalized form, it's clearly a side chair.

All these classifications are correct, and none are mutually exclusive.

* Terminology is a beast. In this book and elsewhere, you'll find the word "baroque" used to identify Queen Anne furniture and the word "rococo" to identify Chippendale furniture. In addition, the term "neo-classical" can be used to identify many pieces in the "Chippendale," "Federal," "Empire," and "Victorian" eras. The terms "baroque," "rococo," and "neo-classical" are terms more commonly used in connection with art and architecture, but they are often useful in the discussion of furniture as well.

** For further information on furniture periods, please see the entries for "armchair," "chest of drawers," "desk," "secretary" and "sideboard."

PART 2

ALPHABETIZED LIST OF AMERICAN FURNITURE FORMS AND THEIR ANATOMICAL FEATURES

Roux sideboard. This Alexander Roux (1813–1886) sideboard, which is dated circa 1853, was shown at the Crystal Palace Exhibition in New York, which led to an order for a pair of sideboards for the Astor family. Because of its arrangement of dinnerware shelves above, this is an example of a sideboard of the étagère type, which was popular in Europe and America in the middle of the nineteenth century. Its most striking feature is the proliferation of high-relief carvings of fish, fowl, fruits, and other edibles encrusting its surfaces. The materials are black walnut—which often lightens as it ages—and pine. *Courtesy of the Metropolitan Museum of Art*

acanthus carving:

Based on the leaves of "acanthus spinosa" or "acanthus mollis" (or both), a stylized carved form that appears on the capitals of Corinthian columns, on the knees of Chippendale casework, and as a decorative element on many other rococo shapes. The leaves of both plants are made up of many lobes, with the lower lobes usually overlapping the lobes higher on the leaf.

accordion-action dining table:

Please see "Federal accordion-action dining table."

acorn finial:

Pointed finial that—descending—swells above a deep cove, appearing at the tops of the back posts of New Lebanon Shaker production chairs lacking cushion rails. On early New Lebanon chairs, these finials taper both up and down from their middle sections. Those early finials are more rounded than pointed at their peaks. In addition, they lack a cove below. Instead they are poised on a downward-tapering shaft about half the diameter of the finial. Then, in the last quarter of the nineteenth century, the finial assumes its mature, semi-bullet-shaped form with a pointed tip and a deep cove below. In the final years of production, in the 1920s, the acorn shape was abandoned on New Lebanon chairs. It was replaced by an elongated ovoid, often with a double cove below. Another style of acorn finial is found on many early country chairs of the New England region. These acorn finials are more naturally modeled than the Shaker examples, with a naturalistic stem and cap over the acorn shell.

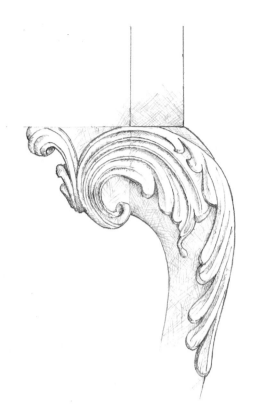

Acanthus leaves carved onto the knee of a cabriole leg

acorn hinge:

Butt hinge with an acorn-shaped knob at the top and bottom of the hinge pin.

acroter:

Small plinth supporting a finial or cartouche, often found between halves of a broken pediment. The term also can denote those ornamental details standing on that plinth.

Acroter used as a plinth for a finial

Adirondack chair:

Simple outdoor chair designed by Thomas Lee in 1903 and patented by his friend Harry C. Bunnell two years later. Traditionally made of rot-resistant cedar, these chairs are built from a small number of flat boards. They are designed to situate users in a near-reclining position with their feet still on the ground. The back is made of flat boards, sometimes fitted into an arced frame to cradle the back of the user. The seat and arms are also constructed from flat boards.

Aeron chair:

Office chair situated on a pedestal that rests on five outstretching legs, each terminating in a heavy castor. The chair back and seat are fashioned from a tough open-weave material known as "pellicle." The arms are cushioned. It has been called "America's best-selling chair."

Adirondack chair. Designed for simplicity and comfort, the Adirondack chair has been a staple of the rural American scene since the beginning of the twentieth century. *Courtesy of Getty Images*

Aeron chair. Designed by Don Chadwick (b. 1936) and William Eugene Stumpf (1936–2006), the Aeron chair was introduced to the American public in the late 1990s by Herman Miller, Inc., of Zeeland, Michigan. The materials are aluminum and pellicle fabric. *Courtesy of the Yale University Art Gallery*

air-dried lumber:

Green material dried outside in covered stacks, with the layers separated through the use of narrow perpendicular sticks, sometimes known as stickers. Many furniture makers then finish-dry this material indoors by restacking and restickering it in a warm, dry environment such as a loft.

altar:

The table-like centerpiece of religious ritual. In the ancient Judeo-Christian world, the altar was the place on which sacrifices were made. Today, the altar is the setting on which the materials of Christian communion are prepared. Although these often-imposing constructions were traditionally built of stone, today most churches celebrate at altars constructed of wood.

ambulante:

French term identifying small, portable table, often used for serving tea.

American eagle:

Symbol of the United States, often appearing as carved or inlaid ornamentation on American Federal furniture, which dominated the high-end American furniture scene from 1790 to 1820.

Amish bentwood rocking chairs:

A rocking chair that combines a bent-twig structure with a seat and back composed of steam-bent strips of milled wood.

ammonia fuming:

A method of darkening tannin-rich wood species like oak, using water and ammonium hydroxide.

American eagle. Sometimes attributed to the shop of Duncan
Phyfe, this eagle table is part of a matching pair, one eagle
facing to the left, the other to the right. Whoever the maker,
this is a supreme example of New York Empire furniture. The
material is mahogany and white pine. The piece is dated
1810–1825. *Courtesy of the Yale University Art Gallery*

amphitheater:

Area inside a desk drop leaf featuring an array of small drawers and cubbyholes arranged on one or more levels, sometimes arcing from one side of the interior to the other. In its most magnificent incarnations, these amphitheaters featured some or all of the following: blocked interiors, a locked central door with split columns on each side, and a shell-carved door or drawer fronts. In some examples, the two split columns flanking the central door are the front ends of a pair of secret compartments that are revealed when the columns are pulled from their housings. In other examples, the entire center section (known as the prospect) can be removed and, when reversed, reveals several small drawers on the backside of this removable center section.

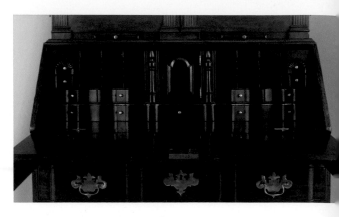

Amphitheater. This amphitheater from a Salem, Massachusetts, block-front secretary, originating in the shop of Nathaniel Gould (1734–1782), has a prospect door in the middle flanked by two half columns. Notice the small carved shells on the two upper outside drawers. *Courtesy of the Metropolitan Museum of Art*

andirons (fire-dogs):

Metal brackets on which logs can be laid in a fireplace so that air may circulate below the logs.

angle brace:

Length of wood, mitered on both ends, used to join or reinforce the corners of a table apron. On modern pieces, this brace is often made of metal.

Andirons. By an unknown maker, these American andirons are made of brass. *Courtesy of the Metropolitan Museum of Art*

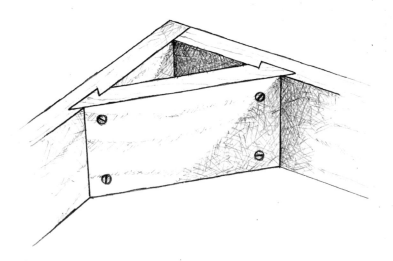

Angle brace securing the corner of a table apron

ankle:

That portion of a cabriole leg just above the foot. Because of the inevitable grain runout, this is the section of a cabriole leg most likely to fail when load stress causes a fracture along the grain.

antefix:

Decorative corner element rising above cornice molding. These are most often found on a tester bedstead.

Antefix standing above a cornice molding

applied molding:

Molding separate from the form it adorns, applied with glue or finish nails or brads, as opposed to the less common molded profile cut into the structural components of a case.

apron:

Wood frame that supports a tabletop and is joined to legs via tenons, dowels, screws, or sliding dovetails. It is often elaborated with scrollwork, fretwork, or molding (or two or more of these). The tabletop is then fastened to the apron either directly (a rarely seen method), with screws or nails driven down through the tabletop into the top edge of the apron, or indirectly through the use of cleats, buttons, or pocket screws hidden underneath the tabletop. Sometimes the ends of the apron components are dovetailed together, and the legs are then attached to that dovetailed frame. In England the term "apron" has a more specific meaning. There it refers only to the often-scroll-sawn piece directly above the kneehole of a desk or dressing table.

anthemion:

Decorative carved form based on the chamomile plant, sometimes referred to as honeysuckle. Like so many details of eighteenth-century furniture, this form has its roots in the architecture of ancient Greece. This form can be traced all the way back to the Erechtheum in the Acropolis, designed by Mnesicles in the fifth century BCE.

antique nail:

Please see "upholstery tack."

Anthemion carved into a surface

aquarium:

A bottle, a bowl, or a case with at least one glazed side in which marine and aquatic life can be displayed. Typically these are equipped with custom-made metal or wood stands to raise them to a convenient viewing height. Please see also "Wardian case."

Arabesque marquetry:

Exceedingly elaborate marquetry style best exemplified in the work of the French genius André Charles Boulle (1642–1732).

architectural cupboard:

A built-in cupboard often without its own back or sides. Please see also "built-in furniture" and "corner cupboard."

architrave:

Horizontal structural member resting on the capitals of two or more columns. The term is also used to identify the moldings around a door or window.

armchair:

Simply a chair with arms. Originally such a construction was reserved for the head of the household or another person of similar importance.

Armchair. This early Massachusetts chair by an unknown maker features an urn-shaped splat, scrolled arms, and Spanish feet. The material is maple. The chair is dated 1720–1740. *Courtesy of the Yale University Art Gallery*

Corner cupboard. This corner cupboard is tricked out in a number of high-style motifs. The gooseneck moldings and the cartouche atop the pediment are nicely done, but the maker chose to use a pair of spindly columns lacking bases or capitals to support the visual weight of a pair of much-larger fluted pilasters. In addition, behind the top panels of glass, where a huge carved shell should appear, this maker chose to cobble up some strips of wood into a vaguely shell-like statement. The materials are walnut, cedar, tulip poplar, and yellow pine. The piece is dated 1760–1780. *Courtesy of the Yale University Art Gallery*

"Modern American" armchair. While I would argue that most mid-twentieth-century manufactured furniture is both uncomfortable and visually unappealing, this chair looks to be reasonably comfortable and—in the right setting—might offer only a minor affront to the eye. Designed by Russel White (1904-1976) and manufactured by the Conant Ball Furniture Company in Gardner, Massachusetts, this armchair is constructed of birch and upholstery. The term "Modern American" was assigned to the piece either by the designer or by someone in the Conant Ball's marketing department. *Courtesy of the Yale University Art Gallery*

armchair, Arts and Crafts:

Typically, an armchair built of oak with a simple straight-forward design.

Roycroft armchair. In 1896, Elbert Hubbard (1856–1915), an American artist, writer, and publisher, founded Roycroft in East Aurora, New York, to further the cause of American craftwork. Among the crafts practiced there was furniture making in the Arts and Crafts tradition. This oak Roycroft armchair from early in the twentieth century includes the distinctive Roycroft brand on the front apron. *Photo by Kari Rene Hall, courtesy of Getty Images*

armchair, Chippendale:

Successor to the Queen Anne with—usually—ball-and-claw feet and often elaborate strapwork on the back. Some are elaborately decorated with rococo carving.

Chippendale-style armchair. Little more than a century before the fabrication of this comfortable chair (1766), Americans were sitting in Pilgrim chairs with straight backs composed of lumpy turnings. This Chippendale example, with Marlborough legs and feet, is attributed to the Philadelphia maker Thomas Affleck (1740–1795). The material is mahogany and white oak. *Courtesy of the Metropolitan Museum of Art*

armchair, Hepplewhite:
Armchair derived from a drawing in George Hepplewhite's 1788 book *The Cabinet-Maker and Upholsterer's Guide*, usually featuring shield backs.

armchair, Queen Anne:
Armchair made during the baroque era, usually featuring spoon or triffid feet (later, ball-and-claw feet), smooth curvilinear lines, and an urn-shaped back splat.

Philadelphia Queen Anne armchair. Made in Philadelphia circa 1755, this gorgeous curvilinear composition with acanthus leaves on the knees, graceful carved strapwork, and carved shell on the crest rail represents the height of late Queen Anne chair making. The maker is unknown. The material is mahogany. *Courtesy of the Metropolitan Museum of Art*

armchair, Sheraton:

Armchair based wholly or in part on the images in Thomas Sheraton's serially published early 1790s book *The Cabinet Maker's and Upholsterer's Drawing Book*. These usually have square backs.

armchair, slat-back:

Armchair having either vertical or horizontal slats between the back posts.

Sheraton-style armchair. Samuel McIntire (1757–1811) was an architect/carver from Salem, Massachusetts. Another Salem resident, Jerathamael Peirce, commissioned McIntire to remodel the parlor of his home, including the design and construction of the furnishings. This chair is one of twelve that resulted from that commission. It's entirely possible that McIntire didn't actually build the chairs, but it seems likely that he did the carving because some of the carved elements are among his favorites. The chair design derived from a plate in Thomas Sheraton's 1793 design book, *The Cabinet-Maker and Upholsterer's Drawing-Book*. The material is mahogany, birch, and white pine. The chair is dated 1801. *Courtesy of the Metropolitan Museum of Art*

Pilgrim-era slat-back armchair. This Pilgrim-era slat-back armchair was made somewhere in New England during the last half of the seventeenth century. The wood is ash. *Courtesy of the Metropolitan Museum of Art*

armchair, William and Mary:

Armchair outfitted with the motifs of the William and Mary period.

William and Mary armchair. This masterpiece of William and Mary chair making features powerful turnings, a boldly carved crest rail, and Spanish feet. Together, they provide a powerful backdrop for anyone lucky enough to occupy this chair. The chair is made of maple and ash with a rush seat. It's dated 1720–1740. *Courtesy of the Metropolitan Museum of Art*

armoire:

A cousin of both the "chifforobe" and the "kas," a large moveable cupboard used to store clothes.

arris:

The intersection of two planes. When a craftsman is sanding between coats of finish, he must pay particular attention to these edges, since it is very easy to sand through the finish on the arrises even when working by hand with a sanding block.

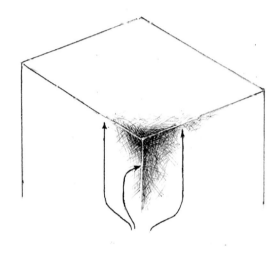

Arrises on a wood block

arrow back:

Windsor chair back in which the spindles are shaped into elongated arrows usually pointed down toward the seat.

arrow foot:

Cone-shaped furniture foot, tapering as it descends toward the floor.

art furniture (artiture):

Furniture having more in common with contemporary sculpture than traditional furniture. This brand of late-twentieth-century work has introduced many exciting forms to modern furniture, including stacked plywood constructions, forms evocative of modern sculpture, and whimsical furniture; for example, the famous "Walking Cabinet" by Wendell Castle (1932–2018), which consists of a gi-raffe-spotted cabinet perched on seven am-bulating legs.

Arts and Crafts pull:

A hand-hammered, usually rectangular copper or iron plate from which is suspended a wrought-iron bail.

ash, white:

Wood of the *Fraxinus americana* tree used for some furniture applications. White ash has a very consistent flat white appearance that many makers find unappealing. However, because of its strength, resiliency, and density, it has long been the preferred material for tool handles and baseball bats, and it has seen some use as flooring and in furniture shops.

astragal molding:

Molding composed of a bead with a filet on each side. Eighteenth- and nineteenth-century astragal-molding planes are among the more common survivors of those eras' molders.

bachelor's chest:

A small chest of usually graduated drawers, often with a handle fixed on each end to give it portability.

backboard:

Board used to back mirrors and large pictures. Today these boards are almost always plywood. Period examples typically employed thin panels of solid wood or—in some cases—thin panels of solid wood overlaid with sheets of veneer.

back ladder:

The assembly of a chair's back posts, back rungs, and horizontal back slats, so named because of its resemblance to a ladder.

back post:

One of a pair supporting the rear of a chair's seat. Usually, these pairs of back posts also provide mooring places for the chair's back slats or back panels.

back slat:

Thin—often only ¼" thick—strip of hardwood connecting a chair's back posts. Typically, these are cut narrow, then steam-bent to better conform to the human back. Slats are features commonly found on country or Shaker chairs. Some lowback examples have just two slats, while others with taller backs may have five or—very rarely—more.

In addition, the Shakers offered for sale a line of panel-back chairs with a single slat fitted above a woven back panel.

backsplash:

Board standing perpendicular to a chest top, with grain running parallel to the grain of the top. In a kitchen or bath setting, such a construction can protect the wall from being splashed during washing or food preparation. Today, on a chest of drawers, the backsplash is simply a design element, a holdover from a time when morning ablutions were performed at a basin resting on a chest or stand in the bedroom.

back stand:

That portion of a chair's back that rises above the seat. The term is used primarily in England.

bail:

Loose half circle of metal—usually brass—suspended from two metal posts bolted through a drawer front. It's intended for grasping with the hand to facilitate the opening of drawers. On high-style American period furniture, the bolts attaching the bail penetrate one large or two small—sometimes elaborately chased or engraved—metal plates.

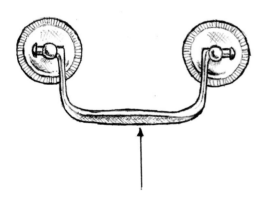

Bail used to open a drawer

ball-and-claw foot:

One of the most distinctive elements of American Chippendale furniture, consisting of a four-taloned claw gripping a ball flattened on the bottom, where it contacts the floor. The concept likely originated in China, where fanciful dragons were portrayed with balls clenched tightly in their taloned feet. In the eighteenth century, the American ball-and-claw foot reached its zenith in the highboys and lowboys made in Philadelphia by craftsmen such as Thomas Affleck (1745–1795) and in the powerful open-taloned feet produced by the Goddard/Townsend families of craftsmen working in Newport, Rhode Island. Ball-and-claw feet were nearly always fashioned from wood, but on some occasional pieces—particularly from the nineteenth century—a metal foot grips a metal or glass ball.

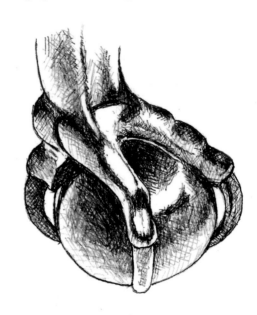

Ball-and-claw foot at the bottom of a cabriole leg

ball-and-nipple finial:

Finial composed of a ball with a small nipple on top. This detail is found on many country chairs.

ball-and-ring pedestal:

Chippendale support column for a tripod table with a turned, sometimes vertically compressed ball, above which are several turned rings or beads.

ball catch:

Catch for cabinet doors, available in several different formats. All are built around one or more spring-mounted balls contained in a metal sleeve or sleeves. On some constructions, a single ball will secure a door by popping into a depression on the strike plate when the door is in the closed position; on others, a post on the strike plate is secured when a pair of balls pop into hollows at the base of the post.

ball foot:

Umbrella term for several different styles of furniture feet. The most basic ball foot is an unadorned turned ball from which a furniture post rises, such as is found on many eighteenth-century Delaware chairs. But also included in this group are the "bun" feet on some William and Mary furniture, and the "onion"/"turnip" feet of some Germanic-American furniture.

balloon back:

A chair back that swells in width as it rises from the seat, becoming a round or ovoid shape, enclosed by a wood frame. Usually, the interior of this shape is left open, but on some chairs the space is filled with a backboard fronted with cushioning covered in fabric or a single rail at the back's pinch point. This particular variant was popular throughout the Victorian era.

balloon chair:

A form consisting of a chair with continuous sides, back, and sometimes a hood that envelope the user.

balloon seat:

Rounded seat style resembling the body of a dreadnaught guitar, most often seen in Philadelphia chairs of the Queen Anne period. This form is sometimes known as a "compass seat."

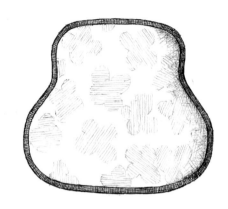

Balloon seat of a chair

ball wall clock:

A clock on which the numeral places are occupied by unnumbered balls at the ends of short spokes emanating from a central hub. The design is attributed to George Nelson (1908–1986).

baluster:

Turned spindle used to support stair rails, although any furniture element resembling a stair spindle can be called a baluster.

baluster-back chair:

Please see "banister-back chair."

balustrade:

Series of balusters capped with a handrail.

bamboo turning:

Turned form meant to mimic the segmented appearance of bamboo. The form is most often seen in square-back Windsor chair components. According to Charles Santore (b. 1935), author of *The Windsor Style in America*, the bamboo

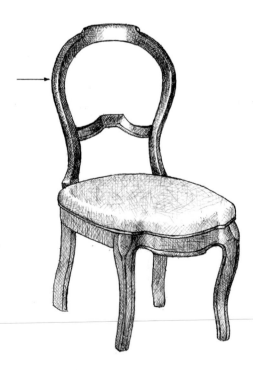

Balloon chair back

turning was inspired by a desire to simplify the process of manufacturing Windsors. The cylinder-and-ball legs appearing on early Windsors required the services of master craftsmen at the lathe. As the popularity of the American Windsor exploded in the late eighteenth century, Windsor chair craftsmen/merchants needed ways to facilitate mass production, and the easiest way to do that was to simplify the form so that less skilled craftsmen could man the lathes. This approach to furniture design—creating forms that can be produced by workmen with little or no skill—remains today as a dominant force in the design of commercially produced American home furniture.

banding:

Inlay made up of many, typically contrasting, woods organized into complex patterns, then sawn into strips. These can be used as edge banding on tabletops or to ornament a table leg. Thin bandings are also used in guitar construction. Please see drawing.

bandy leg:

A term used in colonial America to denote cabriole legs.

banister-back chair (bannister-back chair):

A William and Mary chair with a back made of four or five split upright turnings. These split turnings are produced by gluing together two boards face to face, turning them into a spindle, then splitting the two boards at the glue joint. The chair features bold turnings on the posts and stretchers as well as an often elaborately carved and fret-sawn crest rail. Typically the seat is rush.

Banister-back side view. This side view of a banister back shows the acute angle that craftsmen achieved on the back posts right at the level of the seat. *Courtesy the Metropolitan Museum of Art*

Banding

Banister-back chair. This New England banister-back chair
by an unknown maker from between 1715 and 1735 features
split turnings, a vigorously carved crest rail, and Spanish feet.
Taken together, these elements present a powerful statement
of the William and Mary aesthetic. The wood is painted maple.
Courtesy of the Metropolitan Museum of Art

banjo clock:

A clock in the general shape of a banjo. Above the dial, there is a finial, often a gilded eagle. The clock is joined to a wood box below it by a tapered transitional section (think banjo neck) usually with ornamental brass-work on both sides. The box and the transitional section are usually fitted with *eglomise* glass. The famed clockmaker Simon Willard (1753–1848) invented and patented the form.

Banjo clock. Aaron Willard Jr. (1783–1864), the maker of this clock, was born into a family of horologists. Both his father, Aaron Willard Sr. (1757–1844), and his uncle Simon Willard (1753–1848) were renowned clockmakers. This banjo clock, made circa 1825, is constructed of mahogany, gilt gesso, *eglomise*, white pine, and tulip poplar. *Courtesy of the Metropolitan Museum of Art*

banquet table:

A large dining table set up for use during a banquet.

baptismal font:

Briefly, a container for baptismal water. In the common parlance, it is also the stand on which the container is placed. In some modern churches, baptismal fonts can be quite plain, but in a more traditional church, they might be elaborate expressions of the cabi-netmaker's or stone carver's art.

bar cart:

Like earlier tea carts, except outfitted for serving liquor.

Barcelona chair:

Lounge chair consisting of two thick upholstered pads—one the back, the other the seat—resting on four chromed legs. The chair was designed by Ludwig Mies van der Rohe (1886–1969) and Lilly Reich (1885–1947).

baroque:

Term applied to seventeenth- and ear-ly-eighteenth-century furniture characterized by often-elaborate decoration. The term is sometimes used to identify furniture of the Queen Anne period.

barrel chair:

An upholstered chair on which the arms and back form one continuous half circle.

barrel-top trunk:

Please see "dome-top trunk."

barrister bookcase:

Stackable enclosed shelves with glass doors that lift up and slide back out of the way. A stack of these units may be placed on a plinth and then topped by a hood to become a more permanent bookcase.

barstool:

Usually backless tall stool designed so that patrons can sit comfortably at a bar while consuming the beverages of their choice. The earliest barstools were made of wood, with perhaps three legs. Today's barstools are more likely to be fashioned from metal, with four legs and comfortable upholstered seats.

basin stand (washstand):

A table with three or four legs designed to hold a washbasin. In the case of Federal examples, when the stand's top is raised, the washbasin is revealed. Basin stands would have been seen in most eighteenth- and nineteenth-century homes, at least in the homes of the moneyed elite.

basket:

A handled wood or wicker construction small enough to be carried.

basket of flowers:

Please see "carved basket of flowers."

basket of fruit:

Please see "carved basket of fruit."

bas relief:

Carving only slightly raised above background surface.

Basin stand. This unusual eighteenth-century basin stand by an unknown Newport, Rhode Island, maker has feet patterned after a cat's paws. The top rim is for the wash basin, the three cutouts below are for soap dishes, and the bottom shelf provides a place for a water jug. The piece is dated 1765–1790. The material is mahogany. *Courtesy of the Metropolitan Museum of Art*

Nantucket basket. This basket was woven from oak circa 1900 by an unknown maker. It was made in Nantucket, Massachusetts. *Courtesy of the Yale University Art Gallery*

bast:

The inner bark of a tree. The bast of hickory, elms, and some other trees may be harvested in the spring for use as a seat-weaving material.

batten:

Name of a narrow, vertically aligned board used to cover a gap between two wider, vertically aligned boards. The term "batten" more generally can refer to any strip of wood used to hold things in place. Please see also "board-and-batten panels."

batwing brass:

Drawer-pull backing plate, usually of brass, with a shape suggesting a pair of batwings.

bead molding:

Class of molding encompassing a wide variety of shapes, all variations of the half-round bead. Among those are the side bead, the cock bead, the center bead, the torus bead, the astragal bead, the Gothic bead, and others. Planes cutting such moldings are among the most common molders found in antique shows and among the inventory of antique-tool dealers. In particular, it's relatively easy to assemble a collection of side-bead planes of various sizes—that is, if you live in the American East. West of the Mississippi, it is more difficult unless you rely on internet auction sites. Electric-powered routers or molding machines can also be used to cut some of these beads.

bed bolt:

Specialized bolts for assembling the wooden components of bed frames.

bed bolt covers:

Small disks of stamped metal used to conceal the heads of bed bolts.

bedside table:

Please see "nightstands."

bedstead:

Bed frame that supports the mattress and box spring. In its simplest incarnation, it consists of four posts connected by single-board stretchers. In early country examples, rope was woven through holes in the stretchers, and a stuffed mattress was placed on that weave. During the eighteenth century, much more grand bedsteads appeared, particularly in urban areas, culminating in canopied tester bedsteads with turned, carved, and reeded posts supporting the tester frame above a thick mattress filled with down or other soft materials.

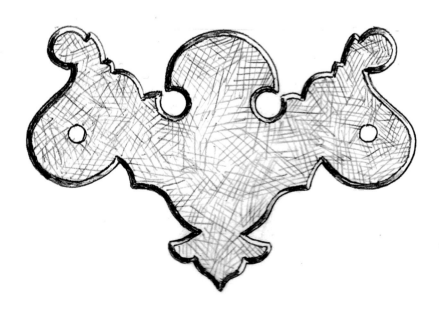

Batwing backing plate for a drawer pull

Lannuier bedstead. Throughout the eighteenth and nineteenth centuries, wealthy Americans were obsessed with all things classical. This bed, by Charles-Honoré Lannuier (1779–1819) and his cousin Jean-Charles Cochois (b. 1776) of New York, is a variation of an ancient Roman daybed, the *lectus*, although the form today would be more likely called a sleigh bed. It is the only piece of signed furniture by Lannuier. The bed is dated 1805–1808. The primary woods are ebony and rosewood, and the secondary woods are ash and tulip poplar. Some areas are gilded over gesso. *Courtesy of the Metropolitan Museum of Art*

bed steps:
    Set of two or three portable steps used to climb into some high beds.

bell-and-trumpet turning:
    Features a bell-shaped turning suspended over and joined to an upward-thrusting, trumpet-shaped turning. This lathe-turned form is one of the signature motifs of William and Mary furniture.

bellflower inlay:
    A five-lobed flower abstracted as a design motif for Federal-era furniture. As an inlaid motif, these flowers are almost invariably shown with only three lobes. The bellflower is typically used as an inlaid chain of blossoms falling down a Hepplewhite-style leg, but it can be seen in other contexts as well.

Bellflower inlay on a Hepplewhite leg

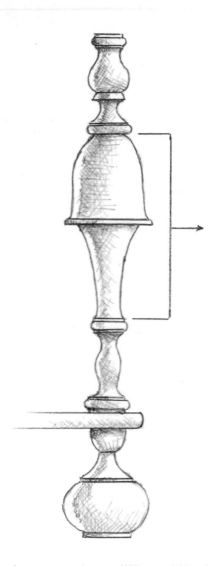

Bell-and-trumpet turning on a William and Mary leg

bellows:
    A device that collects air and then forces it through a narrow tube to oxygenate a fire. Traditionally, these were made of leather and wood, but today they're often made of various metals and synthetic materials.

Bellows. This wood, brass, and leather bellows was made somewhere in the United States between 1810 and 1820. *Courtesy of the Metropolitan Museum of Art*

bellflower-drapery chain:
    Chain of inlaid-bellflower blossoms looping across Federal-era table apron.

bench:

A simple piece of seating furniture, often without a back.

bench, four-board:

Bench made up of only four boards: a top, two ends, and one stretcher connecting the sides. This form was a favorite of country and Shaker makers.

bench-made furniture:

Term is usually taken to mean furniture built one piece at a time by a single craftsman.

bench, piano:

Please see "piano bench."

bevel:

Filet between two surfaces that are 90 degrees apart.

bevel-top trunk:

Rare 1870s form featuring a trapezoidal shape when seen from the side.

Bible box:

A small—Bible-sized—wooden box, usually ornamented with carving. In the seventeenth century, these were used most often to hold Bibles, although some were used to carry documents and writing supplies. Some had slanted lids with a raised lip on the bottom so that the box could be placed on a table and used as a lectern.

billiard chair:

Armed chair with a seat elevated high enough for the user to follow the action on a billiard table.

billiard table:

A large, flat-topped table surrounded by a raised frame, cushioned with rubber on the inside. The top is usually slate covered with felt. The table is used as a platform on which any of several varieties of billiards can be played. Most billiards games require holes in the table at each corner, as well as holes midway on each side along the length of the table.

bin pull:

Stamped metal pull often in the shape of a half cup, used to open the drawers of storage bins.

Bench, Shaker. This severely simple bench by an unknown maker with a one-board seat and a one-board back, both with half-radiussed edges, likely originated in the Hancock Shaker community in Hancock, Massachusetts, sometime in the second quarter of the nineteenth century. The wood is pine. *Courtesy of the Metropolitan Museum of Art*

Bible box. This pine-and-maple Bible box is the work of an unknown maker in Massachusetts somewhere between 1640 and 1680. *Courtesy of the Yale University Art Gallery*

Billiard table. This 1869 Currier and Ives lithograph shows a group of men in action around a billiard table. *Courtesy of the Yale University Art Gallery*

THE DEATH AND REBIRTH OF AMERICAN HAND-TOOL WORK

The work pictured in this book was built over a span of four centuries. Some pieces date from the mid- to late 1600s. Others are from the twenty-first century. The earliest pieces are the result of human-powered hand-tool work, and I don't mean only the cool hand-tool work that we see portrayed in today's pricey hand-tool catalogs. I mean the entire furniture-making process, from the felling of trees to the application of the last coat of finish.

In the seventeenth and eighteenth centuries, trees were taken down by using axes and two-man crosscut saws. The fallen trees were then bucked into usable lengths, again with human-powered saws. After the logs were dragged behind oxen or horses to the sawpit, boards were taken from raised logs by two-man crews operating pit saws (often called whipsaws), one above pulling on the saw's handle as he inched down the log and one poor soul who—as a rain of sawdust pelted his face—pulled down from below, and since pit saws were raked to cut only on the downward stroke, the man below was the one who did most of the work. The water-heavy fresh-cut boards were then loaded by hand into wagons, then unloaded by hand and stacked at the drying site. And, of course, once the dried boards were taken into the shop for use, the material was resawn and thicknessed by hand, surfaces were smoothed by hand, joints were cut by hand, and, of course, any decorative elaborations were executed using handheld tools. Of course, the brutish work wasn't done by master craftsmen. It was done by whatever apprentices, indentured servants, or slaves were available to the master craftsmen.

Eventually, sawmills were constructed in the American colonies, removing one of most arduous tasks from the furniture-making process, but inside the woodshop itself, work was still accomplished through the use of hand tools alone. Rough lumber was converted into usable boards of a consistent thickness by using long hand planes, winding sticks, a discriminating eye, and—of course—generous measures of human muscle power. Material was ripped to width and cut to length with handsaws. This last task might have been accomplished by the most skilled of the servants, apprentices, or slaves. Then the fussy work of cutting joinery and creating ornamentation was accomplished by the master craftsmen. This approach continued throughout the seventeenth and eighteenth centuries, a period that saw the creation of some of the greatest furniture ever built in this country.

The Industrial Revolution was slow to have an impact on most woodshops, because a means of powering individual woodworking machines was not devised until very late in the nineteenth century, although earlier in that era, large shops could power saws, planers, lathes, boring machines, etc. with waterpower directed to these machines via an overhead lineshaft and a complicated system of pulleys and leather or rubber-impregnated cotton-duck belts.

The beginning of the third quarter of the nineteenth century saw the introduction of small foot- and hand-powered woodworking machines. But the real revolution in small woodshop operations occurred at the beginning of the twentieth century, when tools driven by individual electric motors became widely available at reasonable prices, an event that marked the beginning of the end for widespread hand-tool work in the American woodshop.

One way to document the end of hand-tool use is to look at the dwindling number of American hand-plane makers. In the mid-nineteenth century, there were thousands of large factories and small shops annually turning out hundreds of thousands of hand planes in an immense variety of forms for an immense variety of applications. One such company, the Auburn Tool Company of Auburn, New

Line-drive machinery in the carpenter's shop at Hancock, Massachusetts. This view of the interior of the carpenter's shop at the Hancock, Massachusetts, Shaker community shows the overhead line drive that powered the individual machines. On the far right, there is a lathe. Behind that, a bandsaw, and behind the bandsaw, a second lathe. In the middle left, there is a wide jointer. The most interesting machine is the one to the immediate left of the jointer. That strange-looking device is a thickness planer, with the cutting edges on the wheel at the bottom of the vertical spindle. *Photo by DeAgostini, courtesy of Getty Images*

York, reported that in 1865, it had produced 35,000 hand planes and another 25,000 dozen irons for hand planes. But less than thirty years later, declining sales forced Auburn to merge with the Ohio Tool Company, another manufacturer of hand planes, which itself was forced, by declining sales, to close in the early twentieth century. By 1930, all the American makers of wooden planes—both big and small—had vanished, leaving in their wake factories that produced small machines powered by electricity that could straighten, flatten, and surface lumber as well as create joinery and moldings.

By the 1950s, the decade of my childhood, the only hand planes available in any store in my hometown of Fostoria, Ohio, were a smattering of Stanley bench planes: #4s, #5s, and a couple of block planes. In that era, if a craftsman wanted to create a molding, he had only two options: choose from the limited number of profiles his electric-powered shaper could produce, or choose from the similarly limited number of commercially produced profiles available in the local lumberyards.

Of course, hand planes weren't the only class of hand tool affected by the arrival of

machinery powered by individual electric motors. Carving chisels, dovetail and tenon saws, good-quality paring and mortise chisels—all these either disappeared from the marketplace or became rare and hard to find.

One of the most unfortunate results of this lack of an abundance of good-quality hand tools was the fact that designer/craftsmen began to design around the limited options available in electric-powered tooling. In fact, one might argue that the rigid simplicity of most mid-century modern furniture was not so much the result of innovative design but was instead a result of the limited capabilities of an electric-motor-powered shop.

Then, in the late 1970s and early 1980s, something miraculous occurred. Furniture makers once again became interested in working with hand tools in a way that was something more than an idiosyncratic anachronism. In part, this change was initiated by the arrival, in the late 1970s, of *Fine Woodworking* magazine, a publication that openly celebrated hand-tool work, but other forces were involved as well. According to Ronald S. Barlow, the author of *The Antique Tool Collectors Guide to Value*, "in 1970, there were less [sic] than a half dozen books on tool collecting in print," whereas today there are hundreds, maybe thousands. This interest in the hand tools with which work was once accomplished meant that the antique tools our grandfathers and great-grandfathers used were being unearthed and studied and, in some cases, being put to use. The natural

next step, then, was for someone to once again turn his energies to making the tools with which hand-tool work is accomplished.

This is a task that Tom Lie-Nielsen took up in 1981 when he founded Lie-Nielsen Toolworks, which has since become the unquestioned leader in the manufacture of high-quality, American-made hand tools. Lie-Nielsen's course has been paralleled by the Canadian Leonard Lee, who, since 1982, has been offering his own line of high-quality hand tools to Canadians and Americans alike. In the shadows of these two industry leaders, a large number of smaller shops are now producing one-off hand tools of extraordinary quality.

Beginning in the mid-'90s and continuing for the next twenty-five years, I spent much of my time writing profiles of outstanding American craftsman for *Woodwork* magazine, *Woodshop News*, and *Woodcraft* magazine. With few exceptions, what I saw in the shops I visited was a sensible compromise between hand and machine work. Most of the craftsmen (and craftswomen) I visited used power tools for the brute work: for the ripping, the cutting to length, the surfacing and thicknessing—in other words, for the work once done by indentured servants, apprentices, and slaves. But for the fussy work of creating smooth surfaces, for cutting and fitting joinery, and for any carving and turning and veneering, most of these craftsmen have turned once again to human-powered hand tools, which is—in my eyes at least—a most welcome thing.

Carpenter/cabinetmaker, 1860–1890. This confident young man standing in a puddle of shavings does both carpentry and cabinetwork. At least that's what the sign on the right says. He's holding a hammer in his left hand and two small handsaws in his right. One of those small saws appears to be a backsaw for cutting miters, tenons, or dovetails. The second small saw has very coarse teeth in a pattern common to firewood saws. Beside his left hand, there is a framing square and a wood jack plane. Beside his right hand, leaning on an upholstered stool, there is a third handsaw, a much-bigger one. While the stool on the left and the rough table on the right are real, the Victorian furniture behind the young man is painted on a canvas backdrop. *Courtesy of the Metropolitan Museum of Art*

birdcage top support:

Construction appearing on some eighteenth-century tripod tables that allowed the top to rotate horizontally and also to rotate from a horizontal position *into* a vertical position. The mechanism that allows these rotations on two different axes is a small "birdcage" consisting of two small wooden plates joined by four short wooden spindles. A hole drilled into the center of the bottom plate, through which the round top of the table's pedestal was fit, allowed a hostess to rotate the tabletop to avoid unseemly reaching. The table's horizontal rotation could be stopped through the use of a wedge bisecting the top of the pedestal. When the table wasn't needed, the top could rotate into a vertical position on a pair of heavy wood dowels formed on the top plate, which were fit into holes drilled in the two battens supporting the tabletop.

bird's-eye figure:

Wood figure highlighted by small swirling dots vaguely reminiscent of birds' eyes. This highly decorative figure is relatively common in sugar maple but much less so in other hardwood species.

biscuit joint:

Joinery style that uses compressed wood biscuits instead of dowels, mortise-and-tenon joinery, or dovetails. A small, specially designed power saw cuts the slots into the two parts being joined. Glue-covered biscuits are placed in these slots, and the parts are brought together, usually under the pressure of clamps.

Birdcage top support for rotating, tilt-top table

Bird's-eye bedstead. The primary wood on this Renaissance Revival bedstead is bird's-eye maple, a variety long prized for its lightly mottled surfaces. The secondary woods are maple and tulip poplar. According to the Metropolitan Museum's website, the carver who worked the surfaces of this bed was probably foreign born, because American furniture in the years leading up to the early 1880s, when this bed was made, featured uncarved surfaces. The makers are unknown. *Courtesy of the Metropolitan Museum of Art*

The moisture in the glue causes the compressed biscuits to expand, filling the sawn slots and providing tight-fitting joints. Invented in 1956 by the Swiss craftsman Hermann Steiner (1913–2005), the biscuit is used in edge-jointing boards or sheet goods and can also be used in the assembly of casework.

black cherry:

Please see "cherry."

Blacker bracket:

A decorative corner bracket used in the construction of Greene and Greene furniture.

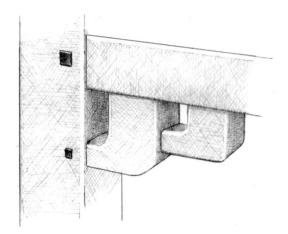

Blacker bracket for Greene and Greene work

blacksmith-made locks:

Large, custom-made locks fashioned of wrought iron by local blacksmiths, usually seen on the doors of buildings.

blanket chest:

A successor to the dower chest, the "blanket chest" is used to hold large pieces of folded fabric such as blankets. Often they are equipped with a pair of drawers below the main cavity.

blanket chest hinge:

Hinge consisting of a long—often a foot or more—iron strap that is hinged to a short L-shaped bracket. In use, the long strap is screwed, unmortised, to the underside of the blanket chest lid, with the L-shaped bracket fitting over the back of the chest screwed to the outside of the back of the blanket chest.

blind dovetail joint:

Please see "dovetail, blind."

blister figure:

A quality of some birches, maples, poplars, and mahoganies to appear to have a blistered surface.

block-and-shell bureau:

A kneehole bureau originating in the Goddard/Townsend shops of eighteenth-century Newport, Rhode Island. It consists of a low bureau with an opening in the middle of its width just spacious enough for one knee.

block-and-shell desk:

Please see "desk, block and shell."

block-and-shell facade:

Variation of the blocked front with large carved shells atop each of the three sections of a blocked front: convex on the outside, concave in the middle. According to Morrison H. Heckschler of the Metropolitan Museum of Art, John Townsend (1733–1809) of Newport, Rhode Island, introduced the block-and-shell facade in about 1765. Please see "block(ed) front."

block-and-shell secretary:

Please see "secretary, block and shell."

block board:

Sheet good composed of solid wood strips bonded to thin plywood sheets on the top and bottom.

block(ed) front:

Casepiece (desk, chest of drawers, secretary) in which the two squared-up outside thirds of the cabinet facade are thrust forward, with the inner third recessed. This movement is expressed in the drawer fronts, as well as in the moldings below and often above those drawer fronts. The thrusting sections are all radiussed on their vertical edges. On some, the radii are quite short, resulting in a nearly square corner, but on most the radii are longer, which produces a flowing set of curves and flats across the width of the facade. Although it was widely practiced everywhere in Massachusetts and Rhode Island, blocked facades on American furniture began in the Boston area. The first signed and dated piece of American block-front furniture was a secretary built by Boston cabinetmakers Job Coit and Job Coit Jr. (1717–1745) in 1738. The blocking on the Coit piece begins with the moldings above the bracket feet and

Kneehole bureau. One of the supreme achievements in American furniture making, this petite kneehole bureau was made in Newport, Rhode Island, by a member of the famed Goddard and Townsend families of cabinetmakers. It features the crisply carved block-and-shell front for which the two families are renowned. This particular bureau is thought to be the work of John Townsend (1732–1809). The circa 1765 bureau is made of mahogany, chestnut, and tulip poplar. *Courtesy of the Metropolitan Museum of New York*

Top drawer from John Townsend kneehole bureau. The top of the Goddard/Townsend block-and-shell facade can be seen in this drawer front from the John Townsend kneehole bureau, which appears above. The two shells on the outside are convex, and the middle shell is concave. Notice that the vertical lobes in the middle of each shell are nearly straight sided. The lobes descending from that center assume ever-more-dramatic cyma curves. *Courtesy of the Metropolitan Museum of Art*

rises through the four drawers of the lower case. On the fourth drawer, the blocking stops, becoming a pair of convex, semicircular domes on the forward-thrusting sections and a concave, semicircular dome on the central inward-thrusting section. This style of blocking was used in much of the blocked furniture produced in Massachusetts. The alternative was the blocking on certain chests of drawers with overhanging tops. On such pieces, the blocking rises all the way to that overhanging top, without the need for terminating elements. In Newport, Rhode Island, the Goddard and Townsend families of cabinetmakers devised a different—and some (for instance, me) would argue—a more aesthetically satisfying style of blocking. In Newport, the blocked facade also rose to the fourth drawer from the bottom, where it terminated not in domes but in energetically carved shells, convex on the forward-thrusting sections and concave on the backward-thrusting section. Blocking of drawer fronts is achieved by bandsawing them vertically. A craftsman who is fortunate enough to have immensely thick material can bandsaw sequentially all four drawer fronts for a single piece of furniture from the same timber.

block-front desk:

Please see "desk, block front."

block-front secretary:

Please see "secretary, block front."

blocking, glue:

Glued blocks used in chairs, tables, and casepieces to reinforce joints. These blocks are concealed from casual viewing. They can be found in a variety of sizes and shapes. In period Massachusetts chairs, many are simple triangles fitted into corners, while on some

Cherry block-front desk. Although Boston, New York, Newport, and Philadelphia are often seen as the places of origin for the greatest high-style American furniture of the eighteenth century, in places such as Colchester, Connecticut, a bit removed from urban America, there were craftsmen producing work that rivaled any produced in America's big cities. The maker of this masterpiece, Benjamin Burnham (ca. 1729–1773), eschewed the mahogany favored in urban centers, and chose, instead, the American species cherry as his primary wood, with white pine and tulip poplar as his secondary woods. The desk is inscribed as follows: "This Desk was maid in the / year 1769 Buy Benjn Burnham, / that sarved his time if Felledlfey (Philadelphia)." However, the details of the desk don't support a Philadelphia connection. Instead, the inlaid star compasses and blocked front are motifs of Massachusetts origin, and the pairing of ball-and-claw feet in front with bracket feet in back suggests New York. *Courtesy of the Metropolitan Museum of Art*

Glue block. Triangular glue blocks are used to reinforce each seat corner of this mahogany side chair. *Courtesy of the Yale University Art Gallery*

Philadelphia balloon seat chairs, the wide glue blocks run from the front of the seat to the back, as well as from side to side. These feature bandsawn edges to match the interior contours of the seat frame.

board-and-batten panel:

Panel sometimes used for cabinet backs, which is composed of boards set in place with ⅛" or more gap between those boards. Narrow strips are then fastened to the backsides of these boards to cover the gaps. The advantage of the board-and-batten back is that it allows for cross-grain shrinkage in the boards without producing visible gaps. This advantage can also be realized through the use of shiplapped boards or tongue-and-groove boards.

boasting:

Rough, incomplete carving.

bolection molding:

Molding rabbeted so that it makes contact with surfaces on two different levels. This allows the molding to hold framed panels in place.

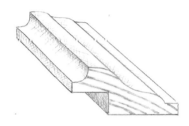

Bolection molding

bolster:

A long, round pillow, sometimes used as the arm on a piece of upholstered furniture.

Sofa with bolsters. This sofa is attributed to the shop of New York City maker Duncan Phyfe (1770–1854). It features a round bolster at each end to provide a cushioned arm support. The materials are mahogany, tulip poplar, cane, and gilded brass. The piece is dated 1810–1820. *Courtesy of the Metropolitan Museum of Art*

bolt-and-barrel fastener:

Fastener used for joining two boards, usually the end of one board to the side of another as in joining a bed rail to a bedpost. A metal "barrel" with a threaded hole piercing it from side to side is fit into a mortise near the end of the bed rail. Then a machine bolt or screw passes completely through the bedpost into the end of the bed rail, where it is turned into the threaded hole in the "barrel." (The stub tenon on the end of the rail fits into a shallow mortise cut into the backside of the post. This stub tenon keeps the rail from twisting in use.)

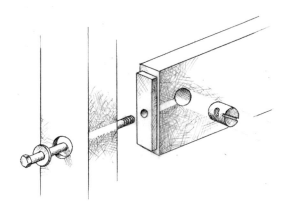

Bolt-and-barrel hardware for attaching bed rails

bombé:

Form of some eighteenth-century casework made in the Boston area in which the sides and front swell outward from the bottom, then taper dramatically inward as the swelling nears the lower case's top drawer. The form is often traced to Thomas Chippendale's 1754 book *The Gentleman and Cabinetmaker's Director*, published in 1754, which includes drawings of bombé pieces, but a bombé secretary signed and dated 1753 by two Massachusetts craftsmen, Benjamin Frothingham (1734–1809) and D. Sprage, predates the publication of Chippendale's book. Gilbert T. Vance, the author of "The Bombé Furniture of Boston,"[1] believes

that "Frothingham probably imitated a bombé casepiece already in Boston," one possibly made by a London-trained cabinetmaker or one imported from England. The 1753 Frothingham/Sprage bombé secretary has drawers with straight sides. This approach to the bombé form appears in many early examples. The interiors of the case sides in these pieces are flat, and the drawer fronts are squared against these flat sides just as they would have been if the case had not featured bombé exteriors. But most bombé casepieces feature bulging sides that are hollowed out, and the drawers were then fit to the interiors of these curving sides. A secretary attributed to John Cogswell (1738–1819), who is sometimes identified as the father of American bombé furniture, features a compromise between these two approaches. The interiors of the cabinet sides are flat—as in the 1753 Frothingham secretary—but the drawer fronts follow the swelling sides of the lower case. As you might imagine, the bombé form is technically difficult to construct, but as the eighteenth century progressed, some makers took the form a step further by combining the bombé and serpentine forms, creating a handful of pieces, several of which are regarded as among the finest cabinetmaking this country has ever produced.

bombé chest of drawers:

Please see "chest of drawers, bombé."

bombé chest of drawers with serpentine front:

Please see "chest of drawers, bombé with serpentine front."

bombé secretary:

Please see "secretary, bombé."

bonnet top:

Top appearing on many tall Queen Anne and Chippendale casepieces in which the shape of the two halves of the broken pediment extends from the front of the highboy to the rear via thin panels usually fastened in place with rosehead nails.

bonnet-top chest-on-chest:

Please see "chest-on-chest, bonnet top."

bonnet-top highboy:

Please see "highboy, bonnet top."

---

1   This essay appears in the book *Boston Furniture of the Eighteenth Century*, edited by Walter Muir Whitehall.

Bombé secretary. The bombé form is one of the most challenging for craftsmen to build. It's probably for that reason that there are fewer than sixty known examples (excluding modern reproductions), all coming from the Boston area. But the bottom section of this secretary goes one step beyond bombé: it is also a block front. It is, in fact, the only known piece to combine these two attributes. The upper case is architectural, with two wide pilasters supporting a broken pediment lined with dentil moldings. Legend has it that this was George Washington's desk during the siege of Boston, and it was exhibited under that description at the 1893 World's Columbian Exposition in Chicago. It is dated 1765–1790. The materials are mahogany and pine. *Courtesy of the Metropolitan Museum of Art*

Bonnet top. This Thomas Townsend chest-on-chest features a bonnet top behind the pediment. *Courtesy of the Metropolitan Museum of Art*

bonnet-top secretary:

Please see "secretary, bonnet top."

bookcase:

A freestanding case with one or more shelves used to store books. This form was of particular interest during the Arts and Crafts era, and some very attractive examples can be found in the Stickley, Roycroft Furniture, and Charles P. Limbert and Company catalogs, including some examples with leaded-glass doors.

bookcase, barrister:

Please see "barrister bookcase."

bookcase, library:

Please see "library bookcase."

bookcase, revolving:

Please see "revolving bookcase."

book-matched veneer or boards:

Two consecutively sawn leaves or boards laid edge to edge so that the figure of one is a mirror image of the figure of the other.

book rack:

A tabletop bookcase popularized during the Arts and Crafts era. These usually consist of one shelf sometimes raised above the tabletop, with ends attached to hold the books in place.

book stand:

A period stand—often designed to be placed on a table—on which an open book might be positioned for reading.

1855 bookcase with Gothic features. Furniture of the Victorian era featured a wide range of design influences, and this bookcase by an unknown New York maker is an expression of one of those: the Gothic Revival style. That can be seen in the Gothic arches on each door and the tracery work at the tops of each of the doors in the upper case. The materials are oak and pine. *Courtesy of the Metropolitan Museum of Art*

boss:

A protrusion on hardware or on a wooden component. The term "boss" is applied to the split turnings on William and Mary casepieces.

Boston rocker:

Solid wood rocker originating in the factories of Lambert Hitchcock (1795–1852). Boston rockers have flat, paint-stenciled crests above a back made of usually round spindles, sometimes bent to conform to the shape of the human back. The seat is machined from a thick plank of solid wood so that it rolls up at the back and down at the front for user comfort. The rockers are notched into turned and splayed legs.

bottle turning:

Spindle turning resembling a bottle, often appearing on table legs or balusters.

Boston rocker in painting. Notice the Boston rocker in this watercolor by Jane Anthony Davis (1821–1855). The chair features a painted surface, a crest rail that arcs across the back with a scrolled top edge, and a back composed of sturdy bentwood spindles. *Courtesy of the Metropolitan Museum of Art*

Bosses. The facade of this William and Mary chest of drawers with doors is studded with bosses, some quite small, some much larger. The case itself is made from a number of woods, primarily red and white oak. The bosses are likely maple or cherry. The piece is dated 1650–1670. *Courtesy of the Yale University Art Gallery*

Boulle marquetry:

A style of elaborate marquetry, often floral, employing exotic species as well as a variety of metals and other materials. This style originated in tenth-century Italy and reached its zenith in the work of the seventeenth-century Frenchman André Charles Boulle (1642–1732).

bow-back Windsor chair:

Please see "Windsor chair, bow back."

bow front:

Term identifying furniture that features a convex arcing across its width.

box corner hardware:

Protective hardware that cups the corners of cases that might receive rough treatment in transport. These are frequently seen on trunks designed to contain a traveler's belongings.

box-corner molding:

Grooved or rabbeted molding that allows the quick assembly of box sides.

box sofa:

A sofa in which the seating area consists of an upright three-sided box, often relieved by pillows.

box spring:

A fabric and wood or metal box containing vertically aligned springs woven together so that they maintain their verticality. This box usually rides on wooden slats that run between bed rails. The box spring assembly provides a resilient foundation for the softer mattress that is placed upon it.

Bow-front chest. This four-drawer chest by an unknown Connecticut maker has a facade that gently arcs from one side to the other. The material is cherry, pine, chestnut, and light-wood stringing. The chest is dated between 1800 and 1820. *Courtesy of the Yale University Art Gallery*

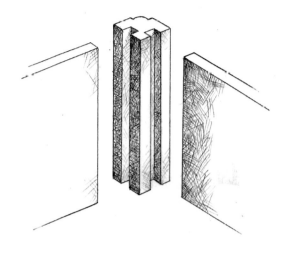

Box-corner molding

Previous page: Marquetry of André Charles Boulle (1642–1732). This is one of two non-American pieces of woodworking in this book, and my reason for including this French piece and another, later, Italian piece is pretty simple: the French and Italians had achieved levels of technical wizardry that Americans of their periods could not match. In fact, although American period furniture brings much-higher auction prices, and although I much prefer it to the work done in England, France, Italy, etc., American work lacks the extraordinary technical mastery of the work being executed in Europe at the same time. This particular armoire is one such example. It features the incredibly elaborate marquetry for which Boulle was known on both sides of the Atlantic. To modern American eyes, such a flurry of marquetry and carving might seem overwhelming, but it is, nevertheless, a triumph of design work and technical skill. The cabinet is dated circa 1700. The marquetry materials are tortoiseshell and brass. *Courtesy of the Metropolitan Museum of Art*

Box sofa. The finest furniture of the American Empire style came from the New York shops of Charles Honoré Lannuier (1779–1819) and Duncan Phyfe (1768–1854). This particular example is attributed to Phyfe's shop. The material is rosewood, brass, gilding, and ormolu. *Courtesy of the Art Institute of Chicago*

brace-back for a Windsor:

An extra pair of shaved spindles that rise from a tailpiece at the back of the seat, which helps support the load the chair's back must carry.

bracket:

A projection from a wall as a setting for displayed valuables or as a shelf support.

bracket clock:

A small clock originating in the seventeenth century that required a bracket on the wall so that the clock's external weights could be hung from that bracket. With the advent of spring-powered movements, the weights were no longer necessary, but the clocks continued to be made in the same compact package.

bracket foot:

Usually mitered, a casework foot consisting of two pieces of wood joined together, often splined and supported by glue blocks on the backside. This foot can also be assembled using blind dovetails. This detail was a favorite of Thomas Chippendale (1718–1779) and is quite common in Chippendale work done both here in the US and in England. Often the outside profile of the two boards is given an ogee shape.

Braganza foot:

Please see "Spanish foot."

brasses:

A generic term for—usually brass—period pulls. The absence of original brasses—even on an otherwise wonderfully preserved antique—can detract significantly from its value.

breadboard end:

Board with grain perpendicular to tabletop planking, attached to the planking through the use of a tongue-and-groove joint. This construction is intended to reduce the likelihood of the tabletop cupping across its width. The tongue is cut on the ends of the planking, and the groove is cut on the inside edge of the breadboard end. If the construction is glued only in the center, the planking on either side of that center can contract or expand in response to seasonal changes in humidity without any cracking.

breakfast table:

Small table, usually, with two drop leaves attached via hinged rule joints. Other forms include circular and oval-topped pedestal tables.

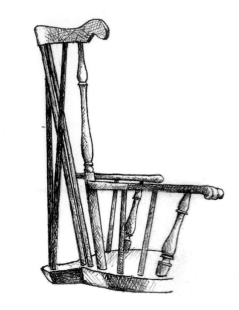

Brace back for Windsor chair

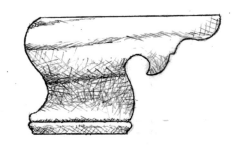

Ogee bracket foot

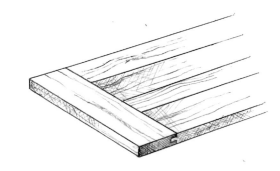

Breadboard end for tabletop

Breakfast table. Pembroke tables like this example have been used as breakfast tables for hundreds of years. This example, with Marlborough legs and Marlborough feet, was likely used for this purpose in the latter part of the eighteenth century. Made in Philadelphia by an unknown maker between 1765 and 1790, the table is made of mahogany, oak, pine, and tulip poplar. *Courtesy of the Metropolitan Museum of Art*

breakfront:

Large Federal-era casepiece with the center section thrust forward. The upper case is divided into—usually—four glass doors with complex geometrical muntin work, with the lower case outfitted with graduated drawers. The shelves behind the glass are used as bookcases or to display china, glassware, or other collectibles. Some examples had desk units revealed by dropping a mock front of the top drawer in the center section. Breakfronts are among the largest American casepieces built during the eighteenth and nineteenth centuries, with some examples nearly 8 feet tall and more than 7 feet long. Those identified as Sheraton stand on short turned feet. Those identified as Hepplewhite typically have sides and fronts reaching all the way to the floor.

Sheraton-style breakfront/secretary. This Federal-era breakfront/secretary, attributed to Nehemiah Adams (1769–1840) of Salem, Massachusetts, is based on plate 52 of Thomas Sheraton's *The Cabinet-Maker and Upholsterer's Drawing-Book.* This handsome composition is unified by the use of elliptical forms in the cornice, the muntin work, and the veneering on the base unit. The piece is dated 1800–1810. The material is mahogany, satinwood, and white pine. *Courtesy of the Metropolitan Museum of Art*

Brewster chair:

Pilgrim armchair with a number of elaborately turned spindles, including two vertical ranks between stretchers in the back, and one vertical rank between stretchers in the front below the seat. The chair, named for the Pilgrim William Brewster (1567–1644), is usually seated with rush.

Pilgrim spindle-back armchair. This powerfully wrought Massachusetts chair by an unknown maker is a type sometimes referred to as a Brewster chair, after William Brewster (1566–1644), who came to America on the Mayflower. Dating to the mid-seventeenth century, this piece of ash seating furniture would have been powerfully uncomfortable for extended periods of sitting. Not only is the back composed of lumpy, unyielding wood spindles, the seat was made of wood as well. Plus, the maker chose to put the seat below the level of the front-seat rung, which means, of course, that the front seat rung would cut into the back's of a user's thighs. Many spindle-back chairs of the period featured much more comfortable woven rush seats. *Courtesy of the Metropolitan Museum of Art*

bride chest:

Please see "dower chest."

bridle joint:

Joint composed of a full-width tenon fit into a mortise of corresponding size.

bridle joint, corner:

Bridle joint used to join the ends of two components at right angles.

bridle joint, mitered:

A bridle joint used to join the ends of two components at a right angle while maintaining the look of a miter on one face.

bridle joint, T:

A bridle joint used to join, at right angles, the end of one component to a second somewhere along the length of the second.

broke front:

Please see "breakfront."

broken-arch pediment:

Broken pediment in which the two halves consist of cyma curves expressed in the form of gooseneck moldings terminating in mitered returns, carved rosettes, or carved scrolls. As in the case of the conventional broken pediment, the space between sections of a broken-arch pediment often houses an acroter (plinth) for a finial, cartouche, or bust. These can also be referred to as gooseneck pediments and swan-neck pediments.

broken pediment:

Pediment with open section at the peak. A finial, cartouche, or bust is often displayed on an acroter or plinth between the two halves of the pediment.

bruise:

Dent in wood caused by collision with something hard. A bruise can often be reinflated by the application of water or steam.

Brumby Jumbo (rocking chair):

A large rocker created by James (1846–1934) and Thomas (1852–1925) Brumby in 1875, composed of a turned red-oak frame and double-woven cane seat and back. President Jimmy Carter brought five of these chairs with him to the White House because of their comfort and possibly, too, because the manufacturer was located in his home state of Georgia. The manufacturer, the Brumby Furniture Company of Marietta, Georgia, was forced to end production of the rocker in 1942

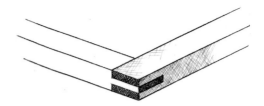

Bridle joint, corner

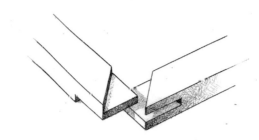

Bridle joint, mitered

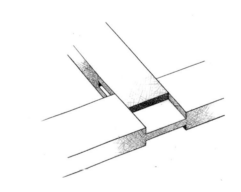

Bridle joint, "T"

This Boston highboy features an early broken-arch pediment. The material is walnut and white pine. The piece is dated 1730–1760. *Courtesy of the Metropolitan Museum of Art*

because of difficulties getting cane out of Asia during World War II. The Jumbo is now being made by the Brumby Chair Co.

buffet:

Please see "sideboard."

built-in furniture:

Casepiece built into or attached to a wall. The overwhelming majority of American furniture is freestanding, but there are some intriguing examples of pieces built into corners or alcoves.

bulb foot:

A usually delicate turned foot often seen in Sheraton-style tables. It features a swelling an inch or two above the floor, surmounted with one or more turned beads. The foot is often reeded.

bun foot:

A turned foot resembling a flattened ball with a cove above, often seen in William and Mary casework.

bureau:

Term often assigned in the United States to a chest of drawers intended primarily to contain clothes. In Europe, the term can also be applied to several types of desks.

Built-in chests of drawers. This monumental forty-five-drawer, built-in unit is constructed in an alcove on the third floor of the Centre Family Dwelling at the restored Shaker community at Pleasant Hill, Kentucky. Each large drawer is assembled with hand-cut dovetails and custom-fit into its opening. The primary wood is cherry; the secondary woods are mixed regional species with tulip poplar predominating. *Photo by Kerry Pierce, courtesy of* Popular Woodworking

Card table with bulb feet. I would prefer to see the legs on this Massachusetts-coast table with a little more curve in their turned profile, but they are reeded, and the table does have a very handsome veneered apron. Plus it stands on four dainty bulb feet. The materials are mahogany, satinwood, ebony, rosewood, maple, pine, and birch. The piece is dated 1810–1820. *Courtesy of the Yale University Art Gallery*

This handsome little block-front bureau is the work of an unknown Massachusetts maker. It's dated between 1750 and 1790. The material is mahogany, pine, and oak. *Courtesy of the Metropolitan Museum of Art*

burl figure:

A unique visual quality of sections cut from burls, which are large amorphous lumps growing on tree trunks or limbs. These sections reveal highly disorganized grain, often mixed with bud formations. This wood is prized by turners.

bust:

A sculpture of a person's head, neck, and often shoulders. Busts sometimes appear on high-style Chippendale work from urban centers of the time, as well as on some later Rococo Revival work done by carvers such as John Henry Belter of New York.

butler tray table:

A small serving table with a removable tray top.

butterfly key:

Please see "dovetail key."

butterfly leaf support:

A hinged wood panel in the shape of a butterfly wing, which—when unfolded from a table base—provides a support for the table's drop leaf.

Bust on Philadelphia highboy. *Courtesy of the Yale University Art Gallery*

Butterfly leaf supports. The two leaves on this early-eighteenth-century table are supported by butterfly leaf supports, which are swung out when the leaves are raised. *Courtesy of the Yale University Art Gallery*

butt hinge:

Simple cabinet door hinges that are fit into mortises, resulting in a hinge that shows only a thin line of metal when the door on which they're mounted is closed. These are commonly made of steel or brass.

butt joint:

Joint in which the components to be joined are mated at squared edges. A butt joint used to join framing components must be reinforced with tenons, biscuits, splines, nails, screws, or other hardware. The most common butt joint used in a cabinet shop is the edge-to-edge butt joint. This is the joint that allows a cabinet-maker to edge-join two or more boards in order to create wide panels. Sometimes these joints are reinforced with splines, biscuits, or dowels, but if the butt-jointed surfaces are carefully prepared, such enhancements are unnecessary. A good edge-to-edge butt joint is perpendicular to the faces of the boards being joined, as well as being straight along its length and without surface irregularities that might impair the tight mating of jointed surfaces. Traditionally these joints were created with a long hand plane. Today, however, most are made with a machine jointer having long infeed and outfeed tables, which allow the easy creation of straight edges on even long boards. Some modern craftsmen further refine the joint by using a long hand plane (a jointer) to remove the faint ripples the machine jointer leaves behind.

butt joint, edge to edge:

Please see "butt joint."

butt joint, mitered:

Simple miter joint used in picture frames and in some box construction. This joint requires reinforcement because end-grain surfaces make very weak glue joints. To compensate, the joint is often reinforced with biscuits or splines and less often with nails or screws.

button:

Small, lipped construction that allows a tabletop to be tightly fastened while still permitting the top to expand and contract across its width in response to seasonal changes in humidity. Shop-made buttons are usually cut from long, rabbeted pieces of cross-grained hardwood. The lip of the button is fit into grooves cut on the inside of the apron components, while a screw is driven up through the main section of the button into the bottom of the tabletop. The lip can slide back and forth in the apron grooves as changes in humidity cause the top to become wider or narrower.

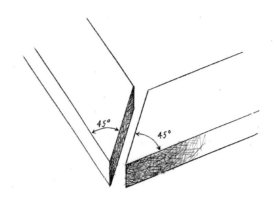

Butt joint, mitered

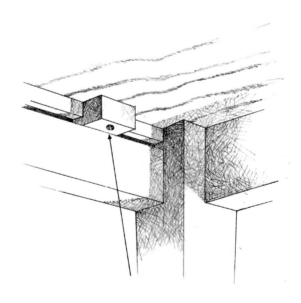

Button for attaching tabletop

Cabinet/cupboard. Only a handful of Pleasant Hill, Kentucky, pieces were signed by their makers, perhaps because the focus on self implied by a signature was antithetical to Shaker ideals. But this charming Pleasant Hill cabinet bears this inscription: "Charles Hamlin Jan 30th 1877." The case is divided into two sections: a chunky, clunky lower case of drawers and a magnificent upper section with three doors, two of which are joined in a bifold construction. The lower case stands on four indifferently tapered legs and is topped by a cherry panel with square unmolded edges. The lower case is so severely rectilinear and plain, the maker might have been working with a copy of the Millennial Laws (rules governing every aspect of Shaker life) open on the bench beside him. The upper case, however, soars, rising almost 8 feet to a wide, graceful cove molding inflected by a pair of narrow filets below. The difference in effect is significant enough to suggest two makers. The material is cherry. (I should add that some scholars believe the 1877 date to be wrong, suggesting, instead, that the piece was made earlier.) *Photo by Al Parrish, courtesy of* Popular Woodworking

cabinet:

Generic name that can be applied to any casepiece containing shelves or drawers (or both).

cabinet lock:

Any of a wide variety of locks used to secure the contents of a cabinet. Traditional cabinet locks are opened and closed with a key, but some modern examples use digital keypads for these functions.

cabinetmaker's samples:

Miniature chests, desks, secretaries, etc. used by cabinetmakers to demonstrate different forms to their clientele in the prephotography era.

cabin trunk:

The nineteenth-century equivalent of today's carry-on luggage. These trunks were small enough to be taken into the cabin of a train.

cable molding:

A half-round molding carved to mimic the appearance of twisted rope.

cabochon:

Semispherical carved or turned ornament.

cabriole chair:

Term originating with George Hepplewhite (1727–1786) to denote a chair with an upholstered back. According to Thomas Sheraton (1751–1806), these chairs should be called "drawing room chairs."

cabriole leg:

Furniture leg designed around the "cyma curve," an ancient motif, which consists of two curved sections: one convex, the other concave. In the case of the cabriole leg so common in eighteenth-century American furniture, the top section of the leg bows outward—the knee—and the bottom section inward—the ankle. For American furniture makers and consumers, this relaxed "S" shape was a welcome break from the rigid verticality of earlier legs. It became the signature design motif of high-style American furniture in the second half of the eighteenth century. The history of

Cabinet. This ho-hum mid-century modern cabinet was designed by Edward Wormley (1907–1995) and manufactured by the Dunbar Furniture Corporation in Berne, Indiana. The materials are walnut and elm veneer over plywood. It's dated circa 1955. *Courtesy of the Yale University Art Gallery*

Cabinetmaker's samples. Collector Wayne Stacey sits with
part of his twenty-five-piece collection of cabinetmakers'
samples from the seventeenth and eighteenth centuries.
Courtesy of Getty Images

the cabriole leg can be traced to ancient Egypt, but like so many other of the ancient world's artistic achievements, the concept of the cabriole leg became lost during the Middle Ages, not to be rediscovered until the early eighteenth century, when it began to appear in France and England, most notably in the furniture built for Louis XV. In American furniture, it appeared first in Queen Anne casepieces married to simple feet; for example, the spoon foot, the pad foot, and the slipper foot. The finest Queen Anne cabriole legs are sawn out of a large blank of wood in two adjacent planes, then shaped with spokeshaves, rasps, scrapers, and sandpaper. An alternative practiced in many country shops was a leg turned on two different tail-stock centers, one to create the knee, then a second to create the ankle and foot. These turned cabriole legs are stiff, lacking the cyma-curved grace of the bandsawn legs, but they are much easier to make. In the eyes of some, the first iterations of the cabriole leg—those that were bandsawn rather than turned—with their unadorned lines and simple feet are the most-magnificent examples of the form. Then as the Queen Anne period gave way to designs influenced by Thomas Chippendale (1718–1779), cabriole legs began to end in—often vigorously carved— ball-and-claw feet. Later versions incorporated acanthus leaves and carved shells on the knee. Simultaneously—particularly in Philadelphia— the cabriole legs on large casepieces became thicker, shorter, and more masculine, a change necessitated by the mass of the 8-foot-tall highboys that these legs were required to support both physically and visually. In addition, these later cabriole legs had less sweep in their cyma-curved profiles. This, too, was necessitated by the load they were asked to carry, because the reduction in sweep reduced the risk of shearing along the short grain exposed in legs with wider sweep. Cabriole legs were used not only in the construction of towering casepieces such as highboys; they were also used in the construction of chairs, tea tables, dining tables, card tables, pedestal tables, etc. In fact, any case or surface that needed to be lifted from the floor could be carried on a structure built around three or

four cabriole legs. Many of these legs—particularly those of the Empire period—terminate in animal feet; for example, hooves, hairy paws, and lion's feet.

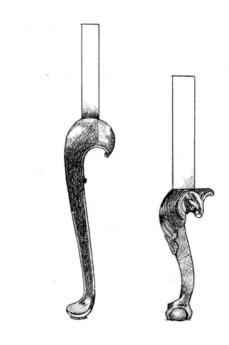

Cabriole leg with knee blocks: Queen Anne on the right, Chippendale on the left

Turned cabriole legs. This soft maple table by an unknown eighteenth-century maker has turned cabriole legs. *Courtesy of the Metropolitan Museum of Art*

cabriole sofa:

Ingenious sofa form originating in a George Hepplewhite (1727–1786) design in which the corners where the back and ends meet have been eliminated. This creates an end/back continuum consisting of one long sweeping curve.

Cabriole sofa in Hepplewhite style. Dating to 1790–1805, this cabriole sofa by an unknown maker is designed in the Hepplewhite style. The material is mahogany and satinwood. *Courtesy of the Metropolitan Museum of Art*

camelback sofa:

Upholstered sofa with a hump in the middle of the back.

Camelback sofa. Camelback sofas, named for the humped midsection, are common eighteenth-century survivors. Stylistic details—the Marlborough legs and feet—suggest a Philadelphia origin for this example. The sofa is dated 1760–1790. The materials are mahogany and yellow pine. *Courtesy of the Metropolitan Museum of Art*

camelback trunk:

Please see "dome-top trunk."

campaign bed:

Small portable bed with hinged folding frame and a half-tester.

campaign desk:

Small portable desk used by military officers while waging war. In the words of Civil War author A. J. Hamler, they are "light, utilitarian, customizable, and eminently portable."

campaign hardware:

Hardware made specifically for the portable desks and storage cases that an officer might need during a military campaign. Traditionally this hardware is made of brass and consists of reinforcing "L" and "T" brackets, box corners, leather trunk handles, and flush pulls.

campeche chair (campechy or campeache):

Named for the Campeche region in Mexico, a kind of sling chair in which the back and seat are one continuous length of fabric hung from a wood frame. Thomas Jefferson favored these chairs, and today there are seven campeche chairs with documented associations with Monticello.

Campeche (campeachy) chair. The simple campeche form, consisting of a frame supporting a one-piece back and seat, was made in New Orleans between 1800 and 1810. It is fashioned of mahogany, mixed inlays, and leather. *Courtesy of the Metropolitan Museum of Art*

canapé:
Upholstered sofa with elaborately carved legs.

candle box:
A small box used to store candles. This form existed in most seventeenth- and eighteenth-century American homes.

candle slide:
Please see "candlestick slide."

candlestand:
Small period or Shaker stand with a top supported by a pedestal base, which is, itself, usually supported by three legs branching out 120 degrees from each other. Most have round, dished-out tops executed on a lathe, but some have square or oval tops. Some examples have tops that tilt into a vertical position. When in use, these small tables hold a lit candle.

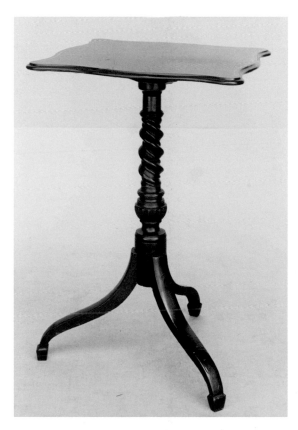

Candlestand. With its molded serpentine-edged top and its spiral-turned pedestal, this Salem, Massachusetts, candlestand conveys a sense of great energy. The materials are mahogany and birch. It is dated 1795–1805. *Courtesy of the Metropolitan Museum of Art*

candlestick (candle) slide:
Narrow slide-out shelf for holding candles, often found on period secretaries. These candles enabled users of the secretaries to read and write in the darkening evening.

Candlestick slide. This secretary from the shop of Nathaniel Gould (1734–1782) has a pair of candlestick slides at the bottom of the upper case. *Courtesy of the Metropolitan Museum of Art*

cane:
A seat-weaving material taken from the hard outer shell of the rattan palm. It was traditionally woven into very complex designs by professionals. Today, however, many cane seats are simply cut out of machine-woven panels of cane, then fixed in place by a spline hammered into a groove cut into the seat frame. (The pith of the rattan palm is split into strips for use in weaving splint chair seats.)

caned chair:
Early-eighteenth-century chair with caned back, rush seat, and Spanish feet. These chairs usually feature elaborately turned posts and carved crest rails. The term is also used to identify nineteenth- and twentieth-century mass-produced American chairs with caned back panels and seats.

Chair with caned seat and back. This American armchair, by an unknown manufacturer, is constructed of walnut with a woven cane seat and a woven cane back. The chair is dated between 1870 and 1890. *Courtesy of the Yale University Art Gallery*

canted corner:
   A chest corner composed of a filet that is 45 degrees from both the front and the side.
canted leg or foot:
   Outwardly inclined leg or foot.
canterbury:
   Originating in the eighteenth century, a small open-topped wood basket for storing sheet music. Some canterburies are equipped with a drawer below the basket, and many stand on castors.

capital:
   The crowning assembly of a pillar or pilaster. The capitals of Corinthian columns with their upwardly surging acanthus leaves were essential models in the evolution of Chippendale furniture.
captain's chair:
   Please see "Windsor, low back."
carcass butt dowel joint:
   Please see "dowel joint, carcass butt."

Canted corner. The two front corners of this gorgeous Jonathan Gostelowe (1745–1795) chest of drawers are canted. Notice that the canting continues in the bracket feet, which adds apparent width to the already enormous chest, which measures 57¼" across. The chest was made for Gostelowe's second wife on the occasion of their marriage on April 17, 1789. The materials are mahogany, tulip poplar, cedar, and yellow pine. *Courtesy of the Yale University Art Gallery*

card table:

Traditionally a table with a hinged top, the leaves of which could be opened to create a larger playing surface. Among the more common forms in late-eighteenth- and early-nineteenth-century high-style furniture, card tables exist in many configurations, ranging from the vigorously formed and very masculine Chippendale card tables wrought by the Goddard/Townsend families of cabinetmakers in Newport, Rhode Island, to the very dainty Sheraton-legged tables of the Federal era. Most early card tables are four- or five-legged constructions (the extra fifth leg was used to support the opened leaf of the tabletop), but in the Federal era, designer/makers such as Duncan Phyfe (1768–1854) in New York began to produce swivel-topped tables fixed on pedestals that rose from three or four arching legs rising from castors to the base of the pedestal.

Card table with lyre pedestal. This exquisite card table with lyre pedestal was made in New York City sometime between 1810 and 1820. It has long been attributed to the shop of Duncan Phyfe, but current thinking is that it might have been made by one of the other supremely skilled New York City makers of the era. The material is mahogany, tulip poplar, and gilded brass. *Courtesy of the Metropolitan Museum of Art*

card table, Chippendale:

Gaming table with a hinged top that unfolds to create a playing surface. This form usually stands on four cabriole legs terminating in ball-and-claw feet, although there are examples with Marlborough legs as well. The finest examples were made in the second half of the eighteenth century in the high-style shops of New York City and Newport, Rhode Island.

New York Chippendale card table. This table's serpentine sides, shaped corners, gadrooned apron, and cabriole legs are signatures of the finest New York card tables. This example by an unknown maker combines those features in a muscular composition that suggests barely repressed energy. The corner extensions are for candlesticks; the dished areas, for game counters. The table is dated 1760–1790. The materials are mahogany, white oak, tulip poplar, and pine. *Courtesy of the Metropolitan Museum*

card table, demilune:

Card table commonly associated with the Federal era, with a top shaped like a half moon. These existed in several different configurations. Some were used in pairs, pushing the straight sides of two tables together to form one large, round playing surface. Others had a hinged top leaf over another demilune leaf and could be opened to provide a large, round playing surface. The opened leaves were often supported by hinged legs that could swing away from the fixed half of the table.

Federal-era card table. John Goddard and John Townsend weren't the only furniture makers of note from their Newport, Rhode Island, families. This Federal card table is attributed to either Stephen Goddard (1764–1804) or Thomas Goddard (1765–1858). Note the inlaid urn and the inlaid chains of bellflowers, as well as the inlaid stringing running down the legs and around the skirt. The table is dated 1790–1804. The materials are mahogany, satinwood, ivory, tulip poplar, and chestnut. *Courtesy of the Metropolitan Museum of Art*

card table, Empire:
Card table with Empire motifs.

card table, Federal:
Federal-era gaming table with top hinged in the middle and folded over when not in use. They stand on four or five dainty, turned Sheraton-style legs or four slender, tapering Hepplewhite-style legs.

card table, modern:
A shabby, usually manufactured, descendant of the great period tables. Most have metal legs that fold into the often pasteboard top. Some are slightly more respectable—but still manufactured—wood examples.

carrier:
A small box usually fitted with a bentwood handle. The Shakers popularized handled bentwood carriers in the nineteenth century.

Card table, Empire. This Philadelphia card table from the first quarter of the nineteenth century is tricked out in Empire motifs: lyre pedestal, ormolu mounts, and castors. The maker is unknown. The materials are mahogany, maple, oak, ormolu, and ivory. *Courtesy of the Art Institute of Chicago*

Federal-era card table. This attractive and well-preserved Boston card table is dated 1785–1815. The materials are mahogany, maple, spruce, and pine. *Courtesy of the Yale University Art Gallery*

cartouche:

A word that originally meant a graphic emblem representing the name of someone of high birth. In the furniture universe, however, it has come to mean a bit of carving occurring between the two halves of a broken pediment.

carved concave shells:

Common eighteenth-century lobed motif, often found carved into the center drawers of both the upper and lower cases of highboys. A smaller form of this shell is also found in the interiors of many desks and secretaries of the period, as well as on the kneehole door of many kneehole bureaus. Please see also "block-and-shell facade."

Cartouche. This marvelous cartouche—that bit of abstraction that sits between the two halves of the broken arch pediment—crowns a cherry highboy, probably made in the shop of Eliphalet Chapin (1741–1807) of East Windsor, Connecticut. The date is 1780–1790. *Courtesy of the Yale University Art Gallery*

Cartouche. This is a great example of a Philadelphia cartouche by an unknown master carver. The highboy and the pediment from which it's taken are on pages 104 and 105. *Courtesy of the Yale University Art Gallery*

carved convex shells:

Lobed shell in which the lobes are carved in relief. This form is one of the signature features of Goddard/Townsend casework. The Goddard/Townsend blocked front features a concave shell atop the middle third and convex shells atop the outer thirds of their widths. Unlike most carved shells of the era, which are made up of stiff, straight lobes, the Goddard/Townsend shells—both the concave and the convex—are composed of cyma-curved lobes at the bottoms of the shells, which straighten gradually as the lobes move upward to the centerlines. Please see also "block-and-shell facade."

carved knee blocks:

Please see "knee blocks."

carved or inlaid basket of fruit:

Often-elongated basket-of-fruit motif found on some high-style casework of the Chippendale and Federal periods. A Sheraton table attributed to Samuel McIntire (1757–1811) of Salem, Massachusetts, includes a noteworthy example of this motif.

carved pinwheel:

Circular, concave, and lobed enhancement found on some rural casework—most often of Connecticut origin— of the late eighteenth century.

carved shell:

Abstracted carved ornamentation found on Queen Anne and Chippendale work. The form is based on the scallop shell.

Carver chair:

Pilgrim chair with four, heavy vertical posts, connected by a series of turned stretchers. There is also a rack of short vertical spindles on the back of the chair. The chair is named for the Pilgrim John Carver (1574–1621). The Carver is the slightly poorer cousin of the Brewster chair.

casepiece:

A construction designed to hold things, built in a boxlike manner, such as, for example, a desk, highboy, or linen press. This is in opposition to chairs, stands, tables, etc., which are designed to provide places to sit and places on which items might be arranged for utility or display.

Carved pinwheel. The top center drawer of this cherry chest-on-chest from Connecticut features a carved pinwheel. This is a decorative touch that is relatively common on period furniture from the Connecticut region. The chest is dated 1760–1790. *Courtesy of the Yale University Art Gallery*

Carved scallop shell. This pediment from a Pennsylvania highboy has a large, concave scallop shell carved into its surface, just above the top middle drawer, and a smaller second scallop carved into the top middle drawer front itself. The unsightly discoloration on the walnut surfaces is likely the result of two conditions. First, this appears to be an unusually soiled surface, and second, it also appears that someone tried to address this with a partial, heavy cleaning. *Courtesy of the Yale University Art Gallery*

Carver chair. This chair by an unknown Pilgrim maker is an
example of a type sometimes known as a Carver chair, which
is named for John Carver (1576–1621), the first governor of
Plymouth Colony, Massachusetts. A kind of predecessor to
the Brewster chair, the Carver chair has only one row of short
vertical spindles, whereas the Brewster chair has two, three,
or more. The material is maple and ash. The chair is dated
1660–1690. *Courtesy of the Metropolitan Museum of Art*

casework:

Please see "casepiece."

casket:

In common use, a large chest made of wood or metal, cushioned and lined with fabric for holding the dead during viewing and later interment. In less common use, the word refers to a usually small chest of wood or metal (or both) in which valuable objects are stored. Please see also "coffin."

castor (caster):

Small wheel affixed to the bottom of a furniture leg. Although rarely employed today on high-style furniture, in the Empire period, castors were common even on the finest work. See also "pedestal base castor."

Animal-paw castor (caster) at the end of a leg

cattail rush:

Rush seating made of twisted cattail leaves. Unlike fiber (paper) rush, which comes in a roll ready to weave, cattail leaves require a fair amount of preparation, since the best results are had when weaving with leaves that have been thoroughly dried over a period of weeks, then soaked for four or five hours just prior to use. In addition, because the leaves are relatively short, a seat weaver must make frequent splices of one piece to another. In contrast, weavers using fiber rush need to make no splices because the material comes in rolls often hundreds of feet in length. But the payoff for using natural rush is a wonderfully variegated color, and the knowledge that the seat is historically correct.

caul:

Catchall term used to identify various pieces of wood used as forms, cleats, or clamping aids.

Cavetto molding:

Please see "cove molding."

cedar chest:

A chest either made of or lined with aromatic cedar, which repels moths.

celebrant's chair:

An often-quite-elaborate chair in which a church's priest or pastor sits during services.

cellarette (cellaret):

Small chest, often lined with metal, raised above the floor on legs, which is used for the storage of alcohol and drinking paraphernalia. According to Wikipedia, these chests date to the fifteenth century in Europe. Some cellarettes contain ice coolers. The term is also used to denote that drawer on a sideboard in which liquors and glassware can be stored.

Cellarette. This North Carolina cellarette consists of a yellow pine case standing on four ash legs. The piece is dated 1785–1820. *Courtesy of the Yale University Art Gallery*

center-bead molding:

Bead formed in the direction of running grain at a distance from the edge of a board or panel. Traditionally, these were cut with center-bead planes guided either by a fence like those found on plow planes or by a fixed batten. Today, except for beads produced by hand-tool Neanderthals like myself, center beads are machine made.

center table:

In the Victorian era, a table meant to be positioned in the center of the parlor.

chafing-dish cabinet:

Cabinet designed to hold a chafing dish (a chafing dish holds food over a low heat to keep it warm during serving). Chests for the containment of chafing dishes became popular during the Arts and Crafts era, with companies such as Gustav Stickley's Craftsman Furniture and Roycroft Furniture offering these in several configurations, usually with windows made up of glass set in copper muntins.

chair:

Furniture form designed to hold the human body in a seated position.

chair-table:

A William and Mary–era construction consisting of a table, the top of which can be tilted into a vertical position to reveal a chair seat underneath.

Rococo Revival center table. In the Victorian era, the parlor became the centerpiece of homes owned by the American well-to-do, and the center table occupied the heart of that room. This Rococo Revival center table with marble top by an unknown maker is constructed of rosewood and ash. It's dated 1850–1860. *Courtesy of the Metropolitan Museum of Art*

Candle chandelier. The earliest chandeliers relied on candles as light sources, such as this early-eighteenth-century tin example with four cups to hold candles. The maker is unknown. *Courtesy of the Metropolitan Museum of Art*

Oil-burning chandelier. This mid-eighteenth-century chandelier manufactured by Clark, Coit, and Cargill of New York has four oil burners and an oil reservoir—as well as lots of little glass doodads. *Courtesy of the Metropolitan Museum of Art*

Chair-table. This unusual Massachusetts form, dating to the second half of the eighteenth century, combines the attributes of a chair and those of a table. The wood is red oak, yellow pine, and white cedar. *Courtesy of the Metropolitan Museum of Art*

chamfer:
Bevel that is 45 degrees from each of two adjacent planes.

chandelier:
Ceiling-hung light fixture, often with many light sources. These light sources could be candles, oil lights, gas lights, or electrical lights.

channel:
Groove or fluting cut into a surface for decorative effect.

chasing:
Use of a hammer and various shaping tools to create surface designs on the front side of a sheet of malleable metal. This results in some areas being sunk while other areas stand proud. This style of ornamentation was common on period brasses. "Repoussage" is the same technique but enacted on the backside of the metal.

cheek:
Please see "tenon cheek."

This very ornate chandelier was designed and built by George Shastey (1839–1894) and Company of New York. It was originally lit by gas, then later switched to electricity. The materials are brass, glass, mother-of-pearl, and semiprecious stones. *Courtesy of the Metropolitan Museum of Art*

cherry:

Wood of *Prunus serotina*, prized for its beauty and workability. After black walnut, this is the premier American primary wood. The heartwood, which darkens dramatically over time with exposure to light, has a red-brown hue. The sapwood is a creamy white. Like walnut, cherry was a primary wood of choice for makers in areas lacking access to the ports that received mahogany shipments in the eighteenth and early nineteenth centuries.

Cherry. This Connecticut chest-on-chest from 1802 illustrates the most desirable look of aged cherry wood. It's a smooth, creamy orangish brown without the striped or plum-pudding appearance of many mahoganies. *Courtesy of the Yale University Art Gallery*

chest:

A box, usually with a hinged lid, in which valuable things are stored and preserved.

Chesterfield:

A stuffed and upholstered couch having arms and back all of the same height.

chest lock:

Lock used to secure chests, usually through the use of a skeleton key. Typically, the steel or brass lock body is mortised into the backside of the chest front, and a mating strike plate is mortised into the bottom of the chest lid.

chest of drawers:

A case containing—usually—graduated drawers. This form was a milestone in the creation of freestanding storage furniture.

Its likely predecessor was the Pilgrim chest, with a large lidded cavity above a drawer or two, which evolved, in the William and Mary era, into the four-drawer unit with which we are so familiar today. The finest examples are arguably the Chippendale chests made in the urban centers of the East Coast during the last half of the eighteenth century and the Federal chests made later in those same locations.

chest of drawers, Arts and Crafts:

Turn-of-the-century chest of drawers, usually made of oak and usually severely rectilinear in design.

chest of drawers, block and shell:

Chest of drawers with Newport-style blocking.

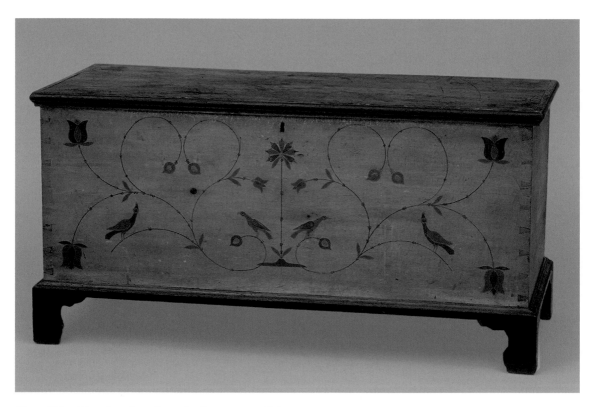

Chest. This white pine chest from the first quarter of the nineteenth century stands on four tall bracket feet and features delicate painting of lacy vines, tulips, and birds. The Pennsylvania maker is unknown. *Courtesy of the Yale University Art Gallery*

Country board chest with drawers. This simple country chest is decorated in the manner of Robert Crossman (1707–1799) of Taunton, Massachusetts. The chest is made of white pine and cedar. *Courtesy of the Metropolitan Museum of Art*

Label from John Townsend chest (pictured on next page). *Courtesy of the Metropolitan Museum of Art*

Drawer dovetailing from John Townsend chest (pictured on next page). *Courtesy of the Metropolitan Museum of Art*

John Townsend chest of drawers. A masterpiece of block-and-shell design and execution, this is one of the most important pieces of eighteenth-century American furniture. It is the work of John Townsend (1732–1809), one of America's most important makers. The material is mahogany, tulip poplar, pine, and chestnut. *Courtesy of the Metropolitan Museum of Art*

chest of drawers, bombé:

Chest of drawers with the characteristic bombé swelling beginning in the second drawer from the top and widening all the way until the middle of the fourth drawer from the top, where the swelling begins to recede. All or nearly all the eighteenth-century bombé chests originated in the Boston/Salem areas.

chest of drawers, bombé with serpentine front:

A eighteenth-century bombé chest of drawers with a facade that includes a serpentine flow across its width. Few of these gems exist today, and—except for modern reproductions—all can be traced to the Boston area.

chest of drawers, bow front:

Chest of drawers with convex arcing across its width.

Serpentine-front bombé chest of drawers. This chest of drawers is not only a serpentine front; it is also a bombé front, one of only six known eighteenth-century pieces having that combination of features. This example was made in Boston, probably by John Cogswell (1753–1819), at the height of the Chippendale era (1760–1790). The material is mahogany and white pine. *Courtesy of the Art Institute of Chicago*

chest of drawers, Chippendale:
    Chest of drawers outfitted with Chippendale-era motifs; for instance, ball-and-claw feet, gadrooning, batwing brasses etc.

chest of drawers, Empire:
    Chest from the Empire era, often with the top drawer thrust forward on corbels or pillars. These can feature animal-paw feet, glass or porcelain knobs, veneering, and some carving.

chest of drawers, Federal:
    Veneered and inlaid chest of drawers, often with French feet or slender turned feet.

Chippendale chest of drawers. Most Boston block fronts are—well, blocky. This small chest of drawers offers a slightly different take on this form. While the center section of the facade is flat across, the two outer sections are gracefully curved. These curves are followed by the base moldings and the top. Together these give the piece great appeal. The materials are mahogany, white pine, and spruce. This piece is dated 1760–1790. *Courtesy of the Yale University Art Gallery*

Federal chest of drawers. This handsome chest of drawers features a serpentine facade, veneers of mahogany and flame birch, and French feet. Although made in a relatively small city—Portsmouth, New Hampshire—it has the high-style look of a construction from a larger urban center. It dates to 1795–1805. The material is mahogany and birch veneers, white pine, and tulip poplar. *Courtesy of the Metropolitan Museum of Art*

Three-quarter view of the chest above, showing a back foot. *Courtesy of the Metropolitan Museum of Art*

chest of drawers, Gilded Age:

Chest of drawers designed for the super-wealthy in the years between the Civil War and the Spanish-American War. The work is typified by high levels of decoration executed by New York makers such as the Herter Brothers of New York.

Close up of floral inlay on chest below. *Courtesy of the Metropolitan Museum of Art*

Gilded Age chest of drawers. Made at the height of the Gilded Age in 1880, this Herter Brothers (active 1864–1906) chest of drawers is decorated with a very precisely arranged pattern of inlaid flowers, a recurrent theme in Herter work. The material is cherry, tulip poplar, and cedar. (For some reason, the color is skewed in this photo.) *Courtesy of the Metropolitan Museum of Art*

chest of drawers, mid-century modern:

Chest of drawers dating to the middle of the twentieth century. Chests of this period usually feature unembellished cases and drawer fronts. Many are assembled from plywood. In addition, they often utilize nontraditional materials, such as steel, plastic, or fiberglass. They are, in general, functional, cheap to manufacture, and utterly devoid of aesthetic appeal.

Mid-century modern chest of drawers. George Nelson (1908–1986), the first design director of Herman Miller, Inc., has probably had more to do with the furniture that surrounded you during your childhood than any other figure in this book. This chest of drawers is walnut-veneered maple plywood, which provides a decent appearance at what I imagine was moderate cost. The design debuted in 1946. *Courtesy of the Yale University Art Gallery*

chest of drawers, Queen Anne:

Relatively uncommon form standing on short cabriole legs and spoon feet. Some chests of the Queen Anne time period are identified as Queen Anne even though they possess motifs associated with other periods; for example, the ball or bun feet of the William and Mary period.

Queen Anne chest of drawers. This Queen Anne chest of drawers is the work of Samuel Dunlap (1752–1830), brother to John (1746–1792), both of whom were highly skilled furniture makers in rural New Hampshire, and both men worked a bit outside the mainstream of then-current high-style furniture-making traditions. For instance, in the construction of this piece, Samuel Dunlap chose soft maple as his primary wood, which would have been an unthinkable choice for an urban maker. In the eyes of urban makers of that era, there was only one proper choice for high-style furniture: mahogany. Notice, too, that this piece is dated 1790–1810. During those years, high-style urban makers had nearly all switched to Federal furniture, leaving behind both the Chippendale and the even-earlier Queen Anne styles. And finally, notice the unusual—but very appealing—scrollwork on the knee blocks and the molding that runs around the base. I should confess that I have stolen shamelessly from this piece. (Full disclosure: I've stolen from many of the pieces in this book, always shamelessly.) *Courtesy of the Yale University Art Gallery*

chest of drawers, serpentine front:

Chest originating in the Chippendale period and continued through the Federal era, with a facade that curves inward on the outside third, then swells outward in the middle. Chippendale examples of this largely urban form stand on ball-and-claw or bracket feet, with Federal examples often standing on French feet.

Serpentine-front chest of drawers. This Federal-era, serpentine-front chest of drawers features mahogany veneers with light-wood stringing and Hepplewhite-style pulls. The maker is unknown. The chest is dated 1795–1810. The secondary woods are cedar and pine. *Courtesy of the Yale University Art Gallery*

chest of drawers, William and Mary:
    Chest of drawers from the early eighteenth century, usually with ball or onion feet and drop pulls. The drawer fronts are often veneered or made up of frame-and-panel assemblies.

William and Mary chest of drawers. The unknown maker of this chest of drawers reached back into the Pilgrim era for his choice of material, using both red and white oaks as his primary woods. The chest also employs white pine and maple. The chest is dated 1700–1730. *Courtesy of the Yale University Art Gallery*

chest-on-chest:

One chest of four or five, usually graduated, drawers stacked on another chest of four or five, usually graduated, drawers. In the hands of unskilled country craftsman, this form is simple utilitarian furniture, but in the hands of master craftsmen, the form can have a breathtaking aesthetic presence. The Stephen Badlam (1757–1815) chest-on-chest (with carvings by Simeon Skillin [1757–1806]) made for the daughter of Elias Hasket Derby in the eighteenth century is one of the finest examples of American furniture making. So, too, is the chest-on-chest made by William Lemon with carvings by Samuel Mcintire (1757–1811) for the personal use of Elias Hasket Derby (1739–1799).

Chest-on-chest. This tour de force of high-style Philadelphia rococo cabinetmaking overwhelms with its size, its magnificently striped mahogany, its balanced composition, and the extraordinary quality of its execution. The material is mahogany, tulip poplar, and yellow pine. It's dated 1765–1775. *Courtesy of the Yale University Art Gallery*

This is one of the truly great broken-arch pediments of the Chippendale era. *Courtesy of the Yale University Art Gallery*

chest-on-chest, bonnet-top:
Chest-on-chest with bonnet top. Please see "bonnet-top" discussion.
chest-on-stand:
Name applied by some academics to the highboy form.
cheval glass:
Tall mirror suspended from two screws or bolts passing through two posts into the mirror's vertical frame members. This suspension makes it possible for the mirror to be tilted down to show the feet or tilted up to show the face.

Cheval glass. This New York cheval glass by an unknown maker is framed in a rather-stiff architectural surround with reeded columns on both sides and a triangular pediment above. A tray for beauty aids stands on a wing projecting from each side. The glass is dated circa 1815. The materials are mahogany, brass, and mirrored glass. *Courtesy of the Metropolitan Museum of Art*

chiffonier:

In the United States, a tall chest of drawers, often with four or more full-width drawers topped by a pair of half-width drawers. Typically a mirror is mounted on the top.

chifforobe:

Large moveable cabinet with, behind doors, a closet rod on one side and a flight of drawers on the other. This is a generally rural and southern term that is often applied, in those areas, to any large piece of furniture intended for clothing storage.

children's furniture:

In general, furniture of reduced sizes—such as the New Lebanon #1 and #2 chairs—appropriate only for children.

chimney furniture:

A catchall term that includes all manner of fireplace accessories: andirons, pokers, wood bins, bellows, etc.

china cabinet:

Cabinet used for the display of china and other collectibles. This form dates to the late seventeenth century in England, when people began collecting oriental china, and has been revived several times since. These are manufactured today in many different configurations.

china closet:

Please see "china cabinet."

Walnut china cabinet. This walnut china cabinet was made in Manheim, Pennsylvania, by a country maker sometime in the eighteenth century. The cornice has high-style aspirations that the maker couldn't quite carry off. Although the dentil molding has some appeal, the lower case is blocky and crude. (Please see "cornice moldings" for a discussion of cornice organization.) The doors swing open on rat-tail hinges. *Courtesy of the Metropolitan Museum of Art*

chip box:

Small, usually handled, box used to hold shavings and kindling for starting fires.

chip carving:

Style of decorative, low-relief wood carving in which precise chips are cut free with a knife or chisel, leaving behind elaborate geometrical designs on the surface of the wood.

Chip carving. The surfaces of this 1737 spoon rack have been decorated with highly organized chip carving. The bright color of its original paint can be seen peeking through the more recently applied dreary brown. *Courtesy of the Yale University Art Gallery*

classical orders:

Design orders dating to ancient Greece and Rome, which are based on five pairings of classical columns and capitals: the Doric, the Ionic, the Corinthian, the Tuscan, and the Composite. The first three were developed in ancient Greece, the last two in ancient Rome. Each of these orders consists of a set of design principles derived from these five pairs of columns and capitals. The orders demonstrate more than instruction for the re-creation of these building elements. They also demonstrate principles of proportion, profile, and elaboration, all of which were central to the home furnishings presented by Thomas Chippendale (1718–1779) and other eighteenth-century furniture and interior designers. In fact, Thomas Chippendale said that the five orders were "'the soul and basis of the cabinetmaker's art." The Doric is the simplest of the classical orders. It is based on Doric columns, which tend to be short and squat, their height being only four to eight times their diameter, with twenty vertical flutes carved around their outside surfaces. The Doric capital consists of only a simple bead. The Ionic order is based on columns with heights eight times their diameters, topped by capitals consisting of two pairs of opposing volutes. The column itself has twenty-four flutes carved around its outside surface. The Corinthian is the most ornate of the Greek orders and, therefore, the most influential to eighteenth-century rococo furniture designers. Its columns were ten diameters tall, with elaborate capitals featuring both a double row of upwardly surging acanthus leaves and a pair of scrolls. Like the Ionic column, the shaft of the Corinthian column has twenty-four flutes. The two Roman additions include both the simplest and most complex of the classical orders. The simplest is the Tuscan, based on plain, unfluted columns rising to a height only seven times their diameter, with similarly plain capitals. The Composite order is the most complex, with capitals consisting of four large volutes set at 45-degree angles from the architrave above, with a double row of upwardly surging acanthus leaves below. Its columns, like the Corinthian columns, are ten diameters high.

Classical designers working within these orders tweaked them to suit the needs of a particular building, adjusting proportions and adding or subtracting details whenever necessary. Similarly, and to an even greater extent, furniture and interior designers of the eighteenth century such as Thomas Chippendale selected details and proportions that suited the pieces they were designing. In the realm of furniture, the use of paired opposing volutes, vertical flutes, and acanthus leaves are the most obvious borrowings from these classical orders.

Doric column and capital. This painting by the Danish artist Constantin Hansen (1804–1880) shows a pair of Doric columns and capitals at the Temple of Neptune at Paestum, south of Naples, Italy. The material is oil on canvas. *Courtesy of the Metropolitan Museum of Art*

Ionic column and capital. While the entire 58-foot height of the column can't be seen here, the capital of this column from the Temple of Artemis at Sardis is fully present. The material is marble. *Courtesy of the Metropolitan Museum of Art*

Corinthian capital. This pair of carved wooden capitals is an American representation of the Corinthian form. The capitals are dated 1810–1825. *Courtesy of the Yale University Art Gallery*

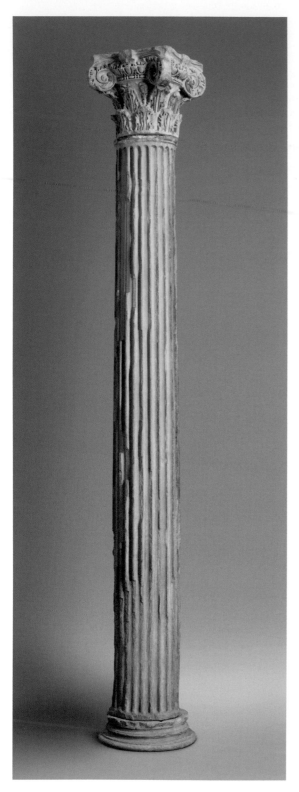

Composite column. The capital of this Composite-type Roman column has the Ionic volutes above and the Corinthian rows of acanthus leaves below, a combination that makes the capital taller and enhances the column's graceful appearance. *Courtesy of the Metropolitan Museum of Art*

cleat:
Generic term for any kind of support, attachment, or batten made from a fairly narrow strip of wood.

clockface:
Paper or metal surface on which the divisions of the hours are marked. Today, clockfaces tend to be quite simple. Some, in fact, use no numbers, relying instead on abstractions at the 3, 6, 9, and 12 positions, with dots or dashes in between. Period clockfaces, however, often feature elaborate lettering, painted scenes, and fret-sawn brasswork, as well as secondary faces showing the phases of the moon.

clothes press:
Please see "press cupboard."

cloud lift:
A feature of some Greene and Greene furniture in which long horizontal lines are relieved by the use of steps. This motif is Asian in origin and is intended to resemble the look of low clouds stacked up just above the horizon.

club chair:
A relatively small chair with the low back and sides enclosing the user in an upholstered "U."

club foot:
Style of "spoon" foot common on Massachusetts Queen Anne casework. It features a round carved or turned pad underneath a radiussed foot bottom.

clustered column:
A furniture component consisting of three or four columns clustered together at one corner of the construction being supported. This feature is most commonly seen in Gothic furniture of the Chippendale or Victorian eras.

Clustered column. The upper case of this Gothic Revival bookcase by an unknown New York maker is flanked by a pair of clustered columns. The piece is dated 1835–1850. The materials are mahogany and pine. *Courtesy of the Metropolitan Museum of Art*

coat or hat rack:

Federal-era invention consisting of a pole whiskered with thin upward angling spindles on which coats and hats can be hung. The poles typically stand on three—usually cabriole—legs positioned 120 degrees apart.

cock(ed) bead:

Thin strips of wood, framing a drawer front or following the curves on a scrolled apron. The forward edges of these strips are rounded, usually with a beading plane, after which the strips are mitered, then fit into a rabbet cut around the drawer front. To be used on a scroll, the strips must be plasticized in steam or boiling water after having the front edge rounded.

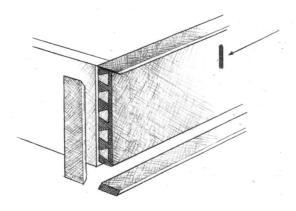

Cock bead

cock bead, scratch stock:

Pseudo cock bead produced with a scratch stock, which cuts through the use of a bit of thin, sharpened metal into which the desired profile has been cut. That strip of metal is fixed into a block of wood shaped for grasping, which the user can hold in his or her hand, scratching out the bead around a drawer front. While this

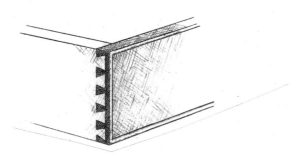

Scratch stock cock bead

tool can be made to produce credible cock-bead shapes in the direction of rising grain, it's very difficult to make it produce clean cross-grain cock bead shapes at the ends of a drawer front.

cocktail cart:

Please see "bar cart."

cocktail table:

A brother to the coffee table, a low table around which seating furniture can be arranged and on which drinks may be placed close at hand.

Cocktail table. The designer of this mid-century modern table, the Dane Finn Juhl (1912–1989), was commissioned by Baker Furniture of Grand Rapids, Michigan, to design a line of "Scandinavian" furniture, and the design of this table was part of that commission. Baker Furniture intended the Juhl line to compete with the Scandinavian furniture that had become so popular in this country in the years following World War II. The materials are walnut, cherry, maple, and tulip poplar. The table was made by the American company Baker Furniture in 1951. *Courtesy of the Yale University Art Gallery*

coconut chair:

Chair composed of a large cushioned surface in the shape of a quarter coconut, standing on a base composed of chromed steel tubes. The form is attributed to George Nelson (1908–1986).

coffee table:

Informal table designed to be placed in front of a sofa or couch. According to Wikipedia, the form can be traced to the English designer E. W. Godwin in 1868, although in the United States the form seems to have evolved alongside the television as a place to support unshod feet, bowls of popcorn, and—on a coaster, of course—the beverage of one's choice. Typically the table is low—less than 18" tall—and perhaps twice as long as it is wide. Some are equipped with a drawer or two. Others consist of a simple top and four legs screwed into the underside of the top or attached to a narrow apron.

Coffee table. This is probably not what most Americans imagine when they think "coffee table"; nevertheless, that is the function cited by the designer Lorin Jackson (1908–1987) and the manufacturer, Rohm and Haas Company of Philadelphia. *Courtesy of the Yale University Art Gallery*

coffer:

A chest, often covered in leather, for storing valuables.

coffin:

A usually wood box in which the dead can be viewed and later interred. There are two significant differences between a "coffin" and a "casket." First, a casket has two sides and two ends, while a coffin has four sides and two ends. The two extra side pieces allow the coffin to widen at the shoulders and narrow at the head and feet, in this manner conserving material. The second significant difference is cost, with the coffin typically selling for less than the casket.

collector's cabinet:

Casepiece fitted with many drawers, and doors with shelves behind, sized to accommodate the objects being collected.

Collector's cabinet. The Herter Brothers firm of cabinetmakers (active 1864–1906) designed and built this Chinese-influenced collector's cabinet as one of the many furnishings they would supply for the New York mansion of William Vanderbilt (1821–1885). The cabinet is dated 1879–1882. The material is cherry, brass, and silk. *Courtesy of the Metropolitan Museum of Art*

column:
 A pedestal supporting a top or a pillar, providing visual support for an overhanging element.

Column. This Empire chest, dated 1820–1840, has a pair of heavily decorated columns providing visual support for the overhanging top drawer. The material is mahogany, pine, tulip poplar, and butternut. The maker is unknown. *Courtesy of the Yale University Art Gallery*

Conestoga wagon toolbox. This toolbox, of tulip poplar and iron, from the first half of the nineteenth century could probably tell a story or two. *Courtesy of the Yale University Art Gallery*

comb-back Windsor:
 Please see "Windsor chair, comb back."
commode:
 A large, usually low bombé casepiece originating in France. It often has a fanciful exterior made up of veneering and marquetry and ormolu enhancements. The interior is divided into doors and drawers. The term "commode" also came to mean a chair containing a chamber pot, usually with a slip seat or a flat, hinged panel covering the opening above the chamber pot. Some of these chamber pot chairs were very respectable pieces of furniture, with a back splat composed of elaborate strapwork, as well as cabriole legs terminating in ball-and-claw feet. Most, however, were relatively plain pieces of furniture. Boxy nineteenth-century versions of the commode were called thunderboxes. Today, of course, the term "commode" identifies a toilet.
compass seat:
 Please see "balloon seat."
Composite order:
 Classical order devised in ancient Rome, which is based on a column combining Ionic and Corinthian elements. Please see "classical order."
Conestoga wagon box:
 A box designed to hang from a Conestoga wagon during the westward migration of the American people.

conference table:
 Large table at which many people can be seated for the discussion of important matters. History's most famous conference table is King Arthur's round table, which—according to legend—was round so that all of Arthur's barons could be seated equally. Today, virtually every corporation, law firm, and educational institution has one or more conference tables.
conoid lounge chair:
 George Nakashima–designed chair with a sculpted solid-wood seat and two trestled legs rising from the floor to the crest rail in one continuous straight line.
console:
 Please see "console table."
console table:
 Long, relatively narrow table used in entryways, sometimes accompanied by a looking glass above. Modern examples can be quite simple, but Empire examples are often elaborately carved and gilded.
Constitution mirror:
 Tall, framed rectangular mirror originating in that period just after the signing of the Constitution. The mirrors often feature all or

Console table. John Belter (1804–1863) of New York was the leading exponent of the Rococo Revival style during the Victorian era. As is typical of his work, this console table is exploding with vegetative carving. The table is dated 1855. The material is rosewood. *Courtesy of the Metropolitan Museum of Art*

some of the following: gilding, broken-arch pediments, fluted pilasters, a roll of balls under the cornice, and a carved bird appearing as a finial.

continuous-arm Windsor:

Please see "Windsor chair, continuous arm."

convex mirror:

Round domed mirror popular during the Federal era. These mirrors feature elaborately carved frames on which the eagle is a common motif. These are also known as "girandoles."

coopered:

Adjective describing the work of a cooper, a maker of tightly fitted wooden tubs, buckets, and barrels, the walls of which are composed of staves.

coopering:

Noun applied to the work of a cooper

copper, pewter, (and precious metals) inlay:

Marquetry or inlay work employing metals as well as wood. The use of metals in marquetry reached its zenith in the late-seventeenth- and early-eighteenth-century work of the Frenchman André Charles Boulle (1642–1732). Pewter was used as an inlay material during the Arts and Crafts era.

coquillage:

Carved shell motif.

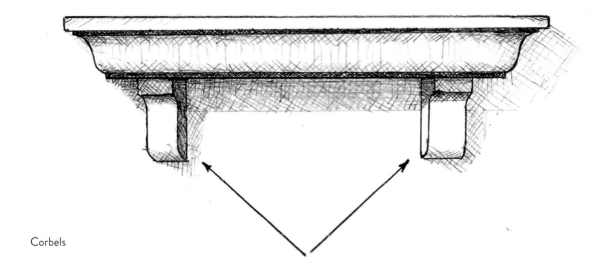

Corbels

corbel:

Originally, in architecture, a structure of wood or stone used to support overhanging weight. In the realm of furniture, corbels carry out the same task, although on a smaller scale. For example, the overhanging width of the arms on some Arts and Crafts chairs have simple corbels to provide visual and structural support for that overhanging width.

Corinthian order:

Last and most complex of the three classical Greek design orders, which is based on the proportions and decorations of the Corinthian columns of ancient Greece, specifically those columns in the Greek city-state of Corinth. Please see also "classical orders."

corner bracket:

Wood or metal bracket used to reinforce a right-angle joint, most notably in chairs or tables

Corinthian capital. This carved wooden capital is an American representation of the Corinthian form. The capital is dated 1810–1825. *Courtesy of the Yale University Art Gallery*

Previous page: Convex mirror / *girandole*. This gilded convex mirror (or *girandole*) by an unknown maker is topped by an eagle with outstretched wings standing on a plinth above a spray of vegetation. The entire cartouche and the mirror's round frame are gilded, as are the four candleholders. This mirror and one like it were made for the Albany home of Stephen Van Rensselaer IV (1786–1868). The mirror is dated 1817. The materials are gilded gesso over white pine. *Courtesy of the Metropolitan Museum of Art*

corner bridle joint:

Please see "bridle joint, corner."

corner chair:

Chair designed to sit in a corner, with one leg positioned between the legs of the occupant. In ordinary hands, this construction is less appealing than a conventional chair, but in the hands of a gifted craftsman, this form can become a beautiful object.

corner cupboard:

Display cupboard designed to fit into a corner, with its slightly projecting facade at an angle from the wall on either side. Some

Corner chair. This corner chair, or roundabout, is probably the work of Joseph Armitt (?–1747) of Philadelphia. The chair is dated 1740. The material is walnut. *Courtesy of the Metropolitan Museum of Art*

Corner cupboard. Many colonial American homes were outfitted with corner cupboards, but most would not measure up to this example from eighteenth-century Lancaster County, Pennsylvania—at least as it must have been originally. It's current very rough condition hides what I suspect was solid execution. The boldly molded cornice features a pair of ogee moldings, one wide at the top and another narrower below. The doors are enclosed in a graceful arch, which is repeated in the muntin work. The wood species is unknown, as is the maker. *Courtesy of the Metropolitan Museum of Art*

are freestanding. Others—called architectural cupboards—are built in and often feature elaborately molded cornices and fluted pilasters flanking the doors. The grandest examples have broken-arch pediments, finials, and sometimes an immense concave shell crowning the interior behind glass doors.

corner lap joint:

Please see "lap joint, corner."

corner table:

Please see "handkerchief table."

cornice:

Strictly speaking, only the molding atop the frieze, but more loosely, it identifies the entire horizontal structure atop a piece of period furniture.

cornice molding:

Horizontal molding applied at the top of a large piece of furniture, usually consisting of several individual shapes. Some makers prefer a simple but wide ogee or cove as a cornice molding. Some combine that wide, simple shape with a molding that includes a narrow clutter of shadow lines. And still others prefer a three-stage cornice molding, having a bottom section with a narrow clutter of shadow lines, then a simpler middle section made up of a wide cove or ogee, and a top section that once again presents several shadow lines.

corn shuck mattress:

Mattress composed of a fabric sack stuffed with the leaves that protect growing ears of corn

cornucopia:

Classical horn of plenty, consisting of a ram's horn from which spills the various products of the harvest. It was a frequently used motif in eighteenth- and early-nineteenth-century carving and inlay work.

counter:

Large-surfaced work table. Author John Gloag suggests that the term might originally have been a table at which a landlord collected rents; hence the name. Today it has many definitions, the most common of which is the kitchen counter on which food is prepared. Another common usage is the counter at which merchants tally up and wrap a customer's purchases. The Shakers also made counters for use in their weaving and tailoring shops.

counter chair:

Tall chair for sitting at a counter, predecessor of the bar stool.

country furniture:

Furniture made outside urban areas, usually by craftsmen less skilled and less knowledgeable than their urban counterparts.

Shaker double counter. This double counter from the New Lebanon, New York, Shaker community provides two columns of three drawers each and a large work surface. The counter is dated circa 1825. The wood is pine, applewood, and pearwood. *Courtesy of the Metropolitan Museum of Art*

cove molding:

Molding consisting of a concave quarter round, nearly always accompanied by a pair of filets: one above the concavity and the other below.

cradle:

Small bed for a baby with crosswise rockers. The name is also applied to baby beds suspended from a frame, the suspension of which allows for side-to-side rocking.

credenza:

Originally a synonym for "buffet" or "sideboard." Today the word has changed from a piece of food-service furniture to a piece of desk-height office furniture for the storage of paper and miscellaneous office supplies.

cresting:

Carved decoration enhancing crest rails.

Cradle. This delightful confection features wavelike undulations along the top of both sides, which are echoed in the movement of the rocker, as well as a wood canopy to protect the child from the sun. The materials are mahogany, rosewood, pine, and brass. The piece is dated 1815–1820. *Courtesy of the Metropolitan Museum of Art*

crest rail:

Top rail of chair back, which connects outside stiles. The crest rails on banister-back chairs of the William and Mary period typically feature vigorous carving. Simpler Windsor crest rails often terminate in carved scrolls, while the crest rails on high-style period chairs are often adorned with fussier shell and vegetative carving.

crib:

Child's bed enclosed all around, typically within rows of spindles set into upper and lower rails. On modern examples, one side can be lowered to facilitate access to the child.

cross lap joint:

Please see lap joint, cross."

crotch grain (figure):

A visual quality of woods sawn vertically from the intersection of trunk and limb. Typically, annular grain lines arc downward, often accompanied by stripes of iridescence. Although the figure can be spectacular, the same features that provide its beauty also make it difficult to dry without planar distortion and checking.

crown molding:

Please see "cornice molding."

C scroll:

Decorative motif based on the shape of the letter "C."

cubbyhole:

Shelf section set off by—usually thin—vertical panels housed in shallow dadoes. In the amphitheaters of period desks, ranks of cubbyholes often fill spaces between drawers and doors.

cube tables:

Mid-century modern form designed by Peter Hvidt (1916–1986) and Orla Molgaard-Nielsen (1907–1993). The tables are each finger-jointed "U"s, which, when correctly aligned, can form a cube.

cup (cupping):

The tendency of some boards or panels to arc across their widths. Top surfaces, being exposed to more light and heat, shrink more quickly than the comparatively sheltered bottom surfaces. This shrinkage differential results in boards or panels cupping. The effect can be restrained through the use of cleats

Crib. This crib was made late in the working life of Duncan Phyfe (1768–1854) when his company was known as Duncan Phyfe and Son, in reference to his son James. The crib is dated 1840–1847. The material is mahogany. *Courtesy of the Metropolitan Museum of Art*

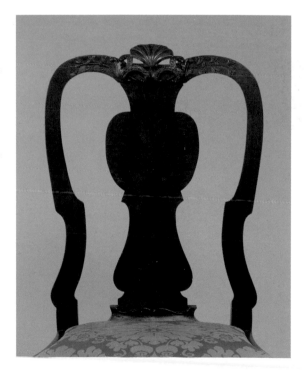

Crotch figure (grain). The back splat from this Queen Anne side chair exhibits spectacular crotch figure. *Courtesy of the Metropolitan Museum of Art*

on the underside or backside of a panel, or—in the case of a tabletop—through the use of breadboard ends. But in some situations—for instance the ⅜" thick tops of some Shaker lap desks—other means are needed as well, the best of which is selecting quarter-sawn material for the panel, then making the reduction in panel thickness in stages, over a week or more, so that stresses can manifest themselves and be corrected a bit at a time.

cup-and-trumpet turning:

Similar to the bell-and-trumpet turning, with one exception: the inverted cup lacks the small lip present on the inverted bell. Like the cup-and-bell turning, this motif is a signature of William and Mary work.

cupboard:

Utilitarian casepiece intended for storage, usually outfitted with doors, drawers, or both.

Shaker cupboard. This little pine cupboard of Shaker origin has four drawers below and a door above. The door is flanked by the extra-wide stiles common to many Shaker cupboards. The cupboard was likely made in the New Lebanon, New York, Shaker community by an unknown maker sometime in the first half of the nineteenth century. *Courtesy of the Metropolitan Museum of Art*

curio cabinet:

Cabinets used to house collectibles.

curly figure:

A visual quality of some woods—in particular maple, cherry, red oak, and ash—to exhibit a surface resembling wavelike undulations.

curved chair-back settee:

Rare form based on a drawing in Thomas Sheraton's early 1790s book *The Cabinet-Maker and Upholsterer's Drawing Book*, which features a long, upholstered, curving seat backed by six shield backs. One example now housed at Winterthur was designed to fit a particular half-round alcove at the base of a spiral staircase.

cushion rail:

Turned rail pierced by small tenons atop the back posts of some New Lebanon production chairs. The ends of this rail were intended to serve as attachment points for a back cushion on Shaker slat-back chairs, which could be, without a cushion, hard on the human back. The term is also used to denote the felt-covered cushions surrounding a billiard table.

cut nails:

Nails sheared from steel strip stock wedge-shaped in profile. Invented at the beginning of the nineteenth century, cut nails (sometimes called square nails) replaced the handmade wrought-iron nails that had preceded them. They were then, in turn, largely replaced by cheaper wire nails at the beginning of the twentieth century. Today, cut nails are sold in small numbers to those who want that square-headed look in their restoration or reproduction work. Additionally, some carpenters and cabinetmakers believe they are superior to wire nails because their blunt tips are less likely to cause splitting (they crush wood fibers instead of wedging them apart) and because their square shanks resist twisting.

cylinder-and-ball legs:

Legs on some Windsor chairs with leg bottoms consisting of a downward-tapering cylinder terminating in a ball.

cylinder desk:

Federal-era predecessor of the rolltop desk, having a partial cylinder of solid wood that can be drawn down and locked to hide the desk cubbyholes, drawers, and work surface. Unlike the rolltop, which could be cheaply mass-produced because of the simplicity of manufacturing tambour slats, the cylinder desk was much more expensive to make because of the difficulty of producing a stable quarter cylinder of solid wood. Sometimes a bookcase rises above the desk.

Phyfe cylinder desk. The cylinder desk is one of the most exacting forms to come out of the Federal era, more difficult to fabricate than its cousin, the tamboured rolltop, and the craftsmanship of that component is equaled throughout this secretary attributed to the New York shop of Duncan Phyfe (1770–1854). The attribution rests upon the fact that the spiral fluted ellipsoids above the tapered legs were found on a Duncan Phyfe–labeled work table. The piece is dated 1815–1820. The materials are mahogany, satinwood, and gilded gesso with tulip poplar and pine. *Courtesy of the Metropolitan Museum of Art*

Cylinder desk with cylinder raised

cyma curve:

A line concave on one end and convex on the other. It is the line on which the cabriole leg and ogee moldings are based.

cyma recta:

Shape of a molding cross section that is concave in its upper section and convex in its lower section.

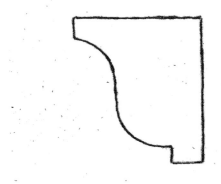

Cyma recta molding in cross section

cyma reversa:

Shape of a molding cross section that is concave in its lower section and convex in its upper section.

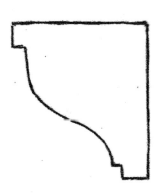

Cyma reversa molding in cross section

dado:

Trench cut across the grain, used as a housing, usually for the end of a shelf. Traditionally, these trenches were cut with a wooden dado plane having two irons: one near the front, which scribed both sides of the trench through the use of two knife points, and a second iron set at a skewed angle at the midsection of the plane. This second iron is the full width of the dado plane's sole and creates the dado by lifting chips between the scribed lines cut by the first iron. Today, dadoes are more likely to be cut with a stack of dado cutters on a table saw or with a router—not a hand-powered tool, but one of those screamers with a cord.

dado joint:

A trench cut across the grain that is intended to serve as a housing for one end of a perpendicular component. By itself, the dado has little holding power, even when the mating surfaces are glued. For that reason, the joint is often reinforced, with nails or screws being driven through the dadoed component into the end grain of the perpendicular component. An even better joint can be created by cutting one or both sides of the dado into a dovetail shape, then creating a corresponding shape on the end of the board to be attached at that location.

dado joint, stopped:

A joint in which the trench is cut short of the full width of one component, with the tongue being cut to match.

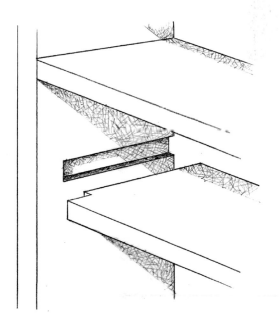

Dado joint, stopped

dado joint, through:

A dado joint in which the tongue and the groove run the full width of the dadoed component.

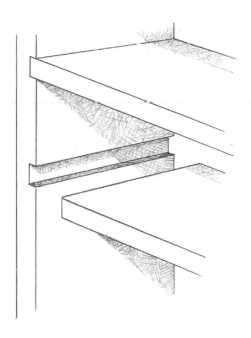

Dado joint, through

dais:

Raised platform on which elaborate beds of the Empire period and beyond were erected. The term originates in the raised platform found in medieval halls, on which the master's/knight's/king's table was situated.

Danish cord:

Three-strand craft-paper cord used to seat chairs.

davenport:

A long, upholstered piece of seating furniture that can comfortably hold three adults. Named for Albert H. Davenport (1845–1905), owner of a turn-of-the-century furniture company, the term today often functions as a synonym for sofa and couch, although many people reserve the term "davenport" for the identification of a wide piece of upholstered seating furniture that can be converted into a bed.

daybed:

Form originating in the William and Mary period, usually consisting of a long, backless bench with a chair back rising from one end. The earliest examples had a turned understructure and were seated with cane and often fitted with banister backs on one end. These were used during the day as seating furniture and at night as a bed. Queen Anne examples could be fancier, with cabriole legs and an end resembling a chair's splat back. Today, most manufactured daybeds have low backs against which pillows are placed to make comfortable pieces of seating furniture.

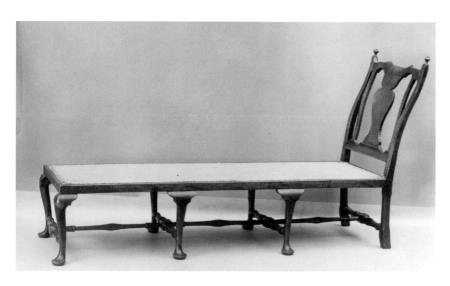

Daybed. Daybeds—like this Rhode Island example from the Queen Anne era—are early examples of lounging furniture. This piece is made of maple and is dated 1740–1790. *Courtesy of the Metropolitan Museum of Art*

deal:

British term used to denote a variety of imported softwoods used in construction and as a secondary wood in some kinds of furniture.

Delaware chair:

A post-and-rung chair that appeared in Delaware and some nearby states early in the eighteenth century and continued virtually unchanged for almost a hundred years. Typically, the front posts and front stretcher are boldly turned in the William and Mary manner. Seats are woven over four seat rungs, using rush or ash splint. The back is composed of five arching slats.

demi-arms:

Narrow or short (or both) chair arms.

demilune table:

Table originating in the Federal era, with a semicircular top. In the hands of a master craftsman such as John Seymour, this simple form achieves iconic status. In the late 1960s, a school teacher, Claire Wiegand-Beckman, bought a "demilune" card table at a garage sale for $25. Thirty years later, the table was appraised on *Antiques Roadshow* for $275,000+, then in 1998 sold for $541,500. The buyer, antique dealer Israel Sack, said at the time that the table was one of six known to have been made by the firm of John Seymour and Son.

dentil:

Small, rectangular, toothlike bit of wood used in spaced lines as molding component.

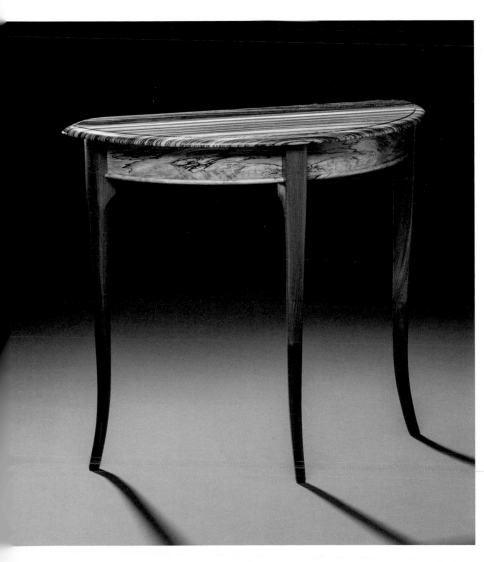

Jeff Lind demilune table. This handsome demilune table is the work of current maker Jeff Lind (b. 1946). Unlike most period makers who relied on carving and inlay work for detail, Lind relies on the dramatic figure of the zebrawood top and the spalted-birch skirt. The material is zebrawood, spalted birch, and mahogany. *Photo by Truslow.com, courtesy of Jeff Lind*

dentil molding:

Molding employing a line of dentils. This is a common detail in Chippendale casework. The moldings are expressed in many different forms, the most common being the standard-block dentil molding and the Greek-key dentil moldings.

desk:

Furniture form that provides a flat writing and work surface. Early examples were boxes with slightly sloping tops. The first true American desks appeared in the late seventeenth century. These consist of an often-dovetailed box with a drawer, and a usually slanted top standing on four turned legs connected by stretchers. Then, in the late William and Mary period, modern desks appeared with multiple drawers, drop-leaf writing surfaces, and cubbyholes to store important papers.

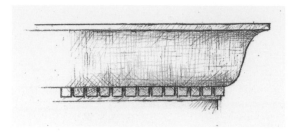

Dentil molding, Greek key

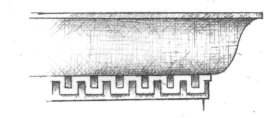

Dentil molding, standard

Art deco desk. Designed by Paul T. Frankl (1886–1958) with an assist from fabric designer Paul Rodier (1866–1958), this attractive example of the Art Deco aesthetic was made in New York circa 1927. The projecting shelves evoke the Prairie-style architecture of Frank Lloyd Wright (1867–1959), whom Frankl admired. The materials are mahogany, cedrela, zebrawood, tulip poplar, pine, ash, and aluminum. *Courtesy of the Yale University Art Gallery*

desk and bookcase:
     Term used by academics as a synonym for "secretary."
desk, Arts and Crafts:
     Compared to earlier period examples, a much-simpler form, usually executed in oak.

Shop of the Crafters desk and chair. This exceptional desk avoids the chunkiness of so much Arts and Crafts work of the era. It has a lightness and elegance that harkens back to Federal-era writing desks. The material is mahogany, cedrela, boxwood, pearwood, mansonia, sycamore, lacewood, brass, and leather. The design is dated 1905. *Courtesy of the Los Angeles County Museum of Art*

desk, Art Deco:
    Desk manifesting the bold geometries and bright colors of the Art Deco period.
desk, block and shell:
    A desk of Rhode Island origin featuring the block-and-shell facade, originating in the work of the Goddard and Townsend families of Newport, Rhode Island.

Art deco desk. Donald Deskey (1894–1989) was one of the leading exponents of the American Art Deco movement. This piece, which Deskey designed in 1929, was probably made in the shop of Schmieg, Hungate, and Kotzian, Inc., active between 1924 and 1933. The material is ebony veneer over tulip poplar, chestnut, ash, plywood, and mahogany. *Courtesy of the Yale University Art Gallery*

Chippendale-era drop-leaf block-and-shell desk. Although
John Townsend and other Newport, Rhode Island, artisans
were the originators and most-renowned makers of block-
and shell furniture, the form was simply too appealing to
escape imitation. An unknown maker, probably from Norwich,
Connecticut, made this cherry and white pine desk in the
second half of the eighteenth century. *Courtesy of the Yale
University Art Gallery*

Cherry block-front desk. Although Boston, New York, Newport, and Philadelphia are often seen as the places of origin for the greatest high-style American furniture of the eighteenth century, in places such as Colchester, Connecticut, a bit removed from urban America, there were some craftsmen producing work that rivaled any produced in America's big cities. The maker of this masterpiece, Benjamin Burnham (ca. 1729–1773), eschewed the mahogany favored in urban centers and chose, instead, the American species cherry as his primary wood, with white pine and tulip poplar as his secondary woods. The desk is inscribed as follows: "This Desk was maid in the / year 1769 Buy Benjn Burnham, / that sarved his time if Felledlfey (Philadelphia)." However, the details of the desk don't support a Philadelphia connection. Instead, the inlaid star compasses and blocked front are motifs of Massachusetts origin, and the pairing of ball-and-claw feet in front with bracket feet in back suggests New York. Burnham probably did spend some time in Philadelphia, but he probably also found opportunities to see work from other urban centers. *Courtesy of the Metropolitan Museum of Art*

Outlier desk. This mahogany desk by an unknown Connecticut maker offers an eccentric take on the tradition of block-front casework. Whereas the blocked facades of high-style Massachusetts and Rhode Island makers had the left and right thirds projecting slightly forward and the middle third receding slightly inward, this unusual piece features right and left sections of the facade that recede slightly inward and a very narrow middle section that projects forward, a reversal of accepted practice. I have to admit that this piece makes me a little uncomfortable. In particular, the blocking resolution in the top drawer front suggests, to me, that the maker had gone slightly off the rails. By comparison, the desk in the above left image with its inlaid stars and its cherry primary wood also offers an eccentric but, in its case, successful take on the tradition of blocked casework. The material of this particular desk is mahogany, pine, tulip poplar, and butternut. The piece is dated 1785–1805, which is very late for a desk of this type. *Courtesy of the Yale University Art Gallery*

desk, block front:

Form originating in Massachusetts and Rhode Island in which the outer thirds of the desk facade project outward. Moldings at the bottom follow this blocking. In the hands of master craftsmen, such as the Goddards and Townsends of Newport, Rhode Island, this form is one of the most exciting produced in the eighteenth century.

desk box:

Box in which writing materials are stored, usually with a slanted lid that serves as a writing surface.

desk chair, swivel tilt:

A rotating chair on rollers. Although modern desk chairs of this type are usually made of metal, Gustav Stickley's catalogs offered examples made of oak with leather-covered upholstery on the seat and back.

desk, Chippendale:

In basic structure, similar to William and Mary and Queen Anne desks that preceded them, with full-length drawers below and a drop leaf above, which conceals an—often—elaborate amphitheater. Some have ball-and-claw feet; others, bracket feet often given an ogee shape.

This block-front, bracket-foot desk is further proof that a period maker didn't have to live in an urban center to produce work that is ingeniously conceived and executed to the highest standards. It is a block front, like so many Massachusetts and Rhode Island desks of the time, but is a block front with a difference. Notice how the blocking extends down the full height of the bracket feet, a detail that is—if not unique—very rare. Notice also the wavelike undulations on the knee blocks of the bracket feet. Again, very rare. And on the front of the bracket feet, those wavelike undulations are given a small bead along their fretsawn profiles. This is a splendidly wrought example of high-style Chippendale work by a maker from Norwich, Connecticut: Felix Huntington (1749–1823). The materials are mahogany, zebrawood, and pine. The desk is dated 1775–1790. *Courtesy of the Art Institute of Chicago*

Boston block-front desk. This handsome block front stands on four powerful ball-and-claw feet. Unfortunately, someone tried to clean the drop leaf and thereby ruined its patina. This is not only unsightly; it also reduces the value of the piece to collectors. The materials are mahogany, cherry, and pine. The desk is dated 1755–1775. The maker is unknown. *Courtesy of the Yale University Art Gallery*

Close-up of left front foot of the desk above. *Courtesy of the Yale University Art Gallery*

desk, drop leaf:

Desk having a hinged wood panel with breadboard ends, which when lowered onto a pair of lopers reveals an amphitheater of cubbyholes and possibly some small drawers.

Desk, drop leaf, Arts and Crafts:

Simple oak desk often with a bookshelf underneath and a drop leaf above, which when lowered creates a writing surface and exposes a modest number of cubbyholes.

desk, drop leaf, eighteenth century:

Any of a variety of period desks with drop-leaf writing surfaces, usually supported on lopers. Chippendale examples are sometimes called "Governor Winthrop desks" or "Governor Bradford desks." These desks often have elaborate amphitheaters that are exposed when the drop-leaf writing surface is lowered.

desk, fall front:

A desk with a drop leaf that is fully vertical when the desk is closed.

Fall-front desk. The Herter Brothers (active 1865–1905) of New York City were among the most prolific high-end furniture designing/making firms in the second half of the nineteenth century. With its taut execution and floral inlays, this fall-front desk is typical of their work. The material is maple, mahogany, tulip poplar, rosewood, and various inlays. The piece is dated 1875–1880. *Courtesy of the Los Angeles County Museum of Art*

desk-on-frame:

A box with a usually slanted writing surface standing on a frame of turned legs connected by stretchers. Often these are equipped with a drawer in which writing materials can be stored.

Desk-on-frame. According to the Metropolitan Museum of Art, this early desk-on-frame could have been made by a Huguenot craftsman in or near New York City circa 1700. The material is sweet gum, possibly mahogany veneer, and tulip poplar. *Courtesy of the Metropolitan Museum of Art*

desk, Queen Anne:
Similar to the William and Mary but with Queen Anne appointments; for instance, short cabriole legs terminating in spoon feet.

desk, Sheraton:
Desk originating in the designs appearing in Thomas Sheraton's early 1790s book *The Cabinetmaker and Upholsterer's Drawing Book*. These desks often stand on petite turned legs.

desk, William and Mary:
The first of the truly modern desks, with full-width drawers below and a drop leaf above, which conceals an amphitheater.

Turned detail of desk-on-frame. *Courtesy of the Metropolitan Museum of Art*

Queen Anne desk. William and Mary was the first grand American style, and the Queen Anne style that followed was a worthy successor. This dainty lady stands on four abbreviated cabriole legs terminating in delicate spoon feet. By an unknown Hartford, Connecticut, maker, the desk has the following inscription on a removable prospect unit: "October 6 (?) 1787." The material is cherry and white pine. *Courtesy of the Metropolitan Museum of Art*

William and Mary desk. This combination of desk box and chest of drawers entered the Boston lexicon early in the eighteenth century, and the form became a mainstay of American furniture for the next one hundred years. This example by an unknown maker is distinguished by the bun feet and the burl veneers on the drop leaf and the drawer fronts. It is dated 1700–1730. The materials are black walnut, ash, white pine, and poplar. *Courtesy of the Metropolitan Museum of Art*

THE VALUE OF A GOOD EDUCATION

In 1770 a young man who wished to become a furniture maker might have sought an apprenticeship with a master craftsman whose work he admired. Then, after six or eight or ten months of doing the shop's scutwork, the master might have allowed the young man to study some of the books in his furniture-making library, which consisted primarily of English design books. In 1770, one of those books was likely to have been a well-thumbed copy of Thomas Chippendale's 1754 book *The Gentleman and Cabinet Maker's Director*. And there, on the pages of that particular book, the young man would have read about Chippendale's interpretations of the classical orders as they pertained to the design of furniture, and he would have seen the plates based on Chippendale's drawings of his own furniture, as well as drawings of furniture built by other London makers Chippendale admired. Eventually, after a seven-year apprenticeship, after the young man had opened his own shop, he might have encountered the design books of Thomas Sheraton (1751–1806) and George Hepplewhite (1727–1786), and if he was successful enough, he might also have traveled to Boston or New York or Philadelphia to see the work of the famed designer/craftsmen of his day. In the eighteenth century, that constituted a thorough education in the cabinetmaker's art and craft.

Now compare that to the educational opportunities available to a young person who wants to learn furniture making in twenty-first-century America. A public library of any size will have over a hundred books devoted to the field, and a university library might have thousands, including every book that a young man in colonial America could have seen. And then, of course, there's the internet, where, in a twinkling, it's possible to find images of the very best work in every furniture-making period in human history. In addition, there are woodworking schools scattered across the country, where one can spend a week or two with a master craftsman who might have flown in from great distances to teach that class. Plus, there are other woodworking schools where one can spend a year or more learning at the benches of a variety of highly skilled practitioners of the cabinetmaker's trade.

This wide-open range of educational opportunities can be a mixed blessing. On the one hand, access to virtually everything in the field can broaden one's education. That twenty-first-century student has opportunities to familiarize himself or herself with the furniture taken from Tutankhamen's tomb, with ancient Chinese furniture, and with medieval and Renaissance furniture, as well as the many styles of furniture popularized in the United States since the Pilgrim era. And on and on.

But too much choice can leave one without direction. Does he or she work in the Chippendale style, which might have been so appealing at first blush? Or how about Art Deco? And the Arts and Crafts movement has so much to recommend it. And Queen Anne.

Where there are no limits, there often is no direction.

That 1770 youth who aspired to make furniture knew he had to build in the rococo idiom if he wished to sell to the wealthy capitalists of the late eighteenth century, so he focused his efforts on creating the most imaginatively conceived and skillfully executed Chippendale furniture possible. Then, when the buying public began to lose interest in rococo ornamentation, he proceeded to work in the new Federal style, once again doing the very best he could within the limits of furniture design in the Federal era.

That eighteenth-century maker might not have had the breadth of educational opportunities available to a twenty-first-century craftsman, but he was never without direction.

dial (clock):
    Please see "clockface."
diamond splat:
    Diamond shape appearing in the strapwork splat of some high-style Chippendale chairs.
dining table:
    Large table intended for dining, with a top 26" to 30" from the floor. Dining tables are typically 30" to 36" wide, with a length that can reach 17 feet in the case of some extreme examples. Please see also "Federal accordion-action dining table."

John Townsend dining table. John Townsend (1732–1809) was arguably the greatest individual designer/craftsman in the Goddard/Townsend families of great American furniture makers. Perhaps as a result of his preeminence, he signed more furniture than any other American maker of the period. This handsome dining table with ball-and-claw feet and rule-jointed leaves was made when Townsend was only twenty-four years old. The table is fashioned from mahogany and maple. There is a signed paper label on the underside of the tabletop. *Courtesy of the Metropolitan Museum of Art*

dipper:

In the seventeenth, eighteenth, and nineteenth centuries, a wood construction for dipping fluids out of pails or buckets. Typically the dipper sides are steam-bent, with an attached bottom and wooden handle. Earlier examples are simply carved from blocks of wood.

display furniture:

Cabinets or tables designed for the display of collectibles, usually with glass doors, sides, tops or combinations thereof. These come in many configurations, the specifics determined by the kind of collectible that will be displayed.

distressed surface:

Originally the slightly torn grain often seen on sliced veneer. The term also has a more modern and more sinister meaning. Today it can mean the creation of what appears to be an aged surface on a freshly made piece of furniture. The distress is caused by rasping corners, scraping surfaces, smacking turnings with a flat board, then covering all with an artificially worn or crazed finish. Sometimes this is done simply to mimic the look of real antiques. At other times, however, it's done as an act of fraud in which antique dealers attempt to sell distressed new furniture as genuine antiques. Some of these criminals go so far as to use old boards for the construction of the piece, to spray color on interior surfaces to mimic oxidation, and to print (and) age paper labels identical to those used by an original maker.

divan:

A type of low sofa without arms or a back, usually placed against a wall.

doctor's box:

A period chest in which a doctor might have carried lancets, drills, trepanning tools, a small bellows for blowing smoke, etc.

document chest:

Small period chest often fitted with a drawer under the primary cavity. These chests were originally used to hold important documents. Many are lockable.

dolphin foot:

Foot in the shape of a head-down dolphin, most often found in Empire and Biedermeier furniture.

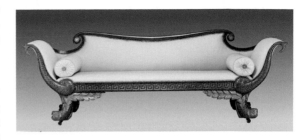

Dolphin foot. The front feet and the fronts of the two scrolled arms on this Empire sofa represent a pair sinuous head-down dolphins. The sofa is the work of an unknown maker from New York City circa 1820. *Courtesy of the Metropolitan Museum of Art*

dolphin hinge:

A drop-leaf hinge, so named because of its supposed resemblance to a dolphin profile.

dome-topped trunk:

A trunk with a top that swells upward across its width and along its length. This characteristic is usually created through the use of thin sheets of laminated wood, but it can also be created with staves. "Dome-topped trunks" is an umbrella term that includes "camel-back trunks," "hunch-back trunks," "hump-back trunks," and "barrel-topped trunks."

door:

Hinged construction made up of one or more framed wood or glass (or both) panels.

door, entrance:

Hinged construction large enough to allow people to enter a building.

Doric column (order):

The earliest of the three classical Greek orders based on early Greek architecture, specifically columns and their capitals. Of the three Greek orders (Ionic and Corinthian being the other two), the "Doric" columns featured the simplest capitals atop its columns, with capitals consisting of nothing more than a quarter bead. Please see "classical orders."

Doric column and capital. This painting by the Danish artist Constantin Hansen (1804–1880) shows a pair of Doric columns and capitals from the Temple of Neptune at Paestum, south of Naples, Italy. *Courtesy of the Metropolitan Museum of Art*

This mahogany double chest of drawers was designed by Paul McNabb (1917–1969) and manufactured by Calvin Furniture of Grand Rapids, Michigan, between 1950 and 1960. I'm no fan of manufactured mid-century modern furniture, and if anybody wonders why, they would only have to look at this particular piece. If it is, in fact, solid mahogany, it is constructed of good material, and I'll concede, without seeing the piece in the flesh, that the construction is adequate. But what else can be said about this double chest of drawers? That it offers a lot of storage space? That it's easy to dust? There is nothing about this sterile block of wood that calls out to the viewer, no detail to seduce the eye, no carving, no turning, no inlay work. There is no testimony of the maker's skill, and that, of course, is because the manufacturer had instructed the designer to dumb it down so that anybody—regardless of skill level—could carry out the steps in its construction. Okay. I feel better now. *Courtesy of Yale University Art Gallery*

double chest of drawers:
   A single long case containing two columns of drawers.
double mortise-and-tenon joint:
   Please see "mortise-and-tenon joint, double."
double tenon joint:
   Please see "mortise-and-tenon joint, double."
dovetail halving:
   A lap joint in which one component ends in a single half-thickness dovetail shape, which is fit into a single half-thickness dovetail housing in the piece to which it is to be joined.
dovetail joint:
   Joint involving the union of one or more dovetail shapes to one or more dovetail housings (the word "housing" here refers to the excavated spaces between "pins" into which the "tails" are fit). Dovetails can be used singly to join together two components (for example, joining drawer rails to a case side), but their most common application is as multiples to join the fronts and sides or backs and sides of box constructions; for instance, drawers. The greatest strength of this joint is not its mechanical resistance to separation. It is, instead, the combination of that mechanical resistance to separation and the extensive glue surface it provides. A dovetail can be used as a part of a lap joint. (Please see "dovetail halving.") A shelf-width dovetail slid into a shelf-width housing can also be used to join the sides of a bookcase or a desk. The dovetail is one of the most ancient means of joining two pieces of wood. Examples have been found on work in ancient Chinese tombs, as well as on objects accompanying 5,000-year-old Egyptian mummies.
dovetail joint, blind (full blind):
   Dovetail joint in which a narrow band of end grain conceals any sign of the dovetails. In the case of a mitered blind dovetail, even

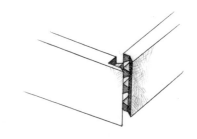

Dovetail joint, blind, mitered

that narrow band of end grain is eliminated, resulting in a completely invisible joint. This joint is sometimes used to connect the two halves of a Chippendale-style bracket foot.

dovetail joint, blind, mitered:
Dovetail joint that is mitered on the outside, then joined with blind dovetails behind that miter.

dovetail joint, half blind:
Dovetail joint in which the tails and pins are visible on one side. This is the preferred joint for attaching drawer fronts to drawer sides. In such a joint, the tails are laid out on the drawer sides, and the pins on the ends of the drawer front.

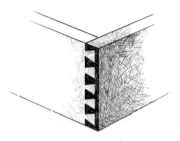

Dovetail joint, half blind

dovetail joint, sliding:
A dovetail joint in which the female half is cut across the width of one component, and the male half is cut across the end of the second component. The male half then slides into the female half to form a powerful joint.

dovetail joint, sliding, stopped:
A dovetail joint in which the female half is cut less than the full width of one component, and the male half is cut similarly short of full width.

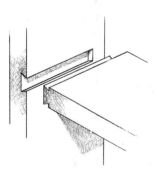

Dovetail joint, sliding, stopped

dovetail joint, sliding, through:
A sliding-dovetail joint in which the male and female components are cut all the way across the boards or panels they're joining.

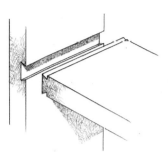

Dovetail joint, sliding, through

dovetail joint, through (and multiple):
A joint often used to connect drawer backs to sides in which the dovetails and pins both penetrate completely through the mating component.

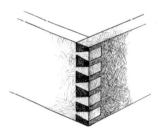

Dovetail joint, through

dovetail key:
A bow-tie-shaped component used to join two pieces of wood. Modern furniture makers employing material with live edges use these dovetail keys to bridge and solidify splits in the material. These keys are often found in the work of George Nakashima.

Dovetail key

dowel(ed) joint:

A joint in which glued dowel pins inserted into drilled holes provide the primary means of aligning and joining two wood components. Although it is possible to align the dowel holes by a combination of measurement and second-person spotting of the drill, the best dowel joints are created using a doweling jig to align the drilling of the holes into which the glued dowels will be placed. It is also important to select dowels of the proper size for a particular job. Ideally, a dowel pin would have a diameter one-third the thickness of the material into which it is to be positioned. In addition, the holes into which dowels are pressed should have at least $^1/_{16}$" of extra depth to use as a reservoir for surplus glue. Although this style of joinery was a favorite of woodworking magazines of the 1950s and '60s, today biscuits are preferred by most woodworkers relying on nontraditional joinery. Most traditionalists eschew the use of either dowels or biscuits, preferring the many variations of classical dovetail and mortise-and-tenon joinery.

dowel joint, carcass butt:

The use of dowels to reinforce a butt joint joining a case side to a case end.

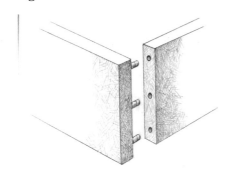

Dowel joint, carcass butt

dowel joint, edge to edge:

Edge-to-edge butt joint supplemented with dowels placed along the lengths of the two edges. Although some craftsmen labor over this joint (or with similarly used biscuits), a well executed edge-to-edge joint needs no reinforcement. A thin spread of glue on mating surfaces and eight hours in a set of clamps provides more strength than necessary, at least in the construction of furniture.

dowel joint, frame:

Joint connecting the end of one component with the edge of another to create a right angle.

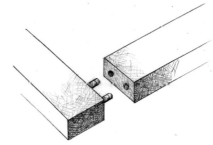

Dowel joint, frame

dowel pin:

Short, round length of dowel, beveled on both ends to facilitate insertion; used to join two pieces of wood. These pins usually feature narrow grooves along their lengths in either straight or spiraling lines to contain excess glue. Preglued pins are also available, although I've never tried them.

dowel rod:

A round length of wood without grooves. These are widely available in diameters of ⅛" to 2", typically in 36" lengths.

dower chest:

A chest in which a bride-to-be collects the linens, silver, clothes, etc. she'll need to start life as a married woman. This construction is sometimes called a glory chest, trousseau chest, or hope chest. Some eighteenth-century Pennsylvania dower chests have bold, often-quite-abstracted imagery painted on their surfaces, imagery in which hearts, tulips, and floral bouquets appear as primary motifs.

drafting table:

Table with large writing/drawing surface that can be tilted for the convenience of the draftsman.

drake foot:

Please see "triffid foot."

draped-swag shield:

Shield back on Hepplewhite chair featuring a double swag of carved drapery.

Painted dower chest. This boldly painted masterpiece of Pennsylvania German culture features unicorns and men on horseback, motifs common to dower chests made in Berks County, Pennsylvania. The chest is dated circa 1780. The woods are yellow pine and tulip poplar. *Courtesy of the Metropolitan Museum of Art*

Painted detail of dower chest, central panel. *Courtesy of the Metropolitan Museum of Art*

Painted detail of dower chest, man on horse. *Courtesy of the Metropolitan Museum of Art*

Painted detail of brass and escutcheon plate. As you can see by the ghost imprint above the brass, the current brass is a replacement. *Courtesy of the Metropolitan Museum of Art*

drapery back:

Back of neo-classical chair with a carved element that resembles a swag of drapery.

draw-bore peg (pin):

Wood peg used to create extremely tight mortise-and-tenon joints through the use of a slightly offset peg hole in the tenon, so that tenon shoulders are forced into a tight alignment against the edge of the mortised component when the peg is driven home. To create the offset peg holes, a craftsman bores a hole through the mortised component and dry-assembles the mortise-and-tenon joint. He then marks the location of the peg hole on the tenon, disassembles the joint, then relocates the peg hole in the tenon incrementally closer to the shoulder. The joint is then reassembled—often with glue—and the peg is driven into its hole.

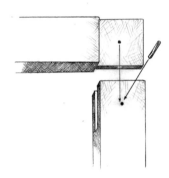

Draw-bore peg

drawer:

A boxlike enclosure with an open top designed to fit into a chest. Traditional drawers have fronts that are either flush with the chest's exterior or equipped with lips on the tops and both ends that lapped the drawer's framing elements. (Usually, drawers have no lip on the bottom because that lip could be broken off if the drawer is placed on the floor.) The inside of the drawer sides and the back of the drawer front are usually plowed with a shallow groove into which a drawer bottom might be fit after passing under the drawer back. High-style drawers are usually dovetailed together with half-blind dovetails at the front and through dovetails at the rear. Rougher, country drawers might have sides that are simply nailed to rabbeted drawer fronts.

drawer-bottom groove:

Grooves cut near the bottom edges of drawer sides so that the edges of drawer bottoms can be slid into place.

drawer guide:

In its simplest form, the sides of a case against which a moving drawer will rub, limiting its side-to-side movement. Drawer guides can also take the form of hardwood strips glued to the outside bottom of the drawer sides to establish the limits of a drawer's side-to-side movement.

drawer lip:

Small lip on top and both sides of a drawer front that provides a stopping point for a closing drawer. This lip is often given a molded shape on the outside. It is typically not found on the bottom edge of a drawer front because the weight of the drawer's contents might break that lip off when the drawer is removed and placed on a hard surface.

drawer lock:

Traditionally, keyed lock for securing a drawer and its contents, often made of brass or steel (or both). The drawer locks found on eighteenth- and nineteenth-century casework are rectangular in shape, housed in either full or partial mortises. When the key is turned, the bolt rises from the lock into a mortise in the strike plate and wood above the strike plate, locking the drawer.

drawer rail:

Wood rail that supports and separates drawer openings in a chest. It can be attached to the case sides with a single dovetail or through the use of a single or double tenon. The back edge of the drawer rail is usually grooved to accept the front edge of a dust panel or tongues at the front of drawer runners.

drawer runner:

One of two wood cleats on which a drawer moves and is supported. These cleats are typically made of secondary wood.

drawing-room chair:

Please see "cabriole chair."

drawing table:

Table with a surface that can be adjusted in height and angle. The form originated in the Federal era based on a design by Thomas Sheraton (1751–1806).

dresser:

In eighteenth-century England, a free-standing piece of kitchen cabinetry with shelves and drawers for china and utensils. In twentieth-century America, however, the term "dresser" has come to mean a bedroom chest fitted with four, six, eight, or more drawers for the purpose of storing clothing and clothing accessories. It is often equipped with a mirror rising above the top.

dressing glass:

Small mirrored unit that is placed on top of a larger casepiece in a bedroom. The dressing glass includes one or more drawers for dressing or grooming accessories, and a wood-framed mirror that rises above the dressing glass's base unit. This form dates to the Chippendale period and continued on through the Federal and Empire eras. These period examples were often exquisitely executed.

dressing mirror:

Please see "cheval glass."

Dressing glass. This Boston dressing glass features bombé front and sides and stands on four small bracket feet. It is dated 1760–1790. The material is walnut, walnut veneer, and white pine. *Courtesy of the Metropolitan Museum of Art*

Dressing table and mirror. This unusual dressing table and
mirror from an unknown maker is constructed largely of
bamboo. The other materials are oak, sycamore, and poplar.
This American construction dates to circa 1880. *Courtesy of
the Metropolitan Museum of Art*

dressing table:

Successor to the lowboy, a table with several drawers standing on four legs, often with a mirror attached. The term is also sometimes seen as a synonym for lowboy.

drop:

Please see "pendant."

drop front:

Please see "fall front."

drop handles:

Term identifying handles that drop flat against the case side when not in use.

drop leaf:

A panel with breadboard ends that conceals the interior of slant-front desks.

When the panel is dropped and supported on a pair of lopers, it becomes the desk's writing surface. The inside of this drop leaf is often covered in leather. The terms "drop leaf" or "drop leaves" can also be used to identify panels hanging from the hinged sides of a table's fixed middle section. These leaves can be raised and supported by a variety of means to increase the table's working or dining surface.

drop-leaf dining table:

Dining table with one or two drop leaves connected to the center panel of the top via hinged rule joints.

Drop-leaf dining table. This unusual variation of the drop-leaf form is made up of two demilune tables, each with a hinged rectangular leaf that can be raised and supported on a swing-out leg. It is the work of an unknown Baltimore, Maryland, maker. The table is dated circa 1800. The material is mahogany, tulip poplar, sycamore, and white pine. *Courtesy of the Metropolitan Museum of Art*

Table with leaf dropped

drop pull:
   A metal teardrop that can be used to open a drawer or door. The drop is suspended from a cotter pin passing through a small, diamond-shaped, often-engraved metal plate. This style of pull is often seen on William and Mary–style casework.

drum table:
   Round table used for writing, usually fitted with drawers.

drying rack:
   Rack composed of slender wood slats used to dry towels or clothing or to air out bedding.

dry sink:
   Small cupboard with a top enclosed on three sides by a low, often-scroll-sawn backsplash. This cabinet, which was usually found in bedrooms in the preplumbing era, was the location at which washing, shaving, and other

Drop pulls. The hanging elements on these pulls are grasped to pull the drawer open. *Courtesy of the Metropolitan Museum of Art*

morning ablutions were carried out. Typically, they were equipped with a large washbowl and a pitcher of clean water, as well as soap and other toiletries.

dust panel (dust blade, dust board):

Frame-and-panel construction placed between drawers and below the bottom drawer of a piece of casework, both to stiffen the case and to prevent dust from reaching the contents of the drawer below. The tongue-and-groove or mortise-and-tenon frame contains one or more floating wood panels that sit in grooves milled on the inside edges of the frame components. The dust-panel frames also function as runners for the drawer above and kicker strips for the drawer below.

Dutch cupboard:

Usually large cupboard with open shelves in the upper section on which plates can be displayed.

Dutchman (Dutchman key, Dutchman joint):

Please see "dovetail key."

duvet:

A quilt stuffed with down or synthetic fibers.

dwarf tall clock:

A tall clock that is between 3 and 5 feet in height.

dye:

A product used to change the color of a wood's surface. Unlike stain, which is composed of relatively large particles, dye imparts color through the use of microscopic particles, producing a more evenly colored surface. Dyes are also available in a wide variety of hues, including many that are never found in wood in its natural state.

Eames chair:

Chair consisting of a fiberglass shell that cups the user. The shell is supported by a slender tubular frame. The chair was designed by Charles (1907–1978) and Ray (1913–1988) Eames.

Dwarf tall clock. This clock is an example of a rare form: the dwarf tall clock. It is thought to be the work of Samuel Mulliken (1761–1847) of Newburyport, Massachusetts, and is dated circa 1780. The material is cherry, white pine, and brass. *Courtesy of the Metropolitan Museum of Art*

Winslow Homer painting of musicians at easels. Homer (1836–1910)—one of the most prolific and accomplished American artists of the nineteenth century—painted this 1867 scene of two musicians playing from music held on a pair of artist's easels. The material is oil on canvas. *Courtesy of the Metropolitan Museum of Art*

Eames lounge:
    Two-part lounge consisting of an uphol-stered cushion cupped in a molded plywood shell, and a second plywood shell containing upholstery, used as an ottoman. The chair was designed by Charles (1907–1978) and Ray (1913–1988) Eames.

early wood:
    The earliest formed portion of a tree's annular rings. This wood is typically less dense and lighter in color than the late wood portion of the annular ring.

easel:
    Upright frame usually angled at approx-imately 20 degrees from the perpendicular, on which an artist might place the panel on which he or she is painting or on which various displays are placed for use in presentations.

easy chair:
    In the common parlance, any upholstered chair that is large and comfortable.

ebonized wood:
    Wood, often walnut or cherry, treated with stains or dyes to give it the deep-black color of ebony.

Easy chair. This easy chair is the work of Newport, Rhode Island, maker, Caleb Gardner (?–1761) in 1758, three years before his death. The chair is made of maple. *Courtesy of the Metropolitan Museum of Art*

ebony plug:

A feature of some Greene and Greene work in which a usually square ebony plug, left proud, is used to reinforce a mortise-and-tenon joint. The proud section of the plug is shaped in a manner called "pillowing," which produces a four-faceted end on the plug.

edge-to-edge dowel joint:

Please see "dowel joint, edge to edge."

egg-and-dart molding:

Quarter-round molding often found on Renaissance and Georgian furniture, which features a vertically oriented egg shape alternating with a vertically oriented dart shape.

egg-and-tongue molding:

Please see "egg-and-dart molding."

eglomise **(églomisé) glass:**

Back-painted glass often seen, for example, on the glass panels of banjo clocks or as tablets on looking glasses.

Eglomise glass panel. The top central panel from a secretary by an unknown maker in Baltimore shows Moses carrying the Stone Tablets. *Courtesy of the Metropolitan Museum of Art*

elbow:

Vertically oriented hinged component that—when opened—supports a leaf of a Pembroke table.

embossed molding:

Molding that mimics the effect of carving by passing under a heated metal wheel of brass or steel engraved with the reverse of the molding pattern. This is the manner in which manufactured egg-and-dart molding is made today.

embroidery frame:

A wood frame on which fabric is held at a comfortable working height so that it can be embroidered.

Embroidery frame. This mahogany and cherry frame was made somewhere in America at some time in the eighteenth century. *Courtesy of the Metropolitan Museum of Art*

EMC:

Please see "equilibrium moisture content."

Empire chest:

Strictly speaking, any chest made during the Empire period fitted with Empire motifs; for example, paw feet, exotic veneers, pillars, gilding, etc. In the general parlance, it has come to mean a tall chest of drawers with the top drawer projecting forward over the other drawers, often supported by pillars or large scrolls.

Empire sideboard:

Please see "sideboard, Empire."

end table:

An occasional table usually placed at the end of a sofa.

en grisaille**:**

Descriptive of decorative furniture painting done only in shades of gray.

En grisaille. Dating from 1690–1720, this New York kas or *kast* has a surface decorated with a lively array of vegetative imagery and festoons, all painted in black and white and blue gray, using a technique known as *grisaille*. Courtesy of the Metropolitan Museum of Art

entablature:

Name given to the assembly of cornice, frieze, and architrave in architecture. The term is used in the furniture field only when discussing the elements that surmount classically inspired casework.

entertainment center:

Large (on the scale of a period breakfront) piece of living room or family room furniture, sometimes built in, which houses a television, a stereo, and gaming systems, as well as storage for DVDs and other entertainment accessories.

equilibrium moisture content:

The moisture content of wood when it stabilizes, in relationship to the moisture content of the environment in which it exists.

ergon chair:

Chair designed in 1976 by the industrial designer Bill Stumpf (1936–2006) after what is described as a ten-year study of the way people actually sit in work situations. The adjustable chair stands on a gas cylinder pedestal capable of adjusting to the user's weight, a pedestal that is itself supported on five outstretching legs terminating in heavy castors. The cushioned seat and back are molded to accept the human body. The arm rests are cushioned as well.

escritoire:

Small writing desk with an arrangement of drawers, pigeonholes, and shelves. The term is sometimes used as a synonym for "secretary."

escutcheon:

Metal or ivory used to protect a keyhole. Some escutcheons are nothing more than a lining for the keyhole, while others are metal plates with keyhole-sized openings that are tacked in place over the keyhole.

Escutcheons. These wrought-iron escutcheons were made somewhere in Pennsylvania in the middle of the eighteenth century. Because of their length—7¹⁄₁₆"—these would have been escutcheons for entrance doors, rather than furniture doors. *Courtesy of the Metropolitan Museum of Art*

étagère:

Connected shelves either hanging from the wall or freestanding (often fitted into corners), used for the display of dishes or collectibles.

Étagère. This immense étagère with the stance and surface of an immense hairy spider was produced in the shop of Alexander Roux (1813–1886) in New York. It's dated between 1850 and 1857. The material is rosewood, chestnut, poplar, and bird's-eye maple. *Courtesy of the Metropolitan Museum of Art*

eye:

The center point of a carved element; for instance, the center point of a carved volute.

facade:

The front face of a piece of casework.

fainting couch:

Upholstered couch with one end and often a back. They are reputed to have been used as massage tables for nineteenth-century women being treated for "female hysteria."

fake furniture:

In the world of real-estate staging, cardboard boxes in the shape of couches, tables, and chairs to give potential buyers a sense of how an otherwise empty house or apartment might look with furniture.

fake furniture, antique:

Furniture intended to fool potential buyers into believing it is real work from an earlier period. This is different than reproduction furniture, which is built with no intention to deceive potential buyers. Probably the most famous piece of fake antique furniture is the Brewster Chair in the collection of the Henry Ford Museum. Built in 1967–68 by master craftsman Armand LaMontagne (b. 1939), the bogus Brewster was then artificially aged through the use of a variety of manual techniques and chemical treatments, resulting in a fake that was so convincing that, after its acquisition by the Henry Ford Museum, a photo of the chair was featured on the cover of a museum publication: *American Furniture, 1620–1720*. In 1977, LaMontagne announced his deception, which was verified by an x-ray photo revealing that the mortises for the spindles had been drilled with a bit having a lead point typical of modern bits and definitely not found on the spoon bits used in the seventeenth century. The chair is now on display at the Henry Ford as an example of a fake antique.

fall board:

Please see "drop leaf."

fall front:

Please see "desk, fall front."

fan-back Windsor chair:

Please see "Windsor chair, fan back."

fancy chair:

Painted and stenciled chair popular with the American middle class in the second quarter of the nineteenth century. Lambert Hitchcock (1795–1852) of Riverton, Connecticut, is credited with igniting the craze for these painted chairs, and he did so by finding ways to offer them to the public at low prices. He streamlined the manufacture of chair parts, making many interchangeable from one design to another. Also he used semiskilled artisans to decorate the chairs, making use of brass stencils cut into the shapes of flowers, leaves, fruit, etc. Unfortunately, when he died of "brain fever" at age fifty-seven, he was nearly penniless.

fan, inlaid:

Lobed, often sand-shaded, fan often appearing as an inlaid ornament on Federal-era furniture. Sand shading is achieved by pushing a veneer fan lobe into a pan of sand heated in a pot or skillet, to darken the inlay by scorching. The amount and darkness of the shading are determined by the depth and duration of the sand scorch, as well as the temperature of the sand.

Inlaid fan. This fan sits in the middle of the pediment on a Philadelphia breakfront constructed by an unknown maker circa 1800. The material is satinwood over mahogany. *Courtesy of the Metropolitan Museum of Art*

fantasy furniture:

Any furniture employing fantastic or whimsical motifs; for example, a tabletop supported by a crouching dragon instead of conventional legs. The terms "art furniture" and "fantasy furniture" share some terrain.

fauteuil:

A seventeenth-century chair, originating in France, with exposed wood undercarriage and exposed wood arms. The back and seat are usually upholstered.

feather banding:

Please see "herringbone."

Federal accordion-action dining table:

Table standing on multiple pairs of legs terminating in casters. Because of the extra pairs of legs, this form has the ability to expand and accept extra leaves. One such table with five pairs of legs, attributed to Henry Connelly of Philadelphia, can expand to 17 feet in length. This table realized a price of $254,400 according to a Sotheby's catalog.

Federal card table:

Please see "card table, Federal."

Federal chest of drawers:

Please see "chest of drawers, Federal."

Federal secretary:

Please see "secretary, Federal."

Federal sideboard:

Please see "sideboard, Federal."

festoon:

A carved, inlaid, or painted loop, usually picturing vegetation, found on some eighteenth- and nineteenth-century furniture. The term can also be used to identify a carved, inlaid, or painted floral wreath.

Floral inlay work like this festoon is typical of Herter Brothers cabinetry. *Courtesy of the Los Angeles County Museum of Art*

fiber rush:

Twisted-paper substitute for traditional cattail rush. Although it's much easier to work with than cattail rush, it lacks the pleasing color variations found in cattail rush. In addition, it's not a natural product, such as splint or caning or hickory bark.

fiddle back:

A chair back with a fiddle- or violin-shaped splat. The term is also used—written as one word—to identify hard curly maple with tight undulations, often on the backs of violins.

field bed:

A bed with a longitudinally arched canopy with relatively short posts.

fielded panel:

In frame-and-panel construction, a panel surrounded by beveled rabbets that fit into grooves cut on the inside surfaces of frame components. Please see panel in "frame-and-panel" drawing.

figure:

A quality of longitudinal wood surfaces that presents the distinctive appearance of curls, flame quilting, blistering, striping or any other similar features.

filet:

A flat, such as a band or a ribbon, used to separate elements of a molding or a turning.

filigree:

Lacy ornamental metalwork employed in some period furniture. The word can also be applied to pierced scroll-saw work in wood.

filing cabinet:

Cabinet in which files are stored. In the era of paper files, offices dealing with high volumes of paperwork needed furniture in which paper files could be quickly and easily stored and quickly and easily accessed. A number of file cabinet variations were manufactured during the twentieth century, of which the most popular made use of what are called hanging files. These are file folders with short metal tabs on their top edges. These tabs then hang from wire racks standing inside a file drawer. This prevents the dreaded "file slouch" so common in earlier file cabinets. Early file cabinets were made of wood. Most recently manufactured cabinets are made of stamped sheet metal, although the growth in electronic storage systems is making the maintenance of voluminous paper files less necessary.

fillet:

Please see "filet."

finger joint:

A substitute for dovetails in the construction of boxes, one that can be quickly and easily cut on the table saw by using a simple-to-fashion jig. The joint is named for the interlocking fingers at the ends of two pieces to be joined at right angles. Like the dovetail joint, the finger joint provides the maker with extensive surfaces to which glue can be applied.

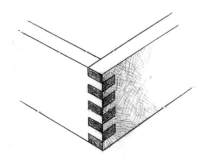

Finger joint

finial:

A turned decorative element at the end of a spindle or a turned or carved one standing at the top of a tall casepiece. In eighteenth-century casework, a finial was often a turned and carved flame, a turned urn, or an urn supporting a turned and carved flame. In the Federal period, carved—and sometimes gilded—eagles were sometimes used as finials. In the field of Shaker chairs, the term is applied to that ornament surmounting the back posts, the best known of which is the acorn finial found at the top of many of the back posts on the chairs made at the chair factory in New Lebanon, New York.

Finial on Thomas Townsend (1742–1827) chest-on-chest. The urn-and-flame finials at the top of this chest-on-chest are typical of high-style eighteenth-century work. *Courtesy of the Metropolitan Museum of Art*

finishes:

Products used to protect wood, to enhance its tactile appeal, and to heighten its inherent visual beauty. The term "finishes" includes paints, stains, and dyes as well as clear topcoats. Please see also "ammonia fuming," "dye," "ebonized wood," "French polishing," "japanning," "lacquer," "linseed oil," "paint," "pickled finish," "shellac," "stain," "tung oil," "varnish," and "wax."

fire-dogs:

Please see "andirons."

fire screen:

Period screen designed to protect a person—particularly one's face—from the harshness of an open fire. Many period examples feature a pole rising from three cabriole legs with embroidered or painted panels that could be raised or lowered on the pole to better protect the face. Others are panels large enough to wall off the entire fire. Today the term "fire screen" is taken to mean either mesh panels to prevent sparks from exiting the fire, or glass doors to reduce the amount of heat entering the home.

fittings:

Metal corners, handles, knobs, etc. applied to casework.

fitting strip:

Hardwood strip glued to the bottom outside of drawers to simplify the drawer-fitting process. Rather than fitting the entire drawer side to the sides of the case into which the drawer is housed, it's necessary only to fit the narrow hardwood strip. Sometimes, these strips are continued under the bottom edge of the drawer side to protect the softer secondary wood from wear.

five-chair-back settee:

A settee with five chair backs, an upholstered seat, and a second narrow band of upholstery designed to fit the user's lower back. The only known example of this form, which is attributed to John or Thomas Seymour (or both), is housed in the Winterthur collection.

flame carving:

Vase-like shape carved into a flame.

Fire screen. This beautifully executed fire screen originated in the Philadelphia shop of Thomas Affleck, although the carving was likely done by professional carvers possibly not in Affleck's shop. Notice the very rare hairy-paw feet. The material is mahogany. The screen is dated 1770. *Courtesy of the Metropolitan Museum of Art*

Flame finial. These flame finials appear atop a William Huston (1730–1791) tall clock. *Courtesy of the Metropolitan Museum of Art*

flame figure:

A quality of some wood species—particularly birch—to exhibit a figure resembling a flame.

Flame figure. The drawer fronts on this Ruben Swift (1780–1843) tambour desk exhibit the flame figure for which certain pieces of birch are renowned. *Courtesy of the Metropolitan Museum of Art*

flat sawn:

Please see "plain sawn."

flat-top:

Please see "steamer trunks."

flat-top highboy:

Please see "highboy, flat top."

flitch:

Section of log to be cut into a bundle of veneer sheets sawn sequentially from a log. The term is also used to identify a bundle of these sequentially cut sheets.

flocking:

Technique for achieving a velvety surface inside (for example, a jewelry box) by spraying the surface with adhesive, followed by finely ground cloth fibers.

floor lamp:

Electric-powered light with a base that stands on the floor. Typically these are 60"–72" inches tall.

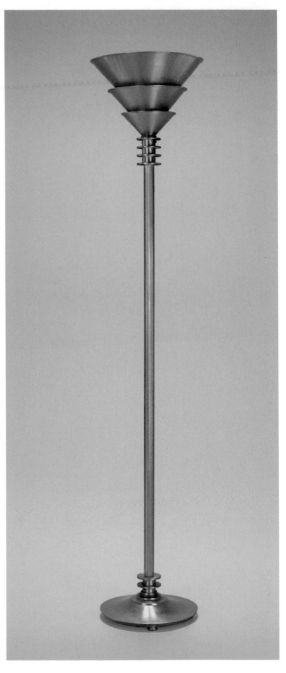

Floor lamp. This floor lamp was designed to bounce light off the ceiling in order to create dramatic effects. The designer was Walter Von Nessen (1889–1943); the manufacturer, Nessen Studio, Inc., founded in 1927, shortly before the release of this lamp into the retail market. The materials are brushed chromium over brass and iron. *Courtesy of the Yale University Art Gallery*

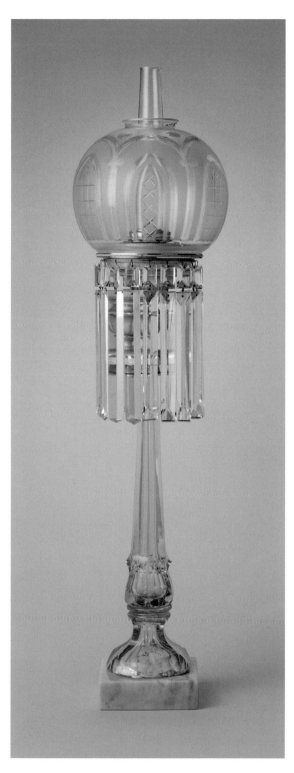

flush-mounted slide bolt:
Bolt mortised into the back of the stile of the left-hand door of a secretary or cupboard.

flush pull:
Pull typically used on travel chests that feature retractable cups or bails so that, when not in use, nothing protrudes beyond the surfaces of case.

flute:
A semicircular or semioval groove—often stopped—usually appearing in multiples, typically on columns or pilasters.

fluting:
The presence or process of making vertical flutes in a column or pilaster. Today, fluting is often done with a router fitted with a round bit and housed in a metal or wood cage traveling the length of a lathe-mounted column or pilaster. In the eighteenth century, fluting was done with carving tools.

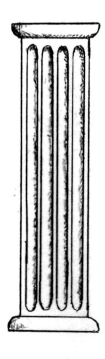

Fluting on a pilaster

Floor/banquet lamp. This lamp's height suggests it might have been used as a floor lamp to illuminate musicians at a concert or perhaps—more conventionally—on a banquet table. The Massachusetts maker is unknown. The lamp is dated 1843–1855. The material is blown, cut, and engraved glass with a marble base. *Courtesy of the Metropolitan Museum of Art*

folding furniture:

Furniture that can be folded to facilitate movement or storage. This idea can be traced to ancient Egyptians, who designed folding chairs and couches that still exist. Few high-style furniture designers since—Thomas Sheraton (1751–1806) being one exception—have worked in this genre.

Folding chair. The Telescope Folding Furniture Company of Granville, New York, was the maker of this circa 1970 folding chair. The materials are beech, canvas, plastic, and aluminum. *Courtesy of the Yale University Art Gallery*

folding screen:

Vertical privacy construction with three or four, or sometimes more, narrow panels hinged together. Typically, these screens stand between 5 and 6 feet in height, with an opened length of 4 to 6 feet.

Folding screen. Mid-century modern designers Charles (1907–1978) and Ray (1912–1988) Eames designed this all-wood screen in which each of the panels resembles a piece of heavily starched, wood-grained drapery. The panels are connected with flexible canvas webbing so that they can be moved into any configuration. The screen was manufactured by Herman Miller, Inc., of Zeeland, Michigan. The materials are fir plywood, ash veneer, and canvas. The design and manufacturing are dated 1946 through 1955. *Courtesy of Yale University Art Gallery*

foliated:

Surface ornamented with carved, inlaid, or painted leaves.

foliate scroll:

Complete or incomplete circles made up of vines and leaves.

folio stand:

A stand with a top large enough to accommodate a folio-sized book, which can range from pages 15" in height (crown folio) to 50" in height (double-elephant folio).

foot:

The terminal part of any leg, that part that rests on the floor. Please see also "ball foot," "ball-and-claw foot," "bracket foot," "Braganza foot," "bulb foot," "bun foot," "canted foot," "club foot," "dolphin foot," "French foot," "hairy-paw foot," "hooved foot," "lion's-paw foot," "Marlborough foot," "monopodium foot," "ogee bracket foot," "open-claw foot," "paw foot," "pad foot," "Portuguese foot," "scroll foot," "spade foot," "Spanish foot," "spoon foot," "tern foot," "triffid foot," and "whorl foot."

footboard:

Arrangement of panel (or turned rails) and posts at the foot of a bed.

foot locker:

A type of trunk used to hold the personal effects of a person in the military.

foot rail:

Front stretcher of a chair.

footstool:

A low stool on which a seated man or woman can rest his or her feet. Often these are simple panels of wood atop four short, turned spindles fit into a narrow apron. Fancier stools are upholstered in order to provide better comfort.

four-board bench:

One of the simplest country constructions, made up of a top, two ends, and a stretcher.

four-poster (four-post bed):

A bed with four turned or bandsawn posts rising above the mattress level. This is an umbrella term that includes, in addition to four-post beds lacking tops, all manner of tester bedsteads.

Footstool. Made of mahogany and brass, this piece has an inscription from the purchaser stating that Duncan Phyfe (1770–1854) made this for him. The legs and apron are decorated with reeding. This footstool is dated 1810–1820. *Courtesy of the Metropolitan Museum of Art*

Four-poster. This unusual four-poster has two turned and fluted posts with Marlborough feet flanking the footboard and two unturned and unfluted tapering posts flanking the headboard. This birch and pine bedstead, which dates to the late eighteenth century, is the work of an unknown maker. *Courtesy of the Yale University Art Gallery*

foxed wedge:

Please see "tenon, foxed wedge."

frame:

Structure consisting of two rails and two stiles within which pictures can be displayed and hung on walls. The term is also used to denote the basic structure of chairs and casework, as well as the rails and stiles surrounding a panel in frame-and-panel construction.

frame-and-panel construction:

Panel construction in which a usually solid-wood central panel is enclosed in a frame consisting of two rails (horizontal members) and two stiles (vertical members). The edges of the panel are reduced in thickness by sawing or planing or through the use of a shaper or router so that they might fit into grooves plowed on the inside edges of the rails and stiles, with the central panel usually floating, unattached, inside this frame. The advantage of this style of construction is that the framed panel can fill a space without developing any visible gaps caused by the inevitable cross-grain shrinkage of the central panel. This is because any shrinkage that does occur is concealed within the grooves cut into the stiles. Larger flat constructions—home doors, for example—feature intermediate rails and stiles housing smaller central panels. Combined, they can make up a panel of theoretically any size in which there will be no apparent shrinkage. A variant of the raised panel consists of a central panel enclosed within two rabbeted rails and two rabbeted stiles. The central panel is then held in place with a bolection molding, which is fastened to the faces of the rails and stile while making unglued contact with the floating central panel. Alternatively, that central panel may be held in place by simple moldings set into the rabbet along with the panel, then held in place by nailing or gluing these moldings to the rabbet wall. Central panels may be flat in external appearance or they may be raised, usually with a beveled border separated from the central section with a shallow filet.

frame dowel joint:

Please see "dowel joint, frame."

freak-figured veneers:

Veneers with exotic figures and colors. The category includes bird's-eye maple, quilted willow, and masur birch, which is a wood marked by dark streaks.

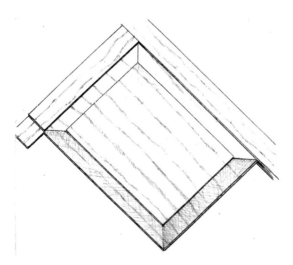

Frame-and-panel construction shown without one rail and one stile, for clarity

WHEN IS A DUNCAN PHYFE REALLY A DUNCAN PHYFE?

We know next to nothing about the shop circumstances of the seventeenth-century craftsmen who constructed the earliest work appearing in this book. We don't know whether they worked in one-man or two-man shops or maybe in shops with a half-dozen craftsmen. We don't know how many apprentices / indentured servants / slaves they might have had to assist them. It's possible, in fact, that some of the very earliest of the Pilgrim-era makers worked completely alone.

But we know something about the shop circumstances of some later furniture designer/makers, and that knowledge can color our view of the work attributed to those individuals. Take the case of early-nineteenth-century New York City master craftsman Duncan Phyfe (1768–1854).

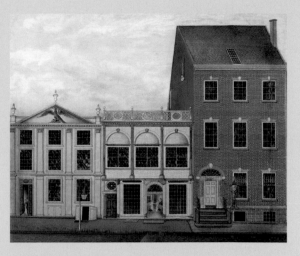

Phyfe shop and warehouse. Between 1800 and 1820, Duncan Phyfe acquired a number of properties on Fulton Street in New York City that became home to his workshops and warehouse. Some of these can be seen in this watercolor-and-ink illustration done by an unknown artist circa 1816–1817. *Photo by DeAgostini, courtesy of Getty Images*

Phyfe portrait. This illustration after a painting by Hiram J. Halle shows nineteenth-century New York City cabinetmaker Duncan Phyfe. *Courtesy of Getty Images*

There is no evidence of wealth accompanying the Fife (the name's original spelling) family when they immigrated to the United States in 1784, but by the time of Duncan Phyfe's death in 1854, his estate was valued at over $500,000, an astonishing sum for the time.

How did he achieve this wealth? It was likely due to a number of circumstances, among them his ability to sell to the rich and famous of his day. But even more, it was the result of his decision to create one of the first furniture factories on the American continent. Between 1800 and 1820, Phyfe purchased a number of Fulton Street properties to house his operation, and according to *The Encyclopedia Britannica*, at its peak that operation employed over a hundred carvers and cabinetmakers.

While there is little doubt that it was Phyfe's oversight that guided these craftsmen through the Sheraton, the Regency, the French Directoire, and finally the Empire styles, we know nothing about whose hands held the actual tools with which that work was executed. We have Phyfe's personal tool chest, a magnificent creation probably made by his own hands, but what

Phyfe sofa. This sofa, attributed to the workshop of Duncan Phyfe (1770–1854), was of a style that became a New York standard in the opening years of the nineteenth century. Like all the furniture attributed to Phyfe's shop, the piece is exquisitely made. It is dated 1805–1815. The materials are mahogany, white pine, and tulip poplar. *Courtesy of the Metropolitan Museum of Art*

about the window seat on page 335 or the sofa on page 61 or the flawlessly executed cylinder desk on pages 123–124? Did Phyfe hold the tools that fashioned any of these pieces? It's possible but not likely. And while his hands probably did hold the tools for his earliest work, it's difficult to identify those earliest pieces because of Phyfe's disinclination to sign and date his work. What we can say with certainty is this: most—the overwhelming majority of the work that left his shop—was not produced by Phyfe's own hands.

So how does this knowledge affect the way that twenty-first-century Duncan Phyfe consumers and admirers see the work that emanated from his Fulton Street factory? In the modern marketplace, there seems to be little effect. According to Christie's Auction House, a recent sale of two Phyfe card tables—possibly made by Phyfe himself but more likely by other hands in Phyfe's shop—brought over $255,000.

That's because to some observers, the name of the actual craftsman is less important than the proximity to the Phyfe shop that can be achieved by running one's fingers across a Phyfe-attributed tabletop or sighting the curving edge of a Phyfe-attributed chair leg or using the fingertips to explore the crispness of a Phyfe-attributed carving. Such intimate contact with work emanating from Phyfe's Fulton Street shop will connect the citizen of the twenty-first century with the work of an early-nineteenth-century craftsman of consummate skill. But was that craftsman Duncan Phyfe? That's impossible to know, and—at least for me—that detracts ever so slightly from the experience.

French cleat:

A two-part cleat system for hanging shelves or cupboards on a wall. One cleat—beveled along its bottom edge—is attached to a cabinet back, then mates with a second cleat beveled on its top edge, which is mounted on the wall.

French foot:

Narrow foot with outward splay found on many Federal-era casepieces.

French foot. Each of the front feet on this Michael Allison (1773–1855) chest of drawers is executed in the French manner. This New York piece is dated 1800–1810. The woods are mahogany, satinwood, ebony, pine, and tulip poplar. *Courtesy of the Metropolitan Museum of Art*

French polishing:

A method of applying a shellac finish through the use of a soft pad and repeated thin coats.

fretwork:

Open work done in a geometrical pattern, traditionally cut with a fretsaw. Today a craftsman is more likely to use an electric-powered scroll saw to produce fretwork. The term can also be applied to low-relief geometric work spread across a flat. Please see "fretwork frieze."

fretwork frieze:

A repetitive fretwork pattern, usually applied to, rather than carved out, on a flat surface underneath a chest cornice or top.

Frieze on Philadelphia highboy. On this highboy, the frieze is that geometrically patterned strip below the dentil molding. *Courtesy of the Metropolitan Museum of Art*

frieze:

Name given to the often highly decorated flat surface between the architrave and cornice of an entablature.

front ladder:

An assembly of front posts and two or more rungs that constitute the front face of a chair below the seat.

fuming:

Please see "ammonia fuming."

futon:

In Japan, a mattress and duvet. A Western-style futon, however, adds a slatted wooden frame so that the futon can be converted into a sofa when not used for sleeping.

gadrooning:

Molding including small curved elements running counter to the grain direction, which are repeated along the length of the molding. It was often used between knee blocks or ankles in work of the Chippendale period.

Gaines chair:

An early Queen Anne chair with Spanish feet and a thick, carved crest rail reminiscent of earlier banister-back chairs. It is seated with rush. The chair is named for John Gaines

Gadrooning. This 1765 New York turret-top card table features gadrooning along the bottom of the apron and around each turret. *Courtesy of the Metropolitan Museum of Art*

II (1677–1748) of Ipswich, Massachusetts, who—according to his tax records—made and sold 1,183 chairs in his working life. His son Thomas Gaines I (1712–1761) then took over his business. An older son, John Gaines III (1704–1743), moved to Portsmouth, where he became a turner and chair maker.

gallery:

Often, fretsawn edging used on top of a piece of casework. It can also consist of a number of short turned elements topped by a molded cap. It can be made of either wood or brass. The term "gallery" is also sometimes used to identify the amphitheater exposed when a desk's drop-leaf is lowered.

gaming table:

Table designed for the play of games: dice, cards, chess, etc.

Garland:

An inlaid or carved wreath, swag, or rope of vegetation.

gateleg table:

William and Mary style of dining table with at least one hinged extra leg that can be opened—gate style—to support a leaf. The finest examples feature bold turning.

gentleman's secretary:

A large Federal-era casepiece with bookcases above and large drawers below. The top center drawer on some examples has a fall front that conceals a writing surface and a variety of cubbyholes, shelves, and small drawers. On others, there is a central drop leaf that is suspended from drop-leaf hardware.

gilding:

Decorative layer of gold, usually applied to a surface in the form of gold leaf.

girandole:

Please see "convex mirror."

Gaming table. In 1876, the American painter Thomas Eakins (1844–1916) painted this scene in which two graying men confront each other over a Victorian-era gaming table set up for chess. *Courtesy of the Metropolitan Museum of Art*

Gateleg table. This gateleg masterpiece is enlivened by a multitude of boldly turned legs and an elliptically curved top. Dating to 1690–1720, this walnut table was made in Boston by an unknown maker. *Courtesy of the Metropolitan Museum of Art*

Detail of gateleg turnings. *Courtesy of the Metropolitan Museum of Art*

glazed door:
   Door having at least one panel of glass.
glazing bar:
   Please see "muntin."
glazing bar lap joint:
   Please see "lap joint, glazing bar."
glazing bead:
   Narrow quarter round used to hold glass panels in a rabbeted doorframe.
glazing points:
   Small triangular metal fastener used to hold glass panels in place before puttying. They are also used to hold pictures and mats within a frame.
glider:
   Chair—often upholstered—suspended from a wood or metal frame with wood or metal components that allow the seat to move forward and backward independent of the chair's stationary base.

globe, globe stand:

An orb, the surface of which is decorated with a geographical representation of the earth or of celestial bodies visible from the earth. The globe is supported by a stand that holds the globe at a comfortable height for viewing and allows the globe to rotate.

Globe and stand. James Wilson (1763–1855) of Albany, New York, was a maker of globes, such as this terrestrial example cradled in a handsome mahogany stand. The globe and stand are dated 1828. The contours of the American landmasses are mapped with astonishing accuracy on the surface of this globe, accuracy achieved without satellite photos and GPS technology. *Courtesy of the Metropolitan Museum of Art*

SHAKER VS. HIGH-STYLE FURNITURE

As a lifelong advocate of Shaker furniture, it's difficult for me to speak this heresy, but here it is: The very best Shaker work is in no way comparable to the very best high-style work of the same era. To most students of American furniture, this statement is so obviously true that there is no need to put it into words, but for those consumers of Shaker originals or reproductions, it might be useful to consider the idea that the magic they see in the Shaker furniture is more a product of their preconceptions than anything actually present in the work itself.

I don't mean that the very best Shaker work lacks aesthetic presence, and I don't mean it isn't—to some extent—a physical manifestation of Ann Lee's[2] teachings. But I would argue that the simplicity that is so often cited as its cardinal virtue is as much a product of incomplete woodworking educations as it is the dictums of the Shaker Millennial Laws.[3]

The men who built the Shaker furniture that became the object of so much twentieth-century admiration were not accomplished high-style makers from the World who simplified their work to conform to Shaker ideals. There were no John Townsends or Duncan Phyfes or John Henry Belters working in Shaker communities. Instead, there were country craftsmen who—in the World—had learned to make muted variations of the high-style work then being done in American urban centers. When these men came into the Shaker universe, they naturally built what they knew: those same muted variations of high-style work, and they passed on that design vocabulary to the Shaker makers who followed them.

Some were highly skilled. The consistent exactitude of the dovetails on the forty-five drawers of the immense U-shaped built-ins on the third floor of the Centre Family dwelling at Pleasant Hill, Kentucky, offers compelling testimony to the quality of some Shaker workmanship.

Some, but unfortunately, not all.

The truth is that in the Shaker woodworking universe, there is a fair amount of indifferent craftsmanship and even some poor craftsmanship. I've examined a number of Shaker casepieces

Shaker basin stand. This pine basin stand from the New Lebanon, New York, Shaker community is plain and severe in the Shaker manner. Only the tapered legs and the bandsawn and slightly radiussed end panels reflect any concern for aesthetics. It is a simple piece of utilitarian furniture, virtually indistinguishable from a washstand that might have been made in the shop of a conscientious country craftsman outside the boundaries of the New Lebanon Shaker community. The piece is dated 1810–1830. *Courtesy of the Metropolitan Museum of Art*

---

2   Ann Lee—or Mother Ann Lee as she was known within the Shaker movement—was the founder and guiding light of that movement.

3   The Millennial Laws, first published in 1821 and later modified and enlarged in 1845, laid out the rules that governed all Shakers in every community. Some of these rules made good sense—such as their fire prevention procedures—but others—such as no eating nuts after 6:00 p.m.—are, well, a little nutty.

Basin stand. By contrast, this period basin stand, which is attributed to William Hook (1777–1867) of Salem, Massachusetts, is a masterpiece of thoughtful design and consummately skillful execution. The legs are not only turned; they are also reeded and carved. In fact, every inch of this small table has been lavished with careful workmanship. The materials are mahogany and white pine. The piece is dated 1810–1815. *Courtesy of the Metropolitan Museum of Art*

in which the top is simply through-nailed into the rails underneath, with turned components sporting flat (incompletely turned) sections, and with chest bottoms simply through-nailed from the sides. Construction errors like these aren't the result of a minimalistic philosophy; they're the result of ignorance or laziness. To a certain extent, ignorance is built into the Shaker method of work allocation. A man who was a brilliant agrarian might have been put to work in the chair shop when the winter fields were frozen. A man who was a highly skilled mason might have been assigned to assemble chests of drawers if there was a need.

And it is also true that gifted Shaker craftsmen lacked the woodworking education available to high-style makers of the period. They may have been unaware of the classical orders that guided Thomas Chippendale (1718–1779) or of the design books of George Hepplewhite (1727–1786) and Thomas Sheraton (1751–1806). They likely hadn't seen the work of urban masters. They knew little of carving, veneering, marquetry, or inlay work. It wasn't until the closing decades of the Shaker movement that Shaker craftsmen such as Henry Green (1844–1931) of Alfred, Maine, began to incorporate previously forbidden decorative touches into the furniture they built, but even those touches lacked the sure-handed mastery of urban makers.

The simple truth is this: the design and execution of the very best Shaker work do not represent the same level of furniture-making accomplishment present in the very best work done in the high-style shops in American urban centers of the day.

And it's not even close.

glory chest:
Please see "dower chest."
glue block:
Please see "blocking."
golden oak furniture:
Mass-produced oak furniture made from the late nineteenth century to the early 1920s.
gold leaf:
Extremely thin sheets of hammered gold (usually 22 carat) that can be applied to flat, carved, or molded surfaces. Since the sixteenth century, bits of gold leaf have also been used in alcoholic beverages intended for the rich.

gooseneck molding:
Longitudinally cyma-curved molding attached to the top front of broken-arch pediments on large casepieces and tall clocks.
gooseneck pediment:
Pediment atop period casework featuring gooseneck moldings. These typically end in mitered returns, carved rosettes, or carved scrolls. They can also be called swan-neck pediments or broken-arch pediments.
Gothic arch:
Arch that comes to a point at its apex.

Gooseneck molding and pediment. The cyma-curved moldings on each side of the pediment of this secretary from the Salem, Massachusetts, shop of Nathaniel Gould (1734–1782) are extended all the way to the back of the case, making this a gooseneck, bonnet-top pediment. *Courtesy of the Metropolitan Museum of Art*

Gothic arch. The Gothic Revival movement brought a variety of Gothic architectural motifs to the creation of furniture. This armchair, made in the New York shop of Joseph Meeks (1771–1868) and John Meeks (?), features several Gothic motifs, including six Gothic arches, the largest of which is the back frame. The chair is dated 1850. The material is mahogany. *Courtesy of the Metropolitan Museum of Art*

Gothic bead molding:

Molding that has a Gothic-arch profile in cross section.

Gothic splat:

Splat composed of strapwork suggesting Gothic windows.

Governor Bradford (1624–1703) desk:

(Although I heard this term used by both of my parents in reference to a drop-leaf desk that my dad, Jim Pierce, had made, I was unable to find any credible origin for the term. My guess is a that "Governor Bradford desk" is essentially the same thing as the "Governor Winthrop desk" discussed in the next entry.)

Governor Winthrop (1587–1649) desk:

A name given to some drop-leaf desks manufactured during the Colonial Revival period in the first half of the twentieth century.

Gothic splat. This mahogany New York chair features a Gothic splat, with strapwork forming Gothic arches. The chair is dated 1770 to 1790. *Courtesy of the Metropolitan Museum of Art*

grain:

The growth lines running along the length of a board.

grain run-out:

Grain lines that don't run parallel to the sides of a board but instead exit on a side of the board. This can create fracture lines in load-bearing components.

grandfather's clock:

Please see "tall case clock."

grandmother's clock:

Please see "tall case clock."

Grecian couch:

Please see *"recamier."*

Grecian ogee molding:

Molding with cyma recta curve in cross section. The same molding shapes can be found under different names in different molding and molding-plane catalogs. In this book, I used those names that I believe to be most common, but if you want to resolve contradictions in molding names, I would recommend John Alexander's book *The Wooden Plane: Its History, Form, and Function.*

Grecian ogee with bead molding:

Grecian ogee with attached bead.

Grecian ogee with bevel molding:

Grecian ogee with attached bevel.

Grecian ogee with quirk-and-bead molding:

Grecian ogee with attached quirk and bead.

Grecian ovolo-and-bead molding:

Grecian ogee with bead and bevel.

 A.

 B.

 C.

 D.

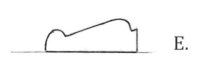 E.

A. Grecian ogee molding in cross section. *B.* Grecian ogee with bead molding in cross section. *C.* Grecian ogee with bevel molding in cross section. *D.* Grecian ogee with quirk and bead molding in cross section. *E.* Grecian ovolo with bead molding in cross section.

grisaille:

Please see "*en grisaille.*"

groove:

A channel cut into a wood surface in the direction of the grain, as opposed to a dado, which is channel-cut across the grain.

gueridon **table:**

Originating in France, a small—often round—table.

Gueridon table. This mirrored Art Deco *gueridon* table by an unknown New York maker dates to circa 1930. *Photo by DeAgostini, courtesy of Getty Images*

Hadley chest:

Frame-and-panel chests originating in western Massachusetts in the very late seventeenth century. They are noteworthy because of their decoration, which consists of abstracted tulips and leaves organized across their surfaces in low relief against stippled backgrounds. Some, such as the celebrated KC chest from Springfield, Massachusetts, also feature ebonized split turnings in the bold William and

Mary style. Author Wallace Nutting, one of the first to attempt to catalog colonial American furniture, had little use for the form, assessing the carving as follows: "There is a considerable difference in the merit of the carving, but it is all poor." More-recent furniture historians have been much kinder to the form, seeing great decorative value in the flat-carved surfaces.

hairy-paw foot:

A type of furniture foot resembling an animal's hairy paw. This form originated in England, then traveled to the United States. A number of pieces with hairy-paw feet were made in Philadelphia. In 1987, one such piece—a wing chair frame without upholstery—was sold for $2.75 million, then a

Hadley chest. The maker of this oak and yellow pine chest from the Connecticut River valley is unknown, one of many now-unknown makers working in that area who had been trained in this style of decorative carving. The chest likely served originally as a dower chest in which the bride-to-be stored the linens, clothes, flatware, etc. she would need in her life as a married woman. The tulip motif had long symbolized perfect love. The chest is dated to the late seventeenth century. *Courtesy of the Yale University Art Gallery*

record for American furniture. When asked why he didn't bid on the hairy-pawed wing chair, Harold Sack (1911–2000), the noted antique dealer, expressed doubt about the intrinsic value of the piece when he asked: "Would it have brought this price if it were not connected with the Cadwaladers?"[4] However, Richard Deitrich, a Philadelphia collector who owns a piece of hairy-paw furniture, said of the chair: "It is the highest expression of Chippendale in the colonies in the high style. I don't think the Cadwalader name added tremendously to the price."

---

4   The John Cadwalader (1742–1786) family of colonial America commissioned a large number of furniture pieces from the greatest Philadelphia makers of his day, including Thomas Affleck (1745–1795) and Benjamin Randolph (1721–1790).

half-blind dovetail joint:
   Please see "dovetail joint, half blind."
half-blind tongue-and-rabbet joint:
   Please see "rabbet joint, half blind."
half-canopy tester frame:
   A wooden or cloth-covered frame supporting a half canopy over the head of the bed, rather than a full canopy over the entire bed.
half-lap joint:
   Please see "lap joint."
half-tester bedstead:
   A bed with a short canopy covering only the head.
hall chair:
   A narrow, shallow (front to back), high-backed chair meant to be placed in a hall.
hall seat:
   A Victorian form that continued to exist throughout the Arts and Crafts era. It consisted

Herter Brothers half-tester bedstead. The Herter Brothers firm (1864–1906) designed interiors and furnishings for the rich and powerful in the late nineteenth century. Their clients included the Vanderbilts and President Ulysses S. Grant. This circa 1880 half-tester bedstead is typical of their work. The material is cherry. *Courtesy of the Metropolitan Museum of Art*

of a combination of a small bench, often a mirror, and hooks for hanging coats.

hall tree:

A stand on which hats and coats are stored.

halving:

Please see "half-lap joint."

handkerchief table:

A drop-leaf corner table with a triangular top and a triangular leaf resembling a man's folded pocket handkerchief. When the leaf is raised, the two triangles form a square. The form originated in the Queen Anne period.

Hans Wegner's "the Chair":

A sleek, sculpted wood frame chair seated with woven Danish cord. The chair won a measure of notoriety when it appeared in the Kennedy-Nixon debates.

hardwood:

Wood sawn from broadleaf trees. Native hardwoods commonly used in American furniture making include walnut, cherry, various maples, tulip poplar, beech, ash, hickory, and oak. Typically, this material is stronger and denser than softwoods, although this is not always true.

harp back:

A distinctive back for some Empire side chairs having a harp with strings integrated into the back. The best-known examples are those attributed to the shop of Duncan Phyfe.

Handkerchief table. This handkerchief table by an unknown Massachusetts maker is dated 1740–1760. The materials are mahogany, white pine, maple, and cherry. *Courtesy of the Yale University Art Gallery*

hasp and staple:

Two-piece hardware construction that allows a chest or door to be secured with a padlock.

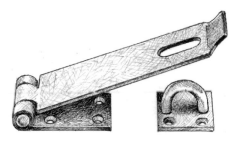

Hasp and staple

hassock:

Footstool with upholstery.

hat rack:

Nineteenth-century form ranging in complexity from a board attached to the wall with pegs on which hats can be hung to an elaborate construction of bench, rack, and mirror.

Horn hat rack. Attributed to Wenzel Friedrich (1827–1902), the best-known and most collected maker of horn furniture, this late-nineteenth-century hat rack is made of horn, velvet, and mirror glass. *Courtesy of the Yale University Art Gallery*

hat trunk (ladies' trunk):

Half-size trunk just large enough to hold a half-dozen stacked hats or bonnets.

haunch:

A short extension of a tenon that fits into a shallow mortise cut in the edge of the mortised component. This addition to the mortise-and-tenon joint prevents any twisting of either the mortised or tenoned component.

haunched mortise-and-tenon joint:

Please see "mortise-and-tenon joint, haunched."

headboard:

Arrangement of panel (or turned rails) and posts at the head of a bed.

heartwood:

The more mature and usually darker wood between the pith and the sapwood. In some species—such as walnut and cherry—the color contrast between heartwood and the sapwood around it can be significant. In others, such as some maples, this contrast is more subdued. Traditional cabinetmakers prefer to use only heartwood, although some makers employ the difference between heart and sapwood to provide a more dramatic surface for their furniture.

Hepplewhite desk:

Please see "desk, Hepplewhite."

Hepplewhite pull:

Oval-shaped, stamped-metal plate to which is fastened a bail with a shape that mirrors the bottom half of the plate to which it is attached.

Hepplewhite sideboard:

Please see "sideboard, Hepplewhite."

herringbone:

A style of banding in which a pair of inlaid strips present grain aligned 90 degrees apart, each set 45 degrees from the edge of the banding. This is also known as "feather banding."

hickory:

Wood of the genus *Carya*, with limited usefulness to cabinetmakers and chair makers. It's strong, resilient, and dense, but to many eyes the bland cream color disrupted by frequent heavy, dark streaks is unappealing. However, it is tough and it can be bent, so some Windsor chair makers have used and continue to use hickory.

hickory bark seat:

Strips cut from the inner bark of a young hickory tree used to seat traditionally made country chairs. Although it is both difficult and time consuming to prepare, it is the most durable of seat-weaving materials. The process begins by selecting and cutting down a 6"–12" diameter hickory tree in the spring when the sap is running. The log is bucked to length, then positioned at a convenient height for working. The hard outer bark is removed with a drawknife. The inner bark, the layer between the cambium and the outer bark (often called the bast), is then cut into strips between ½" and 1" in width. The strips are pulled from the cambium, sometimes split in thickness, and stored in coils until they are needed. The coils are then softened in water before weaving.

high-backed Windsor chair:

Please see "Windsor chair, high backed."

highboy:

Form originating in the William and Mary period that consists of an upper case of drawers positioned over a lower case of drawers.

highboy, bonnet top:

Highboy with bonnet top. Please see also "bonnet-top" discussion.

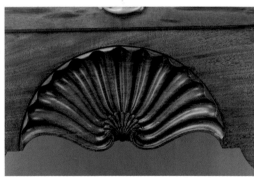

Bonnet-top highboy. This Newport highboy from 1760–1790 features a bonnet top constructed of thin panels of wood running from the front to the back following the contours of the broken-arch pediment. The maker is unknown. The materials are mahogany and chestnut. *Courtesy of the Metropolitan Museum of Art*

Detail of carved shell. *Courtesy of the Metropolitan Museum of Art*

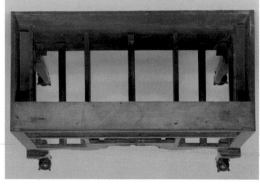

Interior of lower case. *Courtesy of the Metropolitan Museum of Art*

highboy, Chippendale:

The apogee of the highboy in the last of the furniture periods to feature the form. In the hands of truly great Chippendale-era craftsmen, the highboy became one of the most powerful and enduring forms in the history of American cabinetmaking, offering a tall and stately canvas on which cabinetmakers and carvers could best display their artistry.

Philadelphia highboy. Philadelphia highboys of the Chippendale era are renowned for their rococo ornamentation, but the carving on this particular example seems excessive—at least to my eyes. The cabriole legs, the apron, the skirt, the quarter columns, and the tympanum are covered with a blizzard of vegetative carving, much of it on the massive pediment. And that immense, looming cartouche—well, that's just too much. The materials are mahogany, tulip poplar, and yellow pine. *Courtesy of the Metropolitan Museum of Art*

Philadelphia highboy. This masterpiece of Philadelphia design and craftsmanship by an unknown maker dates to 1762–1765. The scroll pediment, the bust, and the cornice moldings originated in the 1762 edition of Thomas Chippendale's (1718–1779) *The Gentleman and Cabinet-Maker's Director*. When compared to the previous highboy, I think it's easy to appreciate the measured restraint used in applying the rococo ornamentation to this particular piece. The primary wood is mahogany, with tulip poplar, white pine, and white cedar used as secondary woods. *Courtesy of the Metropolitan Museum of Art*

Drawer detail of Philadelphia highboy. This is the middle bottom drawer front of the highboy above. According to the Metropolitan Museum of Art, the serpent-and-swan imagery on this drawer front is taken from a design by a London designer/carver Thomas Johnson (1714–1778). *Courtesy of the Metropolitan Museum of Art*

Eliphalet Chapin highboy. Eliphalet Chapin (1741–1807) was one of the most important American furniture makers in the second half of the eighteenth century. At age twenty-six, Chapin moved from his home of East Windsor, Connecticut, to Philadelphia, where he worked for and learned from the Philadelphia makers of the day. Then at age thirty, he returned to East Windsor and established a shop that quickly became known for the design and execution of high-style work in the Philadelphia manner, but with a difference: Chapin favored a cleaner, more subdued style of surface ornamentation. The cabriole legs on this highboy, for example, are powerful and masculine in the Philadelphia manner, but there is considerably less carving spread across the surfaces of this piece. Also, Chapin chose a native wood, cherry, rather than the inevitable mahogany of Philadelphia work of the period. The piece is dated 1780–1790. *Courtesy of the Yale University Art Gallery*

highboy, flat top:
  Highboy with a flat top supported by a
(usually) wide cornice molding.

Flat-top highboy. Christopher Townsend (1701–1773), one
of the famed Newport, Rhode Island, Townsends, made this
flat-top Queen Anne highboy from mahogany, chestnut, and
white pine. Inscribed on the bottom board of the upper case
is this: "Christ Townsend Made 1748." *Courtesy of the
Metropolitan Museum of Art*

highboy, Queen Anne:

Highboy with a lower case, standing on four cabriole legs terminating in spoon or slipper feet (a few Queen Anne highboys stood on ball-and-claw feet). The drawer configuration is similar to that of the William and Mary highboy with one exception: a narrow (top to bottom) full-width fourth drawer is added to the lower case above the other three drawers. Early examples are usually flat-tops, but in the middle of the eighteenth century, bonnet-tops became quite common.

Japanned Queen Anne highboy. This is a masterpiece of Boston japanned furniture of the Queen Anne era, with its graceful pediment, its gilded shells, and its overall stately bearing. This maple, birch, and white pine chest by an unknown maker is dated 1730–1760. *Courtesy of the Metropolitan Museum of Art*

highboy, William and Mary:

Highboy with a lower case rising on six turned legs connected by flat stretchers. The upper case typically features three full-width drawers topped by a pair of half-width drawers. The lower case usually has three drawers, with the center being much narrower (top to bottom) than the two outside drawers to accommodate the profile of the scroll-sawn apron.

Japanned William and Mary highboy. Japanned furniture made its American debut in Boston early in the eighteenth century. Even without its lively japanned surfaces, this William and Mary highboy would be a handsome piece with its six boldly turned legs, connected by energetic stretchers and projecting cornice and waist moldings. The material is maple, birch, and white pine. *Courtesy of the Metropolitan Museum of Art*

high chair, modern:

Manufactured high chair made of wood or plastic or metal (or combinations of these), used to seat small children at mealtime.

high chair, period or Shaker:

High chair designed to seat small children at the dining table. Period examples typically have four turned posts canting inward as they rise from a wide, stable base.

high chest:

A generic term sometimes applied to any tall chest of drawers.

high chest of drawers:

A single chest standing 60"–70" with a stack of six, seven, or eight drawers. The top drawer is often broken into two or three narrower drawers. This term is also used as a synonym for "highboy," particularly by academics.

Period high chair. This period high chair was made somewhere on the Eastern Seaboard by an unknown maker circa 1700. Notice the handsome finials and the splayed and raked legs, which give this top-heavy (in use) construction its essential stability. The wood is maple and hickory; the seat, rush. *Courtesy of the Metropolitan Museum of Art*

high-style furniture:

Au courant period work done in urban areas. During, for example, the Federal era, furniture makers in urban centers were executing designs based on the recently published books of Thomas Sheraton (1751–1806) and George Hepplewhite (1727–1786), while, at the same time, makers in rural areas were often still working within the Queen Anne or Chippendale styles.

hinge:

Two-leaved construction usually made of metal for the controlled opening and closing of cabinet doors and chest lids.

Hitchcock chair:

"Fancy" chair designed and manufactured under the direction of Lambert Hitchcock (1795–1852) in Riverton, Connecticut, later named Hitchcocksville, Connecticut. These chairs featured mass-produced parts and stenciled decoration. Please see "fancy chairs."

Painted Hitchcock side chair. The name "Hitchcock chair" still resonates today with antique fanciers despite the fact that they were mass-produced and marketed to the American middle class. This example is dated 1825–1828. The wood is an unknown species. *Courtesy of the Metropolitan Museum of Art*

hock leg:

Cabriole leg with an abrupt C curve below the knee.

hood:

That section of a tall clock that houses the movement.

hoof foot:

Hoofed animal foot shape at the terminus of a furniture leg. It first appeared in the late seventeenth century and continued to make occasional appearances throughout the William and Mary and Queen Anne periods and on into the late nineteenth century.

hoop-back Windsor bench (settee):

Please see "Windsor settee, hoop back."

hope chest:

Please see "dower chest."

horn furniture:

Furniture style that evolved in the nineteenth century employing animal horns as structural components. The leading exponent of American horn furniture was imported Texan Wenzel Friedrich (1827–1902), a cabinetmaker trained in Bohemia, who in 1880 decided to make furniture with animal horns. The list of customers for his horn furniture included both Queen Victoria and Otto von Bismarck. Today, Wenzel's work can be found in museums throughout the United States.

horsehair:

Material often used to stuff slip seats in the eighteenth and nineteenth centuries and later to stuff upholstered furniture.

horseshoe hunt table:

Period form rarely seen in America, with a horseshoe-shaped top supported by four or more legs. These tables were used to serve drinks, often outdoors, during a hunt.

Hood. The hood of this John Townsend (1732–1809) clock houses a movement by the British clockmaker William Tomlinson (1699?–1750?). *Courtesy of the Metropolitan Museum of Art*

Upholstered horn chair. This Texas horn chair by an unknown maker in the 1870s looks comfortable despite the material from which it's framed, not because of it. And this was the dilemma faced by nineteenth-century makers of horn furniture. In order to produce furniture that was both comfortable and pleasing to the eye, it was often necessary to hide the unyielding shape of the eponymous framing elements. The materials are horn, silk, and brass. *Courtesy of the Art Institute of Chicago*

Hudson River valley side chair:

A country chair consisting of turned cabriole legs on the front and straight turned legs on the back, which rise above the seat to frame a back splat. The front stretcher typically includes bold William and Mary–style turnings. The seat is woven from rush.

humpback trunk:

Please see "dome-top trunk."

hunchback trunk:

Please see "dome-top trunk."

huntboard:

Taller, narrower, and plainer relative of the sideboard. The name is derived from its earliest function; that is, as a serving table for hunters who might have muddy boots and, therefore, can't be served in the dining room.

hutch:

A storage or display cabinet standing on legs, with open shelves above a base fitted with doors or drawers (or both).

incurvate arm:

Chair arm on some Queen Anne and Chippendale chairs, with dramatic inward curve.

inlaid fan:

Please see "fan, inlaid."

inlay:

The placement of contrasting/exotic woods into routed-out areas on primary surface. For example, narrow stringing is often inlaid in Federal furniture, as well as bandings, sand-shaded shells, and bellflower decorations. (For information about sand shading, please see "fan, inlaid.")

inlay bandings:

Please see "banding."

inlay stringing:

Very narrow strips of contrasting wood, often holly, inlaid into darker primary wood.

Ionic column (order):

One of the three classical Greek design orders (the others being the Doric and the Corinthian). The Ionic column was surmounted by a capital consisting of a pair of volutes on either end of a series of egg-and-dart carvings. Please see also "classical orders."

intaglio:

Style of carving in which the design is incised into the surface, as opposed to designs carved in relief.

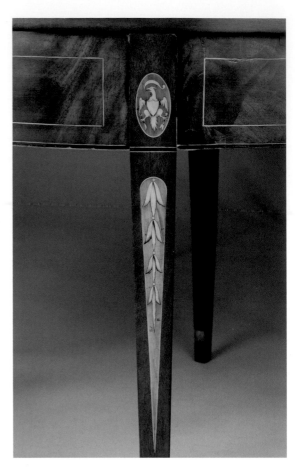

Inlay work. The leg of this Federal-era dining table is embellished with inlay work showing an eagle in a medallion above a row of descending bellflowers. *Courtesy of the Metropolitan Museum of Art*

Ionic capital. While the entire 58-foot height of the column can't be seen here, the capital of this column from the Temple of Artemis at Sardis is fully present. The material is marble. *Courtesy of the Metropolitan Museum of Art*

Japanned surface. This section of a Boston Queen Anne highboy reveals a three-hundred-year-old japanned surface. Please note the oriental fauna and oriental architectural details. *Courtesy of the Metropolitan Museum of Art*

Intaglio carving. The knees of this John Goddard (1724–1785) card table feature intaglio carving. This Newport, Rhode Island, table dates to the second half of Goddard's life. The material is mahogany. *Courtesy of the Metropolitan Museum of Art*

intarsia:

Style of ornamentation in which the design is created by cutting out pieces of wood, ivory, and metal, then sometimes shaping and coloring them, and finally inserting them into routed cavities in the primary wood. The practice began in Italy in the thirteenth century, and it continues today in the shops of some American makers.

japanning:

A multilayered finish with a base coat of black over which a panoply of oriental images was executed in paint and gilding. The purpose of these finishes was to imitate oriental lacquerwork in an era when all things oriental had captured the minds of the buying public. Although

the practice existed in New York, Boston was the epicenter of eighteenth-century japanning in America. According to Dean A. Fales Jr., the author of "Boston Japanned Furniture,"[5] at the time of the Revolutionary War, Boston was home to more than a dozen japanners.

Jenny Lind trunks:

Trunk with hourglass shape when seen from the side, named for the nineteenth-century Swedish singer Jenny Lind.

joinery:

The process of creating mechanical or glue-reinforced means of joining one piece of wood to another. In classical furniture making, the options included—but were not limited to—butt joints, dovetail joints, and mortise-and-tenon joints.

kas (*kast*):

Large storage chest of Dutch origin, standing on bun feet, with two frame-and-panel doors and several drawers, some of which are inside the doors and some of which are below the doors. This form is noted for its often-massive size, its heavy and elaborate cornice, and its distinctive bun feet.

---

5 This essay appears in the book *Boston Furniture of the Eighteenth Century*, edited by Walter Muir Whitehall.

Kas/*kast*. This magnificent kas (or *kast*) sports the enormous cornice molding and the bold frame-and-panel front and sides for which these pieces of Dutch origin are known. It was made by an unknown maker in Ulster County, New York, and is dated 1740–1770. The materials are cherry and white pine. *Courtesy of the Metropolitan Museum of Art*

kettle:

Please see "bombé."

kettle stand:

A small table designed to hold a teapot. Often the tops of these tables are surrounded by a low fretwork gallery.

key:

Please see "keying."

keying:

The use of small wood keys to strengthen a miter joint. Some keys are in the shape of dovetails; others, in the form of splines glued into saw kerfs cut into the joint.

kicker strip (kicker):

Strip of wood secured on the inside of a cabinet's walls to keep the front ends of drawers from dropping when they are pulled forward.

kidney shaped:

Shape modeled on the human kidney, which was a common profile for mid-century modern coffee table tops.

kiln-dried material:

Material that has been prepared for use by stacking and stickering in a kiln (a heated enclosure) under conditions of controlled heat and humidity, which can produce lower moisture contents than traditional air drying. This material is reputed to be more dimensionally stable than air-dried material. Please see also "air-dried material."

kitchen table:

Informal twentieth-century table existing in many different configurations used for dining in the kitchen.

Kettle stand. In New York City during the opening decades of the nineteenth century, there were an estimated three hundred cabinetmakers at work, many of whom were highly skilled, but the shops of Duncan Phyfe (1770–1854), Michael Allison (1773–1855), and Charles Honoré Lannuier (1779–1819) were the best of the lot. As a result, whenever an extremely well-executed New York piece from that era is described, it will likely be attributed to the shop of one of these men, particularly if that association is bolstered by stylistic similarities to pieces known to have originated in that shop. This particular example is attributed to the shop of Duncan Phyfe. The materials are mahogany, tulip poplar, pine, and marble. The stand is dated 1810–1820. *Courtesy of the Metropolitan Museum of Art*

Kitchen table. Raymond E. Patten (1897–1948) designed this kitchen table in the late 1930s. It was manufactured by Mutschler Brothers in Nappanee, Indiana. The material is Monel metal, sheet metal, chrome tubing, tulip poplar, and cardboard. *Courtesy of the Yale University Art Gallery*

klismos chair:

A chair with saber legs on the front and back. This form, which dates to ancient Greece, became quite popular in nineteenth-century America.

Klismos chair. This chair was part of a drawing-room suite designed by Henry Latrobe for a Philadelphia merchant in 1808. The materials are tulip poplar, oak, white pine, and gesso. *Courtesy of the Metropolitan Museum of Art*

knee:

The outwardly projecting portion of a cabriole leg. Typically the knee was extended on the inside through the use of small knee blocks, which were glued in place, then carved to conform to the knee section of the cabriole leg.

knee block:

Shaped block glued either to the side of the cabriole leg knee or to the apron or to both, which extends and completes the downward arc on the inside of the knee. Knee blocks appeared on both sides of the front cabriole legs and—usually—only on the sides of the back cabriole legs.

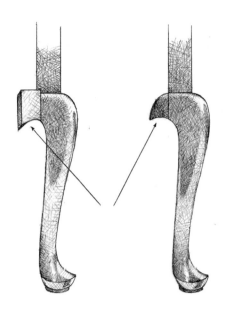

Knee block on cabriole leg, uncarved on left, carved on right

kneehole:

Signature feature of Chippendale kneehole desks or bureaus. Although some examples had kneeholes wide enough for two human legs, many specimens had kneeholes large enough for only one knee, which required the user to sit sidesaddle to work at the desk. The best-known kneehole bureaus are the magnificent block-and-shell bureaus made by the Goddard and Townsend families in the mid- to late eighteenth century.

kneehole bureau:

Small writing desk with two flights of small drawers flanking a kneehole, usually with a locked door at the back. Some kneeholes are wide enough for two knees, but most are wide enough for only one, necessitating a sideways writing posture with one knee in and one knee out. The finest examples were the forty or so known specimens of the Goddard/Townsend block-and-shell kneehole bureaus.

Kneehole bureau with prospect door. The narrow door at the back of the kneehole of this walnut kneehole bureau is called a prospect door. According to the Metropolitan Museum of Art, this bureau was probably made in the second half of the eighteenth century by an unknown Massachusetts maker. *Courtesy of the Metropolitan Museum of Art*

kneehole desk:

Any desk with an area between columns of drawers for the user's knee or knees.

knee return:

Please see "knee block."

knife box (urn):

A companion piece to the Federal sideboard, often veneered to match. Knife boxes typically stand on the sideboard, with their lids closed. When the lid is raised, an array of knife handles are exposed, with the blades sunk into custom-fit cavities in a block of wood.

Knife box (urn). This handsome knife chest (urn) offers an imaginative take on a form that is most often a lidded box. According to the Metropolitan Museum of Art, stylistic details tie the piece to Baltimore. The box is dated circa 1820. The material is mahogany, mahogany veneer, tulip poplar, and white pine. *Courtesy of the Metropolitan Museum of Art*

knob:

A device that provides for the easy opening of doors and drawers. In contrast to pulls, knobs have no bail, relying instead on a protrusion that fingers can grasp. Knobs can be fabricated from many materials: wood, glass, metal, ceramic, etc. In the seventeenth and eighteenth centuries, high-style furniture sometimes employed small brass knobs for small drawers and doors within the amphitheater of a desk or secretary. Wood knobs typify most Shaker work, while some high-style work in the nineteenth century featured metal or glass knobs.

knockdown furniture:

Furniture that can be broken down for ease of storage or transport. Disassembly is accomplished either through the use of joinery designed for this purpose, such as the tusked through-mortise-and-tenon joint, or through the use of hardware designed for quick disassembly.

knuckle:

That portion of a hinge leaf through which the hinge pin passes.

knuckle joint:

Wood hinge joint made by cutting rounded interlocking fingers at the mating ends of two boards, which are joined by a metal pin or wooden dowel inserted into holes drilled vertically through the fingers. This joint is used to connect the leaf support (swing leg) to the table apron on a drop-leaf table.

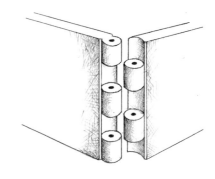

Knuckle joint

kylix:

A shallow bowl with two handles. An abstracted version of this form sometimes appears in the splats of Federal-era chairs, particularly those of Rhode Island origin.

labels:

The most important tool for verifying the creator and the antiquity of antique furniture. Beginning in the eighteenth century, some makers began writing their names on hidden surfaces such as drawer bottoms or backs. Eventually these scrawled marks were replaced by printed paper labels on the work of some makers, such as John Townsend (1733–1809) of Newport and—to a lesser extent—John Seymour (1738–1818) of Boston.

Label. This paper label appears on the underside of a Pembroke table made in 1795 by the Newport, Rhode Island, master John Townsend (1732–1809). *Courtesy of the Metropolitan Museum of Art*

lacquer:

Originally a finishing material made from the sap of a tree: *Toxicodendron vernicifluum* (Chinese lacquer tree). Now, however, most lacquers are synthetics. Many of these are water resistant, and many are capable of producing surfaces ranging from matte to high gloss.

ladder-back chair:

A chair so named because the arrangement of back posts and perpendicular slats and rungs resembles a ladder.

lady's desk:

Diminutive desk with drawers that appeared during the Federal period.

lady's secretary:

Smaller version of the gentleman's secretary, originating in the Federal period. The writing surface often unfolds onto lopers.

lady's trunk:

Please see "hat trunk."

lady's writing table:

Small Federal-era desk with bookcase above a writing surface, a surface that opens to rest on lopers. A single drawer is often found below the writing surface.

lambrequin:

Drapery around the top of a canopied bed.

lambrequin knee carving:

A carving meant to resemble a simple bit of drapery covering the knee of a cabriole leg.

laminated materials:

Materials consisting of multiple thin layers bonded together with glue. In the case of wood laminates, each layer is usually arranged perpendicular to the one above and the one below, which produces panels of great dimensional stability.

lamp:

A device that produces artificial light through the use of electricity, gas, or oil.

Pewter lamp. This pewter, brass, and leaded-glass lamp was made by Roswell Gleason (1799–1887) of Dorchester, Massachusetts, sometime between 1835 and 1860. The lenses on either side of the wick magnify and direct the light of the oil flame. *Courtesy of the Yale University Art Gallery*

lap desk:

A small desk designed to be held in the lap when in use. Typically, the top consists of a hinged panel that, when raised, reveals a small array of cubbyholes in which paper, pens, and ink can be stored.

lap joint:

A joint for bringing together two framing pieces at right angles, in which the end of one piece is reduced to a thickness half that of the parts being joined, and a matching half-thickness reduction is cut in the second piece. The components are then glued and lapped and often reinforced with nails or screws driven into the backside of the joint.

lap joint, corner:

Joint created when two components with matching half-thickness excavations are brought together to form a single right-angle joint. Because with only glue the joint is quite weak, it is usually reinforced with metal fasteners on the backside.

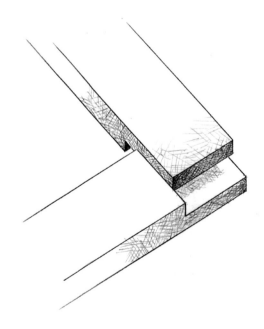

Lap joint, corner

Double-plated lamp. The size of this lamp—almost 39" tall—suggests it might have been used for banquet lighting. The bold surface was created by overlaying the lamp with thin platings of colored metal, then cutting the metal away to reveal the glass underneath. The maker was the Boston and Sandwich Glass Company of Sandwich, Massachusetts. The materials are glass, gilt bronze, and marble. The lamp is dated circa 1865. *Courtesy of the Art Institute of Chicago*

lap joint, cross:
Joint created when two components with matching half-thickness excavations are brought together at some point between the ends of both components. Glued, this joint offers marginal strength. As a result, it is often reinforced with metal fasteners on the backside.

lap joint, "T":
Joint created when a half-thickness excavation on the end of one component is fitted into a half-thickness excavation cut somewhere along the length of the second component. Glued, the joint is very weak, so it is usually reinforced with metal fasteners on the backside.

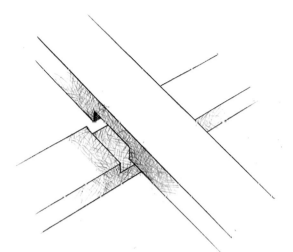

Lap joint, cross

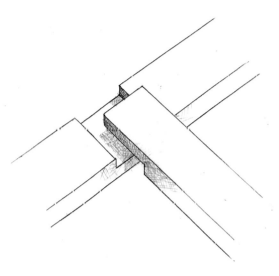

Lap joint, "T"

lap joint, glazing bar:
A lap joint for two glazing bars.

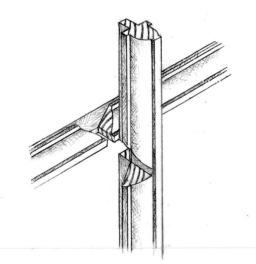

Lap joint, glazing bar

late wood:
The darker, denser portion of a tree's annular rings. Late-wood lines are those that are counted when determining the age of a stumped tree.

lattice:
A crisscross pattern achieved through the use of carving, scroll sawing, or simply laying strips of wood crosswise on top of each other.

lawn (outdoor) furniture:
Furniture intended to be used in gardens or on patios, porches, or decks. The history of American outdoor furniture goes all the way back to the log rolled near the outdoor fire, but the first example of formal American outdoor furniture was probably the painted Windsor, a form brought to the United States from early-eighteenth-century England. In the three centuries since, the universe of lawn/outdoor furniture has expanded to include

materials other than wood—primarily metal and plastic. For the most part, wood furniture intended for outdoor use has been made of weather-resistant species such as teak, redwood, or cedar. More recently, these have been supplanted by pressure-treated yellow pine. But metal-framed (and sometimes seated) outdoor furniture is now more common, and in recent years single-piece molded plastic chairs and tables have dominated the market, with millions sold across the country. And the number of forms of outdoor furniture has expanded so that it mirrors the many forms of indoor furniture. What suburban yard is complete without a picnic table and a bench swing? What patio or deck is complete without an umbrellaed table and chairs, as well as a few benches made of pressure-treated lumber? And wherever there are chairs, there must be small tables close at hand, made of metal, plastic, or wood. Plus, there are outdoor cooking centers rivaling the working quarters of professional chefs.

lazy Susan:
A round wooden disk rotating on a central shaft fixed in the middle of a dining table so that it could be turned to make condiments accessible to anyone seated at the table. The term is also applied to a stack of disks rotating on an axis. This construction is used to make shelf space easily accessible in a corner cupboard having only a narrow door. If you want something on the backside of a shelf, you simply turn the lazy Susan until the proper section of the shelf has been rotated to the front.

leaded glass:
Glass panels often made up of many pieces of art glass contained within strips of lead, brass, zinc, or copper.

leaf:
Wood panel used to lengthen table or to create a writing surface for a desk. Some leaves are hinged from the primary section of a tabletop. Others are stored and laid across telescoping extensions between the two halves of a tabletop.

lectern:
Originally, a desk or stand on which a Bible was placed so that it might be read to the congregation. In common modern parlance, it is any stand behind which a speaker might be positioned.

leg:
Usually one of four or six components used to support a chair, table, or casepiece.

leg caps:
Metal cups encasing the feet of turned, tapered legs on much mid-century modern furniture.

leg rake:
Please see "rake."

leg splay:
Please see "splay."

library bookcases:
Bookcases built to a grand scale, often with glazed doors.

Library bookcase. This neo-classical bookcase of possible New York origin is constructed of mahogany, white pine, and basswood. The maker is unknown. The bookcase is dated 1830–1850. *Courtesy of the Yale University Art Gallery*

Library bookcase. Breakfronts like this handsome New York example are often called library bookcases. The materials are mahogany, pine, tulip poplar, and glass. The piece is dated 1790–1815. *Courtesy of the Yale University Art Gallery*

library ladder:

A ladder used to access books on high shelves.

library steps:

Sets of steps used to access shelves of books too high to otherwise reach. These are made of wood or metal. Some ingenious nineteenth-century examples could be folded so that when not in use as steps, they could be used as chairs or tables. These are referred to as "metamorphic library steps."

library table:

Large table used for research and writing, typically found in libraries and studies.

Library table. This powerful library table was the centerpiece for the library of William Henry Vanderbilt (1821–1885), the son of Commodore Vanderbilt. Although its large—35" × 60"—surface could have been used for study, the table was probably intended more as a monument to the man who owned it, then the wealthiest man in America. The wreath-enclosed stars are a reference to Napoleon; the lion's-paw feet, to ancient Rome; and its massive scale is a testament to Vanderbilt's nineteenth-century power. This Herter Brothers (1864–1906) table is dated 1879–1882. The material is rosewood, mother-of-pearl, abalone, and brass. *Courtesy of the Metropolitan Museum of Art*

Library tabletop. Commodore Vanderbilt was so driven by ego that he had the Herter Brothers create on this tabletop a celestial map of the heavens over the Northern Hemisphere on the night he was born: May 8, 1821. *Courtesy of the Metropolitan Museum of Art*

Stickley library table. Probably a Harvey Ellis (1852–1904) design, this simple library table features the inlay work characteristic of the period during which Ellis worked with Gustav Stickley (1858–1942). The materials are oak, lemonwood, sycamore, exotic woods, copper, pewter, and brass. The table is dated 1903–1904. *Courtesy of the Los Angeles Museum of Art*

THE GREENE AND GREENE STYLE

Greene and Greene furniture is a bit of an anomaly in the history of American furniture making. At the time it was being practiced in Southern California in the opening decades of the twentieth century, the Greene and Greene universe was quite small, with Peter and John Hall producing the furniture that Charles (1868–1957) and Henry (1870–1954) Greene designed for the homes they were creating. The Greene and Greene style was then not of widespread national interest to the furniture-making world in the way of the Queen Anne or Federal or Empire styles in their eras. But as the twentieth century progressed, as other Arts and Crafts genres receded into the past, the subtle qualities of Greene and Greene design work drew more and more attention both from furniture makers and furniture buyers. And now, in the opening decades of the twenty-first century, Greene and Greene furniture is far more popular than it was during the design lives of Charles and Henry Greene.

Greene and Greene side chair. Charles Sumner Greene (1868–1957) and his brother Henry Greene (1870–1954) have proven to be two of the most influential designers of the late Arts and Crafts era. Like Frank Lloyd Wright, they designed furnishings for the homes they'd designed. This exquisite side chair, built in the shop of John and Peter Hall, was created for the Robert Blacker house of Pasadena, California. The materials are mahogany, ebony, oak, silver, copper, abalone shell, and leather. *Courtesy of the Yale University Art Gallery*

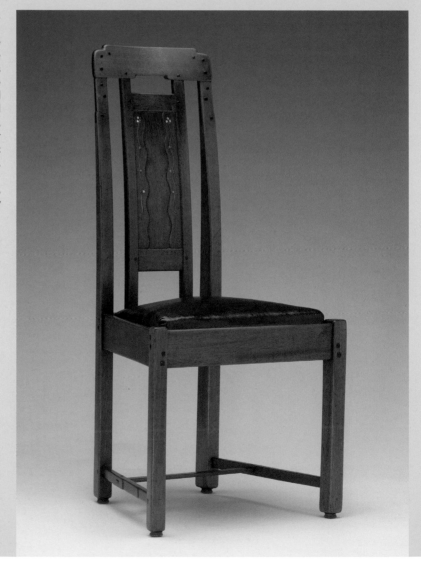

lid stay:

Originally, a wood spindle used to prop open a chest lid. Today, however, that wood spindle has been replaced by a usually brass construction that permits box and chest lids to remain open so that a person can have unencumbered access to the interior. Most depend on a plastic friction washer to maintain the correct tension, although stays fitted with small pneumatic tubes are also available.

liftoff butt hinge:

Hinge with fixed half pin that allows the door to be lifted off without removing the hinge pin.

lighthouse clock:

A creation of Simon Willard (1753–1848) that resembled a lighthouse, with the clock itself housed under a glass dome rising from a pillar that was usually mounted on a base.

line:

Please see "stringing."

linenfold panel:

Feature of medieval and Jacobean furniture in which the wood—usually oak— is carved to resemble a partially unfolded piece of linen. This motif was resurrected on some Arts and Crafts work.

Lighthouse clock. This "lighthouse clock" was originally called an "alarum timepiece" by its maker Simon Willard (1753–1848) of Roxbury, Massachusetts. However, because of its shape, the name "lighthouse clock" has stuck. The clock is dated 1825–1830. The clock case is made of mahogany, white pine, brass, and glass. *Courtesy of the Metropolitan Museum of Art*

linen press:

Originally, this term referred to a construction with two boards that could be brought together via wooden screws to smooth damp cloth. Later the term was used to identify a casepiece having two doors at the top, concealing a number of sliding trays on which folded linens could be stored. A variable number of drawers are located below the doors.

Below and next page: Period linen press. The unknown maker of this Boston block-front linen press decided to give monumental status to a utilitarian piece of furniture. Standing over 7 feet in height, with an unusual but very striking pediment, this press was intended, simply, for the folding and storage of linens and clothes. Behind the doors of the top case, there are six graduated drawers, including a top drawer with a front shaped to conform to the pediment. Also, at the waist, there is a slide-out panel enabling users to fold items before storage. The material is mahogany, red oak, and white pine. The piece is dated 1740–1760. *Courtesy of the Yale University Art Gallery*

Linen press with doors open. *Courtesy of the Yale University Art Gallery*

lining:

Please see "stringing."

linseed oil (flaxseed oil, flax oil):

An edible oil taken from flax seeds, which is an important component in some wood finishes. Used by itself, boiled linseed oil (a combination of linseed oil and chemical dryers) can be an attractive—if time consuming to apply—wood-finishing product. Unlike varnishes, which build a protective layer on the surface, boiled linseed oil soaks deeply into wood pores.

lion's-paw foot:

Style of furniture foot seen (rarely) on Chippendale and Empire furniture, carved to resemble the hairy paw of a lion's foot. It is sometimes known as a "hairy-paw foot."

lip molding:

Quarter-round form surrounding some drawers of the Queen Anne period and later. It is often separated from the surface of the drawer front by a narrow filet.

lipping:

Thin strips of solid wood used to conceal the edges of plywood, often attached with a glued tongue. At other times, it's simply edge-glued to the plywood.

listing:

Name often used by Shakers to identify the woven fabric tape they used to weave seats and panel backs. Its machine-woven equivalent is sold today by a number of vendors.

liturgical furniture:

Furniture associated with worship; for example, a lectern, a baptismal font, a Bible stand, a kneeler, a celebrant chair, etc.

live edge:

Term used to denote an unsawn edge of a board, an edge that reveals a bit of the tree's natural outside diameter. A "live edge" can be one with or without a bark covering.

Lion's-paw foot. The lion's-paw foot can be traced back as least as far as the Assyrian culture in the eighteenth century BCE. There are several hairy examples known from the American Chippendale period, but the Herter Brothers (1864–1906), the makers of this library table, chose to go with simple, unhaired feet. *Courtesy of the Metropolitan Museum of Art*

Living-room case. In the twentieth century, as the living room supplanted the parlor as the center of American middle-class domestic life, designers began to create furniture and accessories for that room. The best known of these is the coffee table, which typically sits in front of a sofa that faces the television. This living-room case designed by Oskar Stonorov (1905–1970) and Willo von Moltke (1911–1987) is another such piece, designed to store the miscellanea that accumulates in the American living room. This is one of the more interesting mid-century modern manufactured forms. It's not a single piece; it's three separate modules resting on a base: the doored unit on the left, the shelves in the middle, and the tamboured section on the right. These modules are interchangeable. The material is walnut and tulip-poplar-core plywood. It is dated 1940. *Courtesy of the Yale University Art Gallery*

living-room case:
    A case with doors, drawers, and or tambour panels for storing living-room materials.
loafer:
    A mispronunciation of "loper" that has become so common it probably should be entered into the language as a synonym. Please see "loper."
lobing:
    Please see "gadrooning."
lock block:
    A block of often-secondary wood glued to the back of the lock stile to provide housing for the door lock.
lock, drawer:
    Please see "drawer lock."
lock (locking) stile:
    Door stile on which a lock is installed.

lolling chair:
    An upholstered chair form with a straight, wingless back and exposed wood arms and legs.

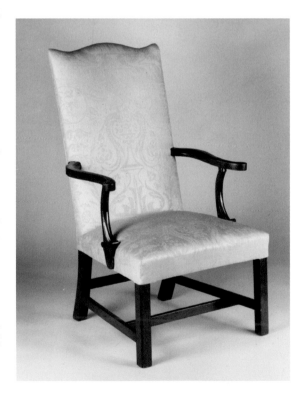

Lolling chair. This Massachusetts lolling chair by an unknown maker dates to 1790–1800. The materials are mahogany and birch. *Courtesy of the Metropolitan Museum of Art*

looking glass:
    Name given to wood-framed period mirrors.
loom:
    Traditionally made of wood, a construction on which weaving fabric from yarn or thread can be done.
loose leaf:
    Please see "table leaves."
loose seat:
    Please see "slip seat."
loose tongue:
    Please see "spline."
loper:
    One of a pair of slide-out arms used to support the drop leaf on a desk or secretary. The term can also be used to identify the slides that support extra leaves on an extension table. In common parlance, this feature is sometimes identified by the term "loafer."
lounge chair:
    Chair designed to put the user in a near-reclining position. These chairs often have adjustable backs.
love seat:
    A usually upholstered form offering seating for just two, sometimes constructed as a tête-à-tête. Please see also "*tête-à-tête.*"
low-backed Windsor:
    Please see "Windsor, low backed."
low-backed Windsor settee:
    Please see "Windsor settee, low backed."
lowboy:
    Formal casepiece resembling the bottom section of a highboy, although usually smaller. It is supported on four legs and is fitted with several drawers, usually one shallow full-width drawer at the top with a line of three drawers below. This form originated in the William and Mary period (although period inventories of household goods usually referred to these as "dressing tables") and continued through the Queen Anne and Chippendale periods. In the post-Chippendale era, pieces of similar size and function were usually called "dressing tables" or "vanities," probably because their bigger brothers, highboys, were no longer in fashion. Please see "highboy" entries for a discussion of period differences.

Looking glass. This Federal-era looking glass features *eglomise* painting on the tablet as well as a Federal eagle, urns, and classical columns. Every framing component is gilded. The mirror is dated 1800–1820. *Courtesy of the Metropolitan Museum of Art*

Loper. This partially extended loper is one of two that are used to support the open drop leaf on a secretary made in the shop of Nathaniel Gould (1734–1782). *Courtesy of the Metropolitan Museum of Art*

Japanned Queen Anne lowboy. This lowboy and its matching highboy by an unknown maker were produced in 1747 at the height of the Boston craze for japanned furniture. This particular example was given its tortoise-shell appearance by "streaking lampblack over a vermillion ground," according to the website of the Metropolitan Museum of Art. It's made of maple and white pine. *Courtesy of the Metropolitan Museum of Art*

Lowboy. This Chippendale lowboy (or dressing table) was made in Lancaster County, Pennsylvania, by an unknown maker in the late eighteenth century. It features a lively surface of rococo vegetative carving. The wood is mahogany and tulip poplar. *Courtesy of the Metropolitan Museum of Art*

Queen Anne lowboy. I believe this cherry lowboy by an unknown maker in the American Northeast is the finest Queen Anne composition in this book (maybe anywhere). It doesn't impress with massive scale like the Stephen Badlam chest-on-chest (page 330) or the architectural grandeur of the Robert Fisher secretary used as the frontispiece of this book. Plus, the lowboy has no carved or inlaid detail to seduce the eye. But it does have—in the Queen Anne fashion—superbly articulated line throughout: in the long unwavering cyma curves of the cabriole legs, in the fluttering profile of the scroll-sawn apron, and, most of all, in the sinuous, molded contours of the overhanging top. It is near perfection in a small package. The secondary wood is pine. The piece is dated 1760–1780. *Courtesy of the Winterthur Museum*

William and Mary lowboy. This early-eighteenth-century lowboy is the work of an unknown maker, probably in Connecticut. Despite its straightforward presence, it features some nifty features not found on all William and Mary casework. Most noticeable is the fifth foot, an extra, located where the cyma-curved X-stretchers cross. It isn't structurally necessary, but is a nice touch that centers the composition. Also, the scroll-sawn apron is finished off with bent cock bead. The strips were probably boiled to make them elastic, then form-dried and tacked into place—at least that's how I do it. In addition, the piece features some particularly well-conceived turnings. The material is cherry, tulip poplar, birch, soft maple, red oak, and ash. *Courtesy of the Metropolitan Museum of Art*

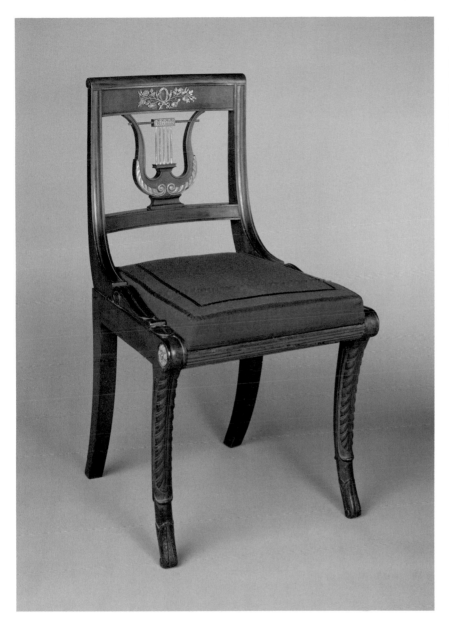

lower case.
    Bottom section of highboy, secretary, or chest-on-chest.
lozenge:
    Usually carved, diamond-shaped decorative element.
lunette:
    Semicircular shape, often decorated with carving, marquetry, or painting.
lyre:
    A structural and decorative motif based on the lyre.

lyre back:
    A chair back with a carved upright lyre centered between the rails and stiles of the back.
lyre pedestal:
    A pedestal—usually for a gaming table—with four legs arcing up to an upright lyre, which supports the gaming top.
magazine rack:
    Shelf unit designed for the temporary storage of magazines. Today a magazine rack can be a very simple utilitarian construction,

Lyre pedestal. The pedestal on this card table, thought to have been the work of Duncan Phyfe's shop, is based on the lyre. The materials are mahogany, tulip poplar, and brass. The piece is dated 1810–1820. *Courtesy of the Metropolitan Museum of Art*

but in the Arts and Crafts era, this form was often a substantial piece of home furniture. Magazine racks of that period typically were tall, narrow, backless shelving units, often tapering as they rose from the floor. One such example, the Roycroft magazine pedestal no. 080, stands 63" tall and can command high prices on the antiques market.

mahogany:

Woods from the *Swietenia* genus, prized for their rich color and workability. Mahoganies are native to the Americas, with two varieties shipped to the United States in large quantities during the eighteenth and nineteenth centuries: Honduran mahogany, native to Central and South America; and Cuban mahogany, native to Florida and the Caribbean. In recent years, wood identified as African mahogany, although from a different genus, *Khaya*, has been heavily imported into the United States as a substitute for mahogany from South America, which has been identified as endangered since 2003. True American mahoganies were the primary woods of choice in the eighteenth and nineteenth centuries.

Maloof rocker:

Rocking chair made by Sam Maloof (1916–2009) or one of his many imitators. The chair is assembled with rough-cut blocks of wood glued and screwed together, then shaped with angle grinders. Please see "Maloof, Sam" in the biography section at the end of this book.

mantle clock:

A clock small enough to be placed on a mantle. This would include lighthouse clocks, pillar-and-scroll shelf clocks, and an Arts and Crafts form identified specifically as mantle clocks.

Mahogany. *Courtesy of the Metropolitan Museum of Art*

Mahogany. *Courtesy of the Metropolitan Museum of Art*

Shelf or mantle clock. Seth Thomas (1785–1859) was one of the best-known clockmakers of the nineteenth century. This petite shelf or mantle clock was made circa 1820 at his Plymouth, Connecticut, shop. The case is mahogany, maple, and white pine. *Courtesy of the Metropolitan Museum*

manufactured furniture:

Furniture that is not bench made. Such furniture is often made in factories with a hundred or more employees, using mass-production techniques. Typically, this furniture is designed so that marginally skilled (and low-paid) workers can execute each step in the manufacturing process.

Manufactured wood furniture. These finished chairs await shipment from the Copeland Furniture manufacturing facility in Bradford, Vermont. Like the Hitchcock chairs of an earlier century, these manufactured chairs are made from solid wood and have a pleasing design—in short, good-quality furniture for the American middle class. *Photo by Shiho Fukada, courtesy of Bloomberg via Getty Images*

map (document) drawer:

Wide, deep (front to back), and shallow (top to bottom) drawer often concealed in a cornice molding of a highboy for the storage of maps or other documents.

maple:

Wood of the genus *Acer*. Worldwide, there are 128 species of maple, but for the discussion of American furniture making, there are only two varieties worthy of discussion: sugar maple (hard maple) and silver maple (soft maple). Hard maple is immensely strong and quite dense, which allows it to stand up to carved and turned detail. This was the favorite material for the Shaker chair factory at New Lebanon, New York. Both hard and soft maples are widely used in furniture making, their figured varieties in particular: fiddleback, curly maple, bird's-eye maple, blistered, and quilted.

marble top:

Slab of highly polished marble used as a tabletop.

Marlborough foot:

Simple foot appearing on some Chippendale work, consisting of four pieces of flat stock mitered around a square leg, usually with a molded top edge. This appearance can also be achieved by cutting away thickness above the foot.

Marble-topped chest of drawers. A marble-topped chest of drawers from the Goddard/Townsend families of cabinetmakers is a rare find. This example, attributed to John Goddard (1724–1785), has a serpentine front and concave sides with ball-and-claw feet at the front and spoon feet at the back. The chest dates to 1755–1785. The materials are mahogany, marble, white pine, and chestnut. *Courtesy of the Metropolitan Museum of Art*

Marlborough leg:

Simple leg, square in cross section, found on some Chippendale chairs, tables, and beds.

marquetry:

Decorative work done in veneer, usually in contrasting woods but sometimes incorporating metals, tortoiseshell, or other exotic materials. This style of ornamentation supplanted carving as the Chippendale period gave way to the Federal era. Individual bits of veneer can be "sand-shaded" using a pan of hot sand to scorch the veneer. Some modern craftsmen use scroll saws or lasers guided by computers to cut their veneers, while traditionalists prefer fretsaws and knives.

marriage:

A combination of two or more furniture parts that were not intended by their makers to be combined. This is most often seen in the cases of highboys, secretaries, and chests-on-chests, which all have upper and lower cases. For example, if the upper case of a secretary is missing or damaged, an owner or an unscrupulous antique dealer might attach an upper case from another source. When an owner does this, it's simply unappealing, but when an antique dealer does this, it can be a criminal act because that dealer can charge far more for a complete secretary than he can for a pairing of two unrelated upper and lower cases.

Marriage. Some marriages are merely ill advised. This one, however, is appalling. With a conventional top, this William and Mary lowboy would be a stunner. It features well-conceived scrollwork and masterful bell-and-trumpet turnings, but the top—likely a Swiss import—has no business riding on this handsome base. Although the website of the Metropolitan Museum, from which these photos are taken, makes no mention of a marriage, it's clear that the craftsman who designed and built the base would never have put this ridiculous top on his work. It's much more likely that the original top was damaged, and the owner of the piece decided—mistakenly—that this top would not be an affront. The material is walnut, birch, spruce, and pine. The base is dated 1715–1735. *Courtesy of the Metropolitan Museum of Art*

Marquetry. This section of a door surround executed by George Shastey (1839–1894) and Company of New York in 1881 features marquetry done in purpleheart and mother-of-pearl against a satinwood background. *Courtesy of the Metropolitan Museum of Art*

The lowboy top from above

marshmallow sofa:

Sofa made up of nine upholstered marsh-mallow shapes for the seat and another nine upholstered marshmallow shapes for the back. The design is often attributed to Herman Miller designer George Nelson (1908–1958), although this is disputed by Irving Harper (1916–2015), a Nelson employee, who claimed the design was his.

Martha Washington armchair:

Known as a Gainsborough chair in England, an upholstered high-backed chair with short, wooden arms and four, usually square in cross section, wooden legs.

Masonic chair:

Chair replete with carved, inlaid, or scroll-sawn Masonic iconography.

mason's miter:

A miter that combines a short miter with 90-degree crosscut. It's most commonly used in stonework and kitchen countertop installs, but occasionally it appears in the construction of furniture.

Massachusetts shelf clock:

Inexpensive alternative to the tall clock, usually equipped with an eight-day movement. A Federal-era invention, these diminutive clocks typically stood on four small French feet.

Masonic chair. Masonic chairs are a class unto themselves, to which this Boston example from between 1775 and 1790 testifies. The undercarriage is pure Chippendale, but the back is a disquieting clutter of uninspiring Masonic iconography. The fluted columns represent King Solomon's temple; the arch, heaven; the compass and square, faith and reason; the mason's level, equality; the tail-swallowing serpent, rebirth; and the trowel, the cement of brotherly love. The chair is made of painted mahogany and maple. *Courtesy of the Metropolitan Museum of Art*

Massachusetts wall clock:

A small wall-hung clock with a wooden case and a simplified brass movement, which originated in the Chippendale period.

masur birch:

Not a species but a birch figure having dark striations against a light background. These striations were once thought to be damage left behind by burrowing larvae, but are now believed to be a genetic sport.

mattress:

A thick quilt-covered case stuffed with soft material on which people sleep.

matched veneers:

Please see "book-matched veneers."

medallion:

Usually small furniture component that has an oval or circular shape.

medicine chest (cabinet, cupboard):

A chest in which medicines can be stored. In the twentieth and twenty-first centuries, medicine chests are wall-mounted units containing several shelves, often with a mirrored door. Period examples are usually freestanding.

Massachusetts shelf clock. This clock was made in Roxbury, Massachusetts, by either Aaron Willard (1757–1844) or Aaron Willard Jr. (1783–1864) between 1805 and 1809. The material is mahogany and pine. *Courtesy of the Metropolitan Museum of Art*

Massachusetts wall clock. Aaron Willard (1757–1844) of Grafton, Massachusetts, was the maker of this wall clock. Aaron had three brothers, and all were horologists, with brother Simon (1753–1848) being the most important. The clock's material is mahogany. *Courtesy of the Metropolitan Museum of Art*

Medicine chest. This mahogany-and-cedar construction includes a number of drawers and cubbies in which medicine might be stored. The two outside drawer sections are hinged and can be closed over the two bottom drawers. The lid can then be closed over the top of all the open cubbies. Notice the carving and the delicate dovetail work on the various cases. The recessed drawer fronts allow the cases to close tight against each other without interference from the hardware. The chest is dated 1775–1795. *Courtesy of the Yale University Art Gallery*

meeting stiles:

In a case with two abutting doors, the stiles that are adjacent to one another when the doors are closed.

metamorphic library steps:

Library steps that can be converted by folding into a chair or table.

miniature furniture:

Scaled-down furniture either for a child or for use as a cabinetmaker's sample.

Miniature furniture. Miniature pieces like this example (11¹¹⁄₁₆" × 21⁷⁄₁₆" × 11½") are sometimes identified as cabinetmakers' samples, which could be used to show a potential client what to expect from the cabinetmaker. This piece, however, could not be scaled up to full size without appearing clunky, so it was probably a toy for a child. The material is walnut, lightwood stringing, and white pine. The piece is dated 1790–1820. *Courtesy of the Yale University Art Gallery*

mirror:

Looking glass in which one can see one's reflection. In the late seventeenth century, these became important pieces of household furnishings. Then in the Queen Anne and Chippendale periods, furniture makers began to surround their—by then quite large—looking glasses with arabesques of finely wrought wood scrollwork, which was sometimes carved and gilded.

miter:

Joint in which a rail and stile are brought together at a 90-degree angle by cutting the end of each piece at a 45-degree angle. This eliminates end grain showing on the edges but requires reinforcement because simply gluing the mating end grain results in an impossibly weak joint. Reinforcement is usually achieved by a glued short-grain spline but can also be achieved with dowels or biscuits or keys.

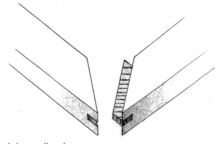

Miter joint, splined

mitered bridle joint:
   Please see "bridle joint, mitered."

mitered butt joint:
   Please see "butt joint, mitered."

miter joint, box:
   A miter that runs vertically up the ends of a box side or a box end.

miter joint, frame:
   A miter joint cut across the widths of framing components. Think of a picture frame.

mitered rabbet joint:
   Please see "rabbet joint, mitered."

miter joint, splined:
   Miter joint reinforced with thin, narrow cross-grain strips used to strengthen an otherwise weak joint.

mitre:
   British spelling of miter.

molding:
   Lengthwise decorative elements used to outline or frame. Traditionally, these were created through the use of molding planes, but today they are most often fashioned by an electric-powered router—or, on a commercial level, with molding machines. The eighteenth- and nineteenth-century molding planes now being brought up out of barns and basements, primarily in the American Northeast, reveal hundreds of different profiles, reflecting the changing tastes of American period furniture buyers and makers. In the same way that carmakers today bring out new models every year, furniture makers of the eighteenth and nineteenth centuries periodically brought out new forms or new interpretations of old forms to stimulate the interest of buyers. And of course these new forms required new molding shapes. The circle-based (in cross section) moldings that predominated in Thomas Chippendale's 1754 book *The Gentleman and Cabinetmaker's Director* shifted to ellipse-based (in cross section) forms in the Greek Revival moldings of the nineteenth century. And during the Federal period, moldings of any kind largely disappeared from high-style casework. The eighteenth- and nineteenth-century molding planes now being unearthed fit into three functional classes. First and most numerous are those planes designed to create simple moldings; that is, those made up of a single shape form (for example, a Gothic bead). Second are the complex molding planes, those capable of cutting moldings containing two or more simple shapes; for example, a Grecian ovolo with bead. John Whelan's book *The Wooden Plane: Its History, Form, and Function* contains a list of nearly six hundred different complex molding planes, each one capable of creating a molding profile distinct from any other. The third class is made up of shaping planes: hollows, rounds, rabbets, and snipe bills. Through the use of these planes, craftsmen could create a theoretically infinite number of profiles, limited only by their imaginations. Most of the planes available today through antique dealers have fairly narrow profiles. The widest is the cornice-molding plane, which might be 5 or even 6 inches across, with several shapes cut into its sole. These planes required two men to operate: one to push and align the plane, and a second to pull through the use of a rope or wooden rod that passed through the nose of the plane. These planes were used to cut the wide moldings that appeared on the exteriors of homes under the eaves or in the interiors of homes at that place where the ceiling meets the walls. By contrast to the almost unlimited number of profiles available to users of antique molding planes, people relying on commercially produced moldings have a much-narrower range of options. In fact, the only advantage of commercially made moldings is their ease of acquisition. (To be fair, modern consumers of moldings can have the owner of a molding machine grind a set of knives to their specifications—at considerable cost.)

monastery table:
   Usually large trestle table typically built of thick wood.

monitor trunks:
   Trunks featuring vertically rounded front corners, so that when viewed from above the profile, they present a "D" shape. These were in use from 1870 to 1910.

monk's bench:
   A low bench that can be converted to a table by pivoting the back into a horizontal position.

monopodium:
 Term identifying a single support column reaching to the floor.

monza chair:
 Contemporary piece of seating furniture consisting of plate steel rolled into a "U" standing on its edge, with a seat panel welded inside the "U."

morocco:
 Fine leather made from goat hides, used as writing surfaces on some Chippendale and later forms.

Morris chair:
 The first adjustable-back armchair, named for the nineteenth-century English Arts and Crafts designer William Morris (1834–1896), who collaborated with architect Phillip Webb (1831–1915) in its design. In some examples, adjustability was achieved by moving dowels from one hole in the inside edge of the arm to another. Other Morris chairs used a wooden bar set between pegs in several different locations on the rear quarter of the arm.

Roycroft Morris chair. The Morris chair, named after William Morris (1843–1896), one of the originators of the Arts and Crafts movement in England, was made by many Arts and Crafts companies, including Roycroft Furniture of East Aurora, New York. In this setting of Roycroft furniture at the Muckenthaler Cultural Center in Fullerton, California, the Morris chair is accompanied by a round Roycroft table and other Roycroft accessories. *Photo by Kari Rene Hall, courtesy of Getty Images*

mortise-and-tenon joint:
 Joint created when a tongue (tenon) on the end of one component is fit into an excavation (mortise) cut into a second component.

mortise-and-tenon joint, double:
 Two tenons—and their requisite mortises—used to join one board's end to another board's edge or face. The joint is created by removing material in the middle of a wide tenon and then cutting two mortises to match the resulting tenons.

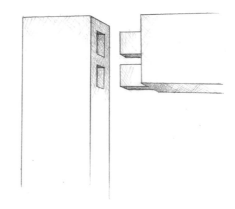

Mortise-and-tenon joint, double

mortise-and-tenon joint, haunched:
 A mortise-and-tenon joint that includes a haunch, a shallow extension of the tenon.

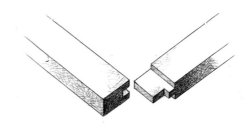

Mortise-and-tenon joint, haunched

mortise-and-tenon joint, stopped:
 Mortise-and-tenon joint in which the tenon doesn't reach all the way through the mortised component.

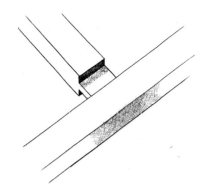

Mortise-and-tenon joint, stopped

mortise-and-tenon joint, through:

A joint in which the tenon penetrates all the way through the mortised component.

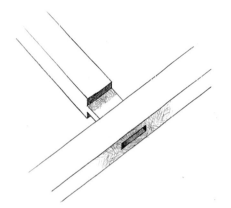

Mortise-and-tenon joint, through

mortise-and-tenon joint, through and tusked:

A projecting through tenon into which a vertical mortise is cut to receive a wedge (or tusk) to keep the joint tight. This joint may be glued, or it may be left unglued in the case of knockdown furniture. This joint is one of

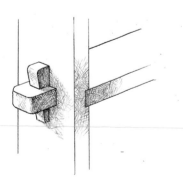

Mortise-and-tenon joint, through and tusked

the signature features of Arts and Crafts design, prominently featured in the Roycroft, Charles Limbert, and Gustav Stickley catalogs.

mortise and tenon joint, wedged, through:

A through tenon into which a wedge is driven into the exposed end grain of the tenon to tighten it in its mortise. To facilitate the installation of the wedge, a narrow notch is cut into the tenon before assembly. This tenon enhancement is usually seen in settings where strength is particularly important, such as in the case of some entrance doors. In such a case, the through tenons at the ends of door rails are often wedged where they pass through the door stiles.

mortise and tenon with foxed wedge:

The use of a wedge with a length calculated so that the bottom of a blind mortise drives the wedge into the tenon to create an exceptionally tight joint.

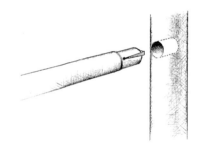

Mortise-and-tenon joint with foxed wedge

mother-of-pearl:

Hard, colorful, and iridescent inner layer of oystershells used in inlay work.

muffin stand, period:

Stand used for tea service. Why "muffin"? I don't know.

muffin stand, modern:

A tabletop stand on which muffins can be displayed. Typically the muffins are placed on graduated plates, with the smallest plate at the top.

mule-ear chair:

An American country slat-back chair with back posts curving toward the back and drawknifed planes on their front sides. Presumably, the flattened back post tops sticking above the top slat resembles a pair of mule's ears.

mullion:

Vertical component that separates panels (lights) in a glazed window.

muntin (muntin bar, glazing bar, sash bar):

Usually thin strip of wood used to separate and support small panels of glass in a door or window. Originally, these were used so that small panels of glass could glaze a large window, in an era when large panels of glass were expensive to manufacture. Today some large panels of glass are decorated with false "muntins" mounted in front of the sheet of glass, because this detail is seen as aesthetically pleasing. In the case of exterior windows, these false "muntins" are usually fitted between panels of double-glazed windows.

Murphy bed (pull-down bed, wall bed, fold-down bed):

A bed, hinged on the headboard end, housed in a wall opening during the day, then pulled down to the floor at night so that it can be used. William Lawrence Murphy (1876–1957) applied for the first of several bed-related patents in 1900. Fold-down beds did exist prior to his first patent application, but Murphy added some important wrinkles to the concept, including a counterbalance to make his Murphy bed easier to bring down and fold away.

mushroom cap:

Thin flattened dome with a cove cut just above its base. These caps house the extensions of the through tenons at the tops of the front posts in many Shaker armchairs and armed rockers produced by the Shaker chair factory at New Lebanon, New York.

mushroom handhold:

Flattened ball appearing at the top of a front post on many Pilgrim chairs; for example, Carver and Brewster chairs.

music cabinet:

Relatively tall and narrow cabinet for the storage of sheet music. These cabinets have a long history in Europe and have been made for at least two hundred years in the United States. Some music cabinets have doors concealing a number of internal shelves. Others have a series of shallow drawers aligned in one or two columns. Often these are decorated with inlay depicting a motif related to music.

music rack:

Like the music cabinet, a piece in which sheet music could be stored. Unlike the music cabinet, the music rack stores them out in the open.

music stand:

Traditionally a simple stand of metal or wood on which sheet music can be displayed for musicians while they play. Some period examples have "candleboards" that provide places for mounting candles. In the 1970s, American designer/craftsmen—Wendell Castle (1932–2018) among them—began building fanciful wooden music stands that were sculpture as much as they were functional pieces.

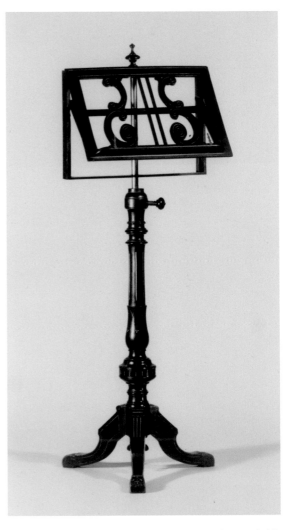

Victorian music stand. This adjustable music stand was probably made in New York City circa 1870. The materials are ebonized maple and brass. *Courtesy of the Metropolitan Museum of Art*

DOES REPRODUCTION FURNITURE HAVE ANY VALUE?

I should begin by admitting that I've made lots of reproduction furniture, rarely exact copies, but many pieces that were clearly descended from either a specific period original or were clearly within the tradition of a particular period. I suppose that approach to my craft could be a result of a lack of design imagination on my part, but even more, I think, it is the result of pure unadulterated love for the many period and Shaker forms I have already built and those I hope someday to build.

Pierce table. This William and Mary–style table built in my shop is characteristic of the period-inspired work I do. Although I'm unaware of any tables of this configuration built in the William and Mary era, this table is clearly descended from that era. The X-stretcher, the bold cup-and-trumpet turnings, the Gothic arches, and the wide-lipped top are all William and Mary signatures. *Photo by Al Parrish,* courtesy of Popular Woodworking *magazine*

Of course, the city closest to my shop—Lancaster, Ohio—is landlocked in what is disparagingly referred to as "flyover country," and many of the men and women who have purchased my reproduction furniture may have had little, if any, exposure to the innovative studio work being made and sold in urban areas on both coasts. Plus, like me, when they think of fine furniture, I suspect they imagine something made by period masters, by Duncan Phyfe or John Seymour or someone in the Goddard/Townsend families of eighteenth-century Newport, Rhode Island. Most of these buyers, I think, would be willing to embrace the live edges of George Nakashima's tables, and they would almost certainly love the sculpted beauty of a Sam Maloof rocker. But a table made of folded metal finished in automobile paint? Probably not so much.

But will a handmade twenty-first-century reproduction of a Queen Anne highboy appear on the twenty-second-century equivalent of the *Antiques Roadshow*? At first blush, the answer would seem to be no. By definition, reproduction work doesn't reflect design innovation representative of the era in which it was created, and that is an important measure of an antique's worth.

But then you have to ask yourself what it is that buyers want when they purchase well-made, handcrafted furniture from an earlier era. Are they hoping to acquire a historically meaningful example of period-specific design innovation? Unquestionably some are. But there are other buyers who are simply looking for something well made, something built in a small shop by craftsmen who care deeply about every step in the process, as opposed to something manufactured in great wheezing factories at a rate of a thousand copies a day. And for these buyers, if that handmade piece evokes the work of an earlier era—well, that's just fine with me.

nails:

Thin-shanked metal fastener driven into wood with blows from a hammer. Although eschewed by most makers of serious furniture (except for secondary applications such as the attachment of some moldings and some hardware), nails have a long history in the realm of furniture making. For example, Shaker craftsmen—like the country craftsmen they were before becoming Shakers—often used through nails to fasten tops to the cases below, driving those nails right through the top. See also "cut nails."

Nakashima key (Nakashima joint):

Please see "dovetail key."

neck:

The narrowest section at the top of a turned vessel.

necking:

Narrow collar near the top of a column.

nested (nesting) tables:

Group of graduated tables designed so that they can be stacked one on top of another.

New Lebanon production chair:

Chairs produced at the New Lebanon, New York, Shaker chair factory under the direction of Brother Robert Wagan (1833–1883). Wagan standardized forms, organized production, and circulated a small catalog that reached all parts of the United States. Today, these distinctive chairs—usually with an acorn finial or a cushion rail atop the back posts—are valued by collectors.

Shaker rocking chair. When people think of Shaker chairs, this is the chair they have in mind. It was made during the peak years of the Shaker chair-making factory at New Lebanon, New York, after the less accomplished models from the middle of the nineteenth century and before the decline in quality that occurred when the Shaker brothers who worked in the chair-making shop had passed away, leaving only two Shaker sisters to run the operation. It has a back that both widens and arches backward as it rises from the seat, mushroom caps at the top of the front posts, gently radiussed arms, and bottom-heavy turned vases on the front posts just below the arms. The material is birch and maple. The chair is dated circa 1875. *Courtesy of the Yale University Art Gallery*

Newport block front:

Block-front constructions of the Goddard and Townsend families of craftsmen in Newport, Rhode Island, in which the tops of each blocked section are crowned with a large carved shell with curving lobes. The Goddard and Townsend designers and craftsmen are arguably the greatest collection of furniture makers this country has ever produced, and their block-front chests, desks, and secretaries represent the pinnacle of their work. These magnificent constructions combine the blocking work found in Boston and elsewhere along the Atlantic Seaboard with superbly carved shells, which are not quite like anything seen elsewhere in eighteenth-century America.

night stand (table):

A small table or drawered case intended to be placed beside the head of the bed so that users have a place to put their personal effects while they sleep.

Noguchi's glass-topped coffee table:

A 1947 design by Isamu Noguchi (1904–1988), who paired a curving plate-glass top with a base of sculpted wood.

nosing:

A rounded front edge, usually on a stair tread. Traditionally, nosings were created with molding planes designed for this singular purpose, but these planes have been supplanted by spindle shapers and routers in most shops.

nulling:

Molding—often with a torus crosscut profile—that features an alternating repetitive carved pattern.

oak, red:

Wood of *Quercus rubra*, with a long history as a construction and cabinet wood. The heartwood is a pale reddish brown, the sapwood a bit darker. Because it's cheaper than white oak, it is the oak often seen in restaurant interiors and similar commercial settings. However, it is prone to splintering when stressed, and does not bend well. The only time I've ever used it was in the construction of a set of liturgical furniture for a chapel outfitted with red-oak furnishings.

Nightstand. The Herter Brothers of New York (active 1864–1906) were a powerful force in the world of Gilded Age interior design. This night table was probably part of a suite for a customer who wanted an entire room done in the same manner. The table's four posts are turned at the bottom just above the castors. The open middle section of the posts is decorated with flower carving, and floral inlay is spread across the drawer front and the apron. The bottom drawer front features an inlaid urn containing a spray of flowers. The material is cherry. The piece is dated 1880. *Courtesy of the Metropolitan Museum of Art*

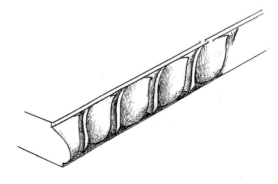

Nulling

oak, white:

Wood of *Quercus alba*, with a long history as a cabinet and chair material. The heartwood is medium brown, with sapwood that is almost the same color. It is immensely strong, and for that reason it has a long history in the fields of cooperage, shipbuilding, and tool construction. If quarter-sawn, it presents an attractive pattern of rays and flecks. Because it takes well to steam bending, it has long been a favorite of Windsor chair makers for the bentwood crest bows. It has been—and continues to be—a favorite of people working in the Arts and Crafts genre. It was Gustave Stickley's wood of choice.

oak-slat trunk:

Trunk composed of a wood frame enclosed with thin oak slats butted tightly one against the next.

occasional table:

A small table in many shapes, used for a variety of household purposes.

octagonal leg:

Eight-sided table or chair leg. Usually, these are fixed in a wooden carriage that allows the leg blank to be turned and locked in 45-degree increments before feeding the blank past a bandsaw or table saw.

ogee arch:

Arch with a pair of ogee curves meeting at the peak.

ogee bracket foot:

A bracket foot made from two mitered pieces of ogee material.

ogee plain:

Any line based on the cyma curve.

ogee molding:

A molding that, in cross section, features a cyma curve.

Ogee molding, in cross section

ogive:

Pointed arch characteristic of Gothic work.

onion foot:

Turned ball-shaped foot, usually slightly flattened. This form is indistinguishable from some of the bun feet of the same period, and it probably didn't matter to the turners of the William and Mary era if they were thinking "onion" as opposed to "bun" when they were working at their lathes.

open-claw (open-taloned) foot:

A variant of the ball-and-claw foot associated with the Goddard/Townsend families of Newport, Rhode Island, in which the powerful talons are separated from the ball by visible gaps.

ormolu:

Gilded metal—usually copper, zinc, and tin—used as furniture mounts and for decorative elements. The use of ormolu reached its artistic and technical zenith in France in the eighteenth and nineteenth centuries.

ottoman:

Upholstered footstool or low seat without arms or back.

Ottoman. This simple ottoman consists of four ogee bracket feet supporting a wide ogee molding, which itself supports an upholstered cushion. The wood is mahogany. *Courtesy of the Metropolitan Museum of Art*

outdoor furniture:

Please see "lawn furniture."

oval-top table:

Table with an oval-shaped top.

ovolo molded edge:
    Convex quarter round bordered on each side by a narrow filet.

Ovolo molded edge in cross section

ovolo shape:
    Convex quarter round bordered by narrow filets; usually encountered in the field of molding, but can be seen in other places as well (for instance, at the corners of tabletops).
oxbow chest front:
    Facade swells outward on both sides, then inward in the middle.

Oxbow-front chest of drawers. During the Chippendale era, cabinetmakers experimented endlessly with chest fronts, hoping to create facades that not only were aesthetically pleasing but would also result in increased prices. The most successful of these chest front variations include the oxbow (seen on this particular chest), the serpentine, the Boston block front, and the Newport block and shell. This particular chest of drawers was made by an unknown New England maker between 1770 and 1780. The materials are mahogany and white pine. *Courtesy of the Metropolitan Museum of Art*

oystering:

Veneers cut as cross sections of whole limbs.

packer:

Please see "steamer trunk."

paddle:

Name given to the small panel of wood attached to the arm of a Windsor chair to make it a writing-arm Windsor.

pad foot:

Type of spoon foot favored by makers of Philadelphia casework in the Queen Anne period. It includes a small, thin pad of wood under the foot, above which is a convexly radiussed second, thicker pad. The cabriole leg rises from the top of this second pad.

pail/bucket/tub:

Round, staved wood construction with a bottom and sometimes a lid. These are constructed for the storage or conveyance of liquids.

paintbrush foot:

Please see "Spanish foot."

painted furniture:

Furniture having the natural color and figure of wood concealed under paint. While the overwhelming majority of fine furniture possesses clear finishes, there are certain forms that have traditionally been covered in paint: the Windsor chair, for example, as well as the japanned furniture of early-eighteenth-century Boston and New York. In addition, some rural makers became experts at painting "mahogany" figure over a painted base, in this manner transforming a pedestrian American species such as soft maple into Honduran or Cuban mahogany. At least, that was their intention.

palmette:

A carved decorative element based on the palm tree.

paint:

Finishing material that imparts layers of color so thick that any trace of the wood below is obliterated. Although the overwhelming majority of fine furniture is given relatively clear finishes, some pieces are enhanced by a painted surface. Please see the Pennsylvania German work illustrating the term "dower chest" entry in this book.

panel:

Flat expanse of wood, often assembled from two or more edge-glued boards. Because of cross-grain shrinkage, unframed panels are used only in applications where that shrinkage can go unnoticed, such as—for instance—a dining-table top without breadboard ends. Otherwise, panels used in the construction of furniture are framed in such a way that the shrinkage is concealed.

panel back:

Term used to identify a chair back made up of a woven panel of splint, Shaker tape, cane, or rush.

pantry latch:

Unmortised door latch consisting of two parts: the catch, which is mounted on one of the meeting stiles, and the receiver, which is mounted on the other meeting stile. Typically, the latch mechanism is housed inside a small metal shell often decorated with relief ornamentation.

parlor (parlour) suite:

A nineteenth-century innovation that consisted of an upholstered sofa or settee (or both) accompanied by several upholstered chairs and maybe a table or two. The parlor was the room in which prosperous people greeted and interacted with guests. It therefore contained a family's very best furniture.

parquetry:

The assembly of contrasting woods to create a geometric pattern, usually in flooring.

partners' desk:

Desk designed so that two partners can work facing one another across the same surface.

patera (paterae):

Small disk of carved or inlaid ornamentation.

patina:

The color and luster that age and use impart to wood. For example, cherry darkens quickly when exposed to bright light, while walnut becomes lighter under the same condition. Also, decades of contact with the human hand can lighten the color of a chair arm or simply wear away the finish. These changed appearances are critical components of the patina of the surfaces on which they're found.

Parlor. This parlor is from the home of early-nineteenth-century lawyer William Clayton Williams (1768–1817), from Richmond, Virginia. It is filled with furniture from the shops of Duncan Phyfe and Charles Honoré Lannuier, the premier New York makers in the opening decades of the nineteenth century. *Courtesy of the Metropolitan Museum of Art*

paw foot:

Please see "hairy paw foot."

pedestal base castor:

A castor attached to a metal cup that receives the ends of the pedestal's legs. The cups are often worked with reeding or fluting to match the leg treatment or the features of animal feet.

pedestal desk:

A desk with a work surface supported on two pedestals, usually two columns of drawers. The desk is typically outfitted with a leather panel as its writing surface.

pedestal table:

Table supported by a pedestal, which itself is supported by three, four, or more legs. This is a category that includes the magnificent piecrust tables with cabriole legs terminating in ball-and-claw feet of the Chippendale era, as well as the Federal-era and Empire-period pedestal tables that followed. And it includes the many pedestal forms created by Shaker craftsmen during the nineteenth century. Some of these last types featured underslung drawers.

Pedestal table. This iconic table is one of a pair: this one in
the Yale University Art Gallery, the other in the Museum of
Fine Arts, Boston. One pedestal eagle faces left, the other
right. Together, these tables would have made a powerful
statement of American patriotism. The pair is sometimes
attributed to Duncan Phyfe. Certainly the quality of the
design and execution makes that a possibility. The material
is mahogany and pine. The table is dated 1820–1825. *Courtesy
of the Yale University Art Gallery*

Previous page: Sheraton pedestal desk. Made of mahogany,
satinwood, and maple, this Baltimore-made secretary is one
of the most striking forms of the Federal period. This circa
1811 masterpiece by an unknown maker was inspired by—but
not a copy of—a design in Thomas Sheraton's cabinet dictionary, which had been published just eight years earlier. *Courtesy
of the Metropolitan Museum of Art*

pediment:

Nonfunctional section atop some high-style eighteenth-century casework, consisting of two triangles rising toward an open center. They are often ornamented with elaborate cornice moldings and sometimes low-relief carving. Some are defined by gooseneck moldings rising toward the open center.

pediment with hood:

Pediment that is extended to the back of a tall casepiece, usually consisting of thin boards held in place with rosehead nails. This form is most often found surmounting Queen Anne highboys. Please see also "bonnet top."

peg:

A shaved dowel used to reinforce mortise-and-tenon joinery. This method of locking joints is not often used today, but it has a long history in the fields of construction and furniture making. Early barns were typically assembled with beefy mortise-and-tenon joinery, then held fast by "pegs" driven into bored holes that pierced both the mortised part and the tenon. To achieve tighter joints, the "pegs" were driven into slightly offset holes (please see "drawbore pegs"). Similarly, "pegs" have a long history in reinforcing mortise-and-tenon joinery in the woodshop. In the absence of effective glues, many early chairs were assembled using only "pegs" to hold mortises and tenons together. Cabinetmakers often used "pegs" to strengthen the frame in frame-and-panel construction. Today, in an era of miraculously strong glues, pegs are usually employed as decorative effects, using—for example—ebony "pegs" to contrast with cherry or maple components.

peg leg:

Turned chair leg that is tapered but otherwise lacking any turned elaboration.

peg-leg stand:

A Shaker stand supported by an extremely plain turned pedestal that is supported by three outwardly reaching dowels.

pellicle:

A thin skin or membrane; in the world of furniture, a name given to a tough woven material used to seat Aeron chairs.

Pembroke table:

A small table with a drop leaf on either side, which is typically joined to the tabletop via a rule joint. These tables were/are often used as breakfast tables.

Federal Pembroke table. The Pembroke table was a mainstay of Federal-era homes. They were often used as breakfast tables, and they were small enough and versatile enough, with their two drop leaves, to be used anywhere else a table might be required. This example by the Newport master craftsman John Townsend (1732–1809) reflects the maker's versatility. Long known for his magnificent Queen Anne and Chippendale-style casework, Townsend shows with this Pembroke table that he could make the switch to Federal styles—even late in his career. The table is dated circa 1795. The materials are mahogany, light-wood inlays, maple, and chestnut. *Courtesy of the Metropolitan Museum of Art*

Peg-leg stand. This pine-and-maple peg-leg seed stand is the work of an unknown Shaker craftsman from the first quarter of the nineteenth century. The stand originated in the New Lebanon, New York, Shaker community. *Courtesy of the Metropolitan Museum of Art*

pencil post bed:

Thin, tapering, often-octagonal bedpost rising to support a tester frame.

pendant:

Small decorative—usually turned—ornament. William and Mary and Queen Anne highboys often have turned pendants hanging from their aprons.

pewter inlay:

Traditionally an alloy of tin and lead, although some modern pewters are made without lead. Its low melting point allows it to be poured into excavations in a wood surface to create very appealing decorative effects. It was/is often used by makers of Arts and Crafts furniture.

Philadelphia chair:

Name commonly given by eighteenth- and nineteenth-century Americans to Windsor chairs. This was due to the huge number of Windsors being made in Philadelphia and shipped all over the country.

Pencil-post bed. This maple-and-tulip-poplar pencil-post bed is dated 1790–1815. *Courtesy of the Yale University Art Gallery*

piano:

Stringed instrument in which the strings are sounded indirectly by hammers connected to keys. Because of the immense tension created by a piano's many strings, instruments made since the mid-1800s have had cast-iron frames. A piano's sound is amplified by a thin panel of Sitka spruce that is connected to the strings via a pair of bridges.

piano bench:

Long, low, backless bench used to seat a musician or musicians at the piano. Modern piano benches are often upholstered.

piano hinge:

A hinge the length of the part to which it is fixed, such as those used to attach piano tops. These hinges typically come in 36" lengths and can be cut to any length.

piano stool:

A stool enabling one musician to sit at a piano.

Piano stool. This massive piano stool was built in New York between 1815 and 1825 by an unknown maker. Like so much animal-footed work of the nineteenth century, it has a powerful—maybe even threatening—stance. The material is mahogany and ash. *Courtesy of the Metropolitan Museum of Art*

Piano. This massive instrument, surfaced with what some might see as a disagreeable encrustation of Renaissance and Rococo Revival ornamentation, was the showpiece of the New York shop owned by British immigrants Robert Nunns (1791–1869) and John Clark (1833–1907). The materials are rosewood, mother-of-pearl, tortoiseshell, abalone, felt, and metal. *Courtesy of the Metropolitan Museum of Art*

pickled finish:

Cloudy white surface achieved by applying, then washing away, part of an undercoat of plaster wood filler.

pictorial marquetry:

The use of marquetry to create portraits, landscapes, still lifes, and *trompe l'oeil* effects. The images are created with contrasting woods, often sand-shaded. The modern craftsman Silas Kopf has created some startlingly real *trompe l'oeil* effects using marquetry.

Pictorial marquetry. Roses done in the most-exacting marquetry are scattered across the top drawer and the two primary doors of this Herter Brothers cabinet. The materials are rosewood, ebonized cherry, maple, walnut, satinwood, marquetry of various woods, brass, gilding, and paint. The cabinet is dated 1878–1880. *Courtesy of the Art Institute of Chicago*

piecrust table:

A tripod table with a top dished out on a lathe so that a wide border remains on the inside of the rim. That border is then sawn and carved into a form reminiscent of a pinched piecrust. The most magnificent of the Chippendale piecrust tables offer a reminder of the majesty of eighteenth-century forests, since some of these tables have piecrust tops over 3 feet in diameter—turned from a single board. Modern manufactured "piecrust tops" of little appeal are made by applying a molding to flat tabletops.

Tilt-top piecrust table. The top of this crisply carved Philadelphia tilt-top tea table is 37" in diameter, cut from a single board. The tabletop can be tilted into the vertical so that it occupies less space. It features a carved border, which identifies this example as a "piecrust table." The table is dated 1765. The material is mahogany. *Courtesy of the Metropolitan Museum of Art*

Tilt-top in the vertical position. *Courtesy of the Metropolitan Museum of Art*

pie cupboard:
Freestanding country-style cabinet usually with pierced tin ventilation panels for the cooling of pies and the storage of other foods.

pierced-brass gallery:
Gallery made of pierced brass used to decorate the tops of some period tables. Most often the brass was in the form of narrow strips of sheet brass, sometimes given a brass cap.

pierced panel:
Panel with decorative piercing, sometimes used to allow air circulation for pantry cupboards. Pierced tracery panels were also widely used in medieval Gothic settings; for example, churches.

pierced work:
Term used to identify scroll saw work in which there are cutouts.

pier glass:
Tall wall mirror often with elaborately molded or scrollworked frame. This form was widely used from the mid-seventeenth to the mid-nineteenth century in the homes of the moneyed elite.

pier table:
A table designed to stand against a wall, often with a large mirror above it. In England, pier tables stand between two windows and often have no back legs and are, instead, fastened to the wall. In America, four-legged versions of these tables were sometimes used in dining rooms and drawing rooms as serving tables. Often these are equipped with marble tops to provide protection against spilled liquids. Thomas Jefferson once referred to "an elegant mahogany drink table with marble top."

Pier glass. This wood-and-marble pier glass was made in New York by an unknown craftsman in the 1870s. *Courtesy of the Metropolitan Museum of Art*

Meeks pier table. In 1797, Joseph Meeks (1771–1868) founded a furniture company in New York City that produced good-quality furniture for the next seventy years. This example of the company's work is distinguished by the energetic Grecian-style scrolls of the pier table's understructure and the marble top. The table is dated between 1829 and 1835. The materials are mahogany veneer, mahogany, pine, ash, and marble. *Courtesy of the Metropolitan Museum of Art*

Meeks advertisement. This hand-colored lithograph from 1833 shows how Joseph Meeks advertised his company's wares. Please notice at the bottom the price list for the pictured items. Only $9 for a mahogany sideboard with pillars and coopered doors? Would someone please direct me to a time machine? *Courtesy of the Metropolitan Museum of Art*

pigeonhole:

Please see "cubbyhole."

pilaster:

Longitudinally split half column—usually rectangular in cross section. These constructions appear, complete with capital and base, on some large Chippendale secretaries. Usually, the pilasters are fluted.

pillar:

A freestanding column, rare in casework, where pilasters are more common. A pair of pillars are sometimes used to support the forward-projecting top drawer of an Empire chest.

pillar-and-scroll shelf clock:

A large dial housed in a small cabinet, with pillars on each side and a delicate scroll across the top. Most rise from the shelf or mantel on four sprightly legs.

pine:

Please see "white pine" and "yellow pine."

pinwheel:

Please see "carved pinwheel."

pipe box:

Colonial-era wall-hung box for the storage of pipes and sometimes matches.

pipe organ:

A musical instrument that produces sound by pushing air into tubes, each of which is tuned to a different pitch. Typically, these are assembled within wood structures that can be quite large.

Pillar-and-scroll shelf clock. This 1820 shelf clock was made by Seth Thomas (1785–1859) in Plymouth, Connecticut. The material is maple and white pine. *Courtesy of the Metropolitan Museum of Art*

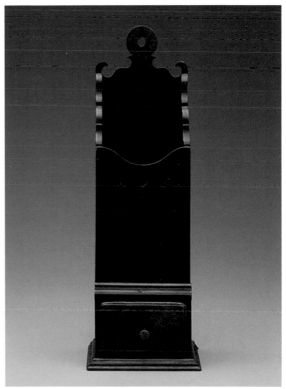

Pipe box. This maple-and-chestnut pipe box from the second half of the eighteenth century features a heart and pipe cutouts, a scrolled top, and molded edges on the base and drawer front. The box is American. *Courtesy of the Yale University Art Gallery*

Next page: Pipe organ. At nearly 9 feet in height, this rosewood encased pipe organ makes a powerful visual statement. The maker is Richard M. Ferris (1818–1858) of New York. The organ is dated to 1850. *Courtesy of the Metropolitan Museum of Art*

pith:

The junk wood at the very heart of a log, prone to checking and splitting. Typically, sawyers cut usable boards around the pith, then sell the pith for use as railroad ties or in other similarly rough applications.

plain sawn:

Identifies the figure that results from the most common method of sawing boards from a log, specifically boards sawn at an angle of 45 degrees or less from the growth rings. Such boards are more prone to warping and cupping than those that are quarter-sawn.

planarity:

State of being in a single plane.

planking:

A construction assembled from long, edge-jointed boards, as in a tabletop.

plant stand:

Traditionally a small table standing 24" or more, on which a plant is placed for display. Today, however, plant stands are available in a myriad of different configurations, including some on which banks of plants are displayed on three or four or more tiers.

plate rack:

A wall-hung construction with grooved shelves for the display of plates and miscellaneous bric-a-brac. The groove on the shelf tops is intended to secure the lip of plates displayed in a nearly vertical position. Some plate racks also have safety bars to keep plates from falling to the floor when the rack is jostled.

platform bench:

A bench designed by George Nelson (1908–1986), with a seat composed of slats standing on edge with spaces in between.

platform rocking chair:

Rocking chair attached to a stationary base. This results in a rocker that doesn't move across the floor when in use.

plinth:

Base on which a cabinet, pedestal, or column stands.

pocket screw:

Screw driven up into tabletop through the apron at an angle. The screw head is typically housed in a drilled pocket larger than the screw, although in some eighteenth- and nineteenth-century work, the pocket is excavated with gouges.

poker table:

Modern version of the card table, usually with a felt top. Unlike period card tables, the tops of most poker tables are not hinged.

pole screen:

A small, usually embroidered screen mounted on a wood pole with tripod base. This form originated in the eighteenth century. The purpose of the screen was to protect the face from the often-harsh heat being broadcast by the open flame in a fireplace. The screen was adjustable so that it could be moved up and down the pole to suit the user.

Pole screen. This pole screen by an unknown eastern Massachusetts maker is dated 1760–1780. The wood is mahogany. *Courtesy of the Art Institute of Chicago*

rabbit-ear armchair:
    A circa 1905 wood-framed armchair with upholstered seat and crest rail, with back posts that rise above the crest rail in a fashion reminiscent of rabbit ears. The chair was designed by J. S. Ford of the Ford and Johnson Company (1867–1913).

racquet-back chair:
    Federal-era chair usually of Philadelphia origin with a back splat resembling a tennis racquet.

Racquet-back chair. Based on a Thomas Sheraton (1751–1806) design, this is a classic Philadelphia racquet-back side chair. The materials are mahogany and ash. The chair is dated circa 1800. *Courtesy of the Yale University Art Gallery*

Rake and splay. Notice the exaggerated rake and splay on this Windsor by an unknown American maker. The seat is white pine, and the other woods are unidentified. The chair was made in the first half of the nineteenth century. *Courtesy of the Yale University Art Gallery*

radiussed edge:

A rounded edge. This can be anything from a slight rounding done with sandpaper to a nosing cut with a nosing plane or an electric router.

rail:

Horizontal component in a frame.

rake:

Outward spread of a chair's legs as they descend from the seat. "Rake" is outward spread when viewed from the side. "Splay" is outward spread when viewed from the front. Windsor chair legs all manifest some degree of "rake" and "splay."

ram's-horn arm supports:

Feature of some early comb-back Windsors in which the two primary arm supports arc forward in a manner suggesting a ram's horns.

rebate:

English term for "rabbet."

***recamier* (*recamier* sofa):**

In early usage, a low sofa with an incomplete back and one end higher than the other. In the hands of John Henry Belter (1804–1863), this became a low sofa with high headrest curving around one end and half of the back, topped with a wide, elaborately carved crest.

Recamier. Because it was made early in the nineteenth century, this piece probably should be called a "Grecian couch," the term in use during Duncan Phyfe's working life. However, because of the notoriety of a painting by the French artist Jacques Louis David (1748–1825) of Mme. *Recamier* lounging on a couch of this type, later in the century the name for this form was changed from "Grecian couch" to *"recamier"* in the common parlance. This 1810–1820 sofa is attributed to the shop of Duncan Phyfe. The materials are rosewood-grained maple, gilding, and ormolu. *Courtesy of the Metropolitan Museum of Art*

IS FURNITURE MAKING ART OR CRAFT?

I have an uncle who—after touring an exhibit of my furniture at The Georgian in Lancaster, Ohio—said to me: "You've raised furniture-making to an art."

It was a deeply uncomfortable moment. I know he meant to compliment, but I also know that nothing made by my hands has ever risen to the level of art. I'm a craftsman, not an artist. My designs are carefully conceived based on traditional forms, and they are constructed with well-executed traditional joinery.

But art? No. Not at all.

But having said that, I should also say that a superbly executed piece of furniture inspires in me the kind of joy I find in a great book, a moving piece of music, or a powerful film. Years ago while browsing in a book about eighteenth-century furniture, I came upon a piece of period work I had never seen before—a tall, narrow spice chest lifted into the air on four improbably slender cabriole legs. The deeply carved talons of the ball-and-claw feet were gathered like a mass of exposed tree roots at floor level, the legs rising from this cluster first in the form of four incredibly delicate ankles, which appeared to be no more than ½" in diameter, then swelling gracefully upward toward the knees. The drawer configuration was carefully composed, and the case enclosing those drawers was topped by a wide cornice with an appealing clutter of shadow lines. It was, in sum, an expertly wrought composition that left me feeling— well, uplifted—in much the same way as might an example of more conventional art.

And it is the same for me with anything made by the Goddard/Townsend families of Newport, Rhode Island, or the finest Boston bombé work, or the massive Philadelphia highboys made by Thomas Affleck in the second half of the eighteenth century.

The truth is, it would be hard for me to see that work as anything less than art.

recessed pull:
Pull that is concealed in a metal or wood housing that sits flush with the panel to which it is attached when not in use. When in use, the pull can be lifted up out of the housing.

recliner:
An upholstered chair designed to allow a user to sit upright or in a reclining position, moving from one configuration to the other through the use of a lever on the side of the chair or, more recently, through the use of small electric motors.

red oak:
Please see "oak, red."

reeding:
Three, four, five, or more beads running adjacent to one another along the length of a part—often a chair or table leg. Reeding was traditionally created with a reeding plane equipped with an iron and a sole cut in the negative reeding shapes. Tapered reeding was carved. Today, reeding is usually created on a molding machine or a router table.

refectory table:
Large, usually heavy, table intended for dining or feasting. It originated in European monasteries, then moved out into castles and other grand residences. The table is often supported on a pair of trestles. Today these tables are more likely to be straining under the weight of books and computers than suckling pigs.

relief carving:
Carving in which the elements stand proud of the background.

reproduction furniture:
Furniture made to mimic furniture of earlier periods. The best-known genre of reproduction furniture is the so-called Centennial

Reeded chair. There is reeding on the bottom back rail and upper back stiles, the outside of the seat rails and stiles, and the lower vase on the arm supports. The chair is attributed to the shop of Duncan Phyfe (1770–1854). The materials are mahogany, cherry, and ash or oak. *Courtesy of the Metropolitan Museum of Art*

Reeding. This detail shows the carving on the crest rail as well as the reeded upper arms. *Courtesy of the Metropolitan Museum of Art*

furniture made in the late 1870s to celebrate the American Centennial. Sometimes, Centennial furniture consisted of accurately replicated Chippendale and Federal forms. At other times, it was simply 1870s furniture on which the maker had emblazoned American motifs, such as the eagle. Today, many makers of fine furniture offer accurate period reproductions or forms consisting of period forms and motifs.

restoration:

The process of restoring antiques to their original glory.

return bead:

A bead seen on some cabinet corners with a quirk on both the front and side. This is traditionally accomplished by using a side bead plane on one side of the corner, then in the opposite direction on the other side.

reverse serpentine chest of drawers:

Please see "oxbow chest front."

revolving bookcase:

Any bookcase that rotates on a center point to present to the user books stored on all sides. This form dates at least to the very early twentieth century.

revolving chair, Shaker:

Form invented by the nineteenth-century Shakers, who made two types of revolvers. The first—dated prior to 1840—consisted of a solid-wood revolving seat backed by a rim of short spindles atop four long turned legs. The second—dated after 1840—consisted of a solid-wood seat backed by a rim of short spindles that revolved above a short turned post atop four bentwood legs arcing down to the floor.

Shaker pedestal revolving chair. This completely successful Shaker design dates to the mid-nineteenth century. The wood is maple, white oak, pine, and birch. *Courtesy of the Metropolitan Museum of Art*

revolving chair, modern:

Manufactured chair in many configurations, the best known of which is the Herman Miller Aeron chair.

riband (ribband) back:

A term denoting a Chippendale chair back featuring carving intended to resemble knotted and intertwined ribbons.

ribbon-and-leaf carving:

Carved sequence in which ribbons alternate with leaves, used in the eighteenth century to adorn table edges.

ribbon stripe:

Bands of darker color stretching along the length of some hardwoods, primarily mahogany and walnut.

ring pull:

Metal finger loop used to open drawers or doors.

rocking chair:

Chair equipped with rockers, which join the bottoms of the posts on each side of the chair to boards sawn or bent into arcs to permit backward and forward rocking. Although it has been suggested that either Benjamin Franklin or the American Shakers originated the form, there are surviving rockers that are thought to predate both Franklin's adulthood and the establishment of Shaker communities. According to Bernice Steinbaum, the author of *The Rocker*, the first rocking chairs were simply ordinary chairs to which craftsmen of the day fastened skates.[6] According to Steinbaum, the first documented rocker was one made about 1760 by a Massachusetts craftsman. Two forces in American furniture

---

6 "Skates" are wide rockers arcing on the bottom but remaining flat on top.

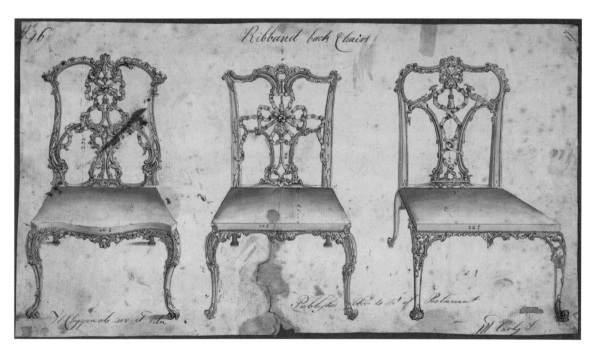

Riband back. These are three preparatory drawings for Thomas Chippendale's book *The Gentleman and Cabinetmaker's Director* (1754), which present three variations for riband-back chairs. *Courtesy of the Metropolitan Museum of Art*

making were most responsible for popularizing this form in the nineteenth century. The first was Lambert Hitchcock (1795–1852), who also popularized "fancy" painted and stenciled chairs. Beginning in 1826, his two companies manufactured huge numbers of rocking chairs. The second force was the Shaker chair factory at New Lebanon, New York, under the direction of Brother Robert Wagan (1833–1883). The chairs made there—including many rockers in different sizes and configurations—were sold to people all across the country as a result of advertisements in *Harper's Weekly* and the *Saturday Evening Post*, in addition to the company's widely distributed chair catalog.

Above: Stickley rocking chair. This chunky oak rocker was made in the Eastwood, New York, shop of Gustave Stickley (1858–1942) circa 1910. *Courtesy of the Yale University Art Gallery*

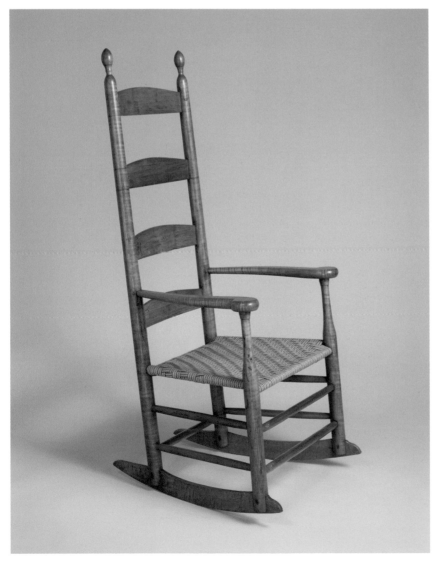

Left: Shaker rocking chair. Originally, in Shaker communities, these chairs were intended only for the old and infirm, but as the nineteenth century progressed, people of all ages began to appreciate the soothing motion of a good rocking chair. This particular New Lebanon example of 1850 predates those sold in Brother Robert Wagan's catalog. The materials are hard maple and birch. *Courtesy of the Metropolitan Museum*

Harvey Ellis rocking chair. Along with Gustav Stickley (1848–1952), Harvey Ellis (1852–1904) was one of the most important figures in the American Arts and Crafts movement. Ellis was first an architect and painter, and then—late in his life—he became a furniture designer. This piece, a handsome Arts and Crafts rocking chair, was built just a year before his death. The material is oak with copper and bronze inlays. *Courtesy of the Art Institute of Chicago*

Eames rocking chair. This stunningly ugly mid-century modern rocker was designed by Charles Eames (1907–1978) and manufactured by Herman Miller, Inc., beginning circa 1955. The materials are steel wire, beech, molded polyester, rubber, and fiberglass nylon upholstery. *Courtesy the Yale University Art Gallery*

rocking horse:

Child's toy in the shape of a horse that creates a rocking motion, either through the use of a pair of rockers into which the legs are mounted or through the use of a stationary frame from which a horse is suspended, like the chair in a glider.

rocking settee:

Rockered construction large enough to hold two or more people.

rococo:

Term assigned to elaborately ornamented, Chippendale-style furniture of the late eighteenth century and of the Rococo Revival period in the late nineteenth century.

rod-back Windsor chair:

Please see "Windsor chair, rod back."

rolltop desk:

Desk with a horizontally tamboured roll covering the writing surface. When the rolltop is raised, it disappears into a housing formed in the body of the desk. This form was popularized during the Arts and Crafts period, a popularity that continued throughout the "golden-oak" era.

rope bed:

A bedstead with holes drilled at regular intervals in the bed frame, through which rope was woven in a simple pattern to provide support for a mattress, usually a fabric sack containing corn shucks. Every year the rope weave had to be removed from the bed frame, boiled, then rewoven. The boiling killed whatever pests might have inhabited the rope, and the reweaving tightened ropes that had grown slack over the course of the year.

rosette:

Round medallion in the shape of an abstracted rose, often used at the termination of a gooseneck-pediment half.

Rose window:

Generally any circular window, but more specifically a window like the rose window on the Strasbourg and Notre Dame cathedrals, which are circles including many rose-petal-shaped sections of leaded glass.

rotary-cut veneer:

Veneer produced by rotating a log past a stationary knife, resulting in a continuous peel of veneer. This is opposed to sliced veneer, in which a veneer log is sawn in the same manner as a board log, the only difference being the thickness of the cuttings and the kerfs. Most consumers of veneer prefer the look of sliced veneer. Rotary-cut veneer is most often used either in the manufacture of interior plys or in the manufacture of construction-grade plywood, although some special plywoods—topped with freak-figured veneers—are the result of rotary cutting.

roundabout chair:

Please see "corner chair."

roundel:

A catchall term including virtually any carved ornament enclosed in a circle.

round *tabouret*:

Small table designed by Gustav Stickley (1858–1942), with four legs, crossed stretchers, and round tops. The word *tabouret* comes from the French and means "small drum." These were available in a variety of diameters from 14" to 20".

rule joint:

A joint used, with hinges, to attach the leaves of drop-leaf tables. The table side of the joint consists of a quarter round topped by a narrow filet. The leaf side consists of a cove with the same radius as the quarter round.

Rosette. This rosette is the terminal element on the gooseneck molding of a secretary by Daniel Spencer (1741–1796) of Providence, Rhode Island. *Courtesy of the Yale University Museum of Art*

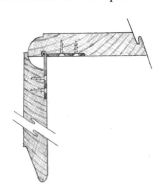

Rule joint with hinge

That cove too is topped by a filet of the same height as the filet at the top of the quarter round. The joint requires special hinges because the pivot point is not at the edge of the tabletop; it is instead centered on a point that is a distance equal to the radius of the quarter round inward from the table edge. Traditionally the two halves of this joint were cut with a matched set of table planes. Today, electric routers or shapers are the tools of choice in most shops.

rung:

Name given to a chair's round stretchers.

run-out:

Please see "grain run-out."

rush (rush seat):

Please see "cattail rush" and "fiber rush."

rustic furniture:

Simply made utilitarian furniture, sometimes made of twigs or cane. Furniture of this type was often used in rural lodges of wealthy nineteenth-century Americans, as well as in the homes of nineteenth-century Americans lacking the wealth to buy manufactured furniture.

saber leg:

Chair leg with a single curve along its length, named for its resemblance to a saber blade. The history of saber-legged chairs dates to the fifth century BCE in Greece. It was then resurrected in the first quarter of the nineteenth century in France and in the United States, where it became a mainstay of Empire-period side chairs.

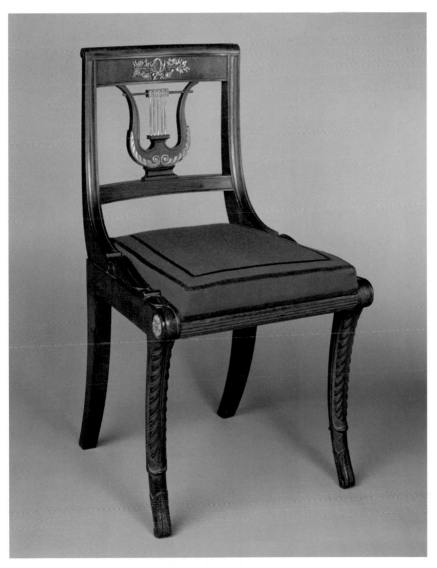

Saber leg. Made in New York by the French immigrant Charles-Honoré Lannuier (1779–1819), this chair with saber legs is an improved version of the Empire chairs Lannuier likely made in France before immigrating to this country. The chair is dated 1815–1819. The material is mahogany, gilded gesso, maple, and brass. *Courtesy of the Metropolitan Museum of Art*

sack-back Windsor chair:
Please see "Windsor chair, sack back."
saddle seat:
Name given to the shaped solid-wood seats of Windsor chairs.
saltbox:
A colonial wall-hung form in which salt is stored.
Sam Maloof–style rocking chair:
One of the most visible forms in twentieth- and twenty-first-century woodworking schools, composed of a vertically slatted back, extra-long rockers, and deeply sculpted seat. The hallmark of a Maloof-style rocker is the smooth flow of one component into another, which is achieved through bandsaw work on individual parts, followed by disk-sanding and rasping after the parts have been joined together.
samples, cabinetmaker's:
Please see "cabinetmaker's samples."
Saratoga trunk:
Large pre-1880s trunk. Typically these were the finest in a manufacturer's list of trunk offerings, featuring the most-complex interiors with a number of compartments and trays.
sash bar:
Please see "muntin."
Saturday table:
A table made on Saturday from wood left over from the week's work, according to legend at the Pleasant Hill Shaker community.

satyr mask:
Carved mask of a satyr[7] found on the knees of some eighteenth-century cabriole legs and later revival furniture.
sausage turning:
Turning modeled after a series of joined sausages, used as stretchers on some Windsor chairs.
sawbuck table:
A tabletop supported on two X-shaped end panels. This type of table is named for the "sawbuck," which looks just like a "sawbuck table," with the tabletop and connecting rails removed so that rounds of firewood can be dropped into the open upper halves of the Xs and held there while being sawn into fire-box-sized chunks.
sawtooth rack:
Set of four cleats, all having one edge cut into large sawteeth into which the ends of shelves can be fit. The long strips are mounted inside a cabinet at each corner. The sawteeth make it possible to position shelves at various heights. This construction was never seen in high-style work, but it was widely used in vernacular (country) work.
scallop shell:
Carved ornamentation on period case-pieces and chairs that resembles the shell of the marine scallop.
scalloped top:
Curvilinear motif repeated around an oversized table or chest top, which became popular in the eighteenth century. In its simplest form, it's just a row of semicircles. More-complex versions involve repeating cyma curves, usually alternating with half or quarter circles.

---

7 A satyr is a half-man, half-horse mythological creature known for its sensuous appetites; in other words, the original party animal.

Saturday table. This unusual table from the Shaker community at Pleasant Hill, Kentucky, features octagonal legs with a swelling taper as the legs descend to the floor. Local legend has it that items like this were made on Saturday, using scraps from the woodshop's weekly assignments. It's possible that the leg facets were planed and chiseled, but it's more likely that the legs were held in a cradle marked in 45-degree increments. They were locked in place, then moved past a bandsaw blade at each incremental stop. Notice the circular saw marks still evident on the top. *Courtesy of* Popular Woodworking

Schrank. This *schrank* is enormous, more than 8 feet high and 7½ feet wide. The two doors—his and hers?—are as large as the entrance doors on most homes, and the whole piece has the feel of an architectural rather than a home-furnishing piece. That feel isn't unique to this example. It's common to all members of the *schrank* species. The case and the doors on this example are tightly fit frame-and-panel assemblies: solid work. But the decorative embellishments are not as crisp as those you might see on a high-style piece of the time. The carved shell is indifferently conceived and executed. And some of the inlay work seems a little vague, as if it's not quite sure where it's headed. But there is one little bit of inlay work that I simply love: the large insect creeping across the bottom of the central door. His body and legs are pieces of inlay, and his lobed feelers are suggested by two rows of shallow—drilled?—indentations. The piece is the work of an unknown maker in the Kutzown, Pennsylvania, area. The materials are walnut and pine. The piece is dated 1781. *Courtesy of the Winterthur Museum*

Schrank:

Related in size and purpose to the kas or *kast*, a large, two-door cabinet for storing clothing and household goods. Drawers and shelves make up one side, while the other side is hanging space for clothes. An immense casepiece with two doors, behind which there is a place for hanging clothes, as well as drawers and shelves. Additional drawers and small doors can be arranged around the primary doors. Since these were often used as dower chest, they were typically designed so that they could be partially disassembled and moved into the bride's new home.

sconce:

A wall-hung holder for a candle. Many of those made by Shaker craftsmen were suspended from a slat drilled with a number of holes large enough to receive Shaker pegs, making their height adjustable when suspended from Shaker peg rails.

scoop (scooped) seat:

Please see "dropped seat."

scotia molding:

Please see "cove molding."

scrap basket:

Circular construction composed of narrow—uncoopered—slats that appeared in Gustav Stickley's craftsman furniture catalogs.

screen, folding:

Please see "folding screen."

scroll:

Spiral feature, used in volutes, as furniture feet, and in many other carved settings.

scroll-back chair:

Chair with a back that arches backward, in which the outside stiles terminate in a carved scroll. This form probably originated in New York during the Federal period.

scrollboard:

Please see "tympanum."

Central door of *Schrank*. Courtesy of Winterthur Museum

Carved shell of *Schrank*. Courtesy of Winterthur Museum

Sconce. This pair of sconces is fashioned primarily of maple. The eagle carvings are typical of Federal-era work. They are the work of an unknown maker in an unknown city. They probably date to the 1790s. *Courtesy of the Metropolitan Museum of Art*

Scroll-back chair. The maker of this chair, Charles Honoré Lannuier (1779–1819), is identified only by a scrap of his printed label. That scrap makes this particular scroll-back chair the only known example of this form that can be tied to any specific New York City shop. The chair is mahogany and dated 1810. *Courtesy of the Metropolitan Museum of Art*

Scroll-top pediment. The gooseneck moldings atop this scrolled pediment are cut from a darker mahogany than the mahogany of the case it surmounts. This secretary is the work of Providence, Rhode Island, maker Daniel Spencer (1741–1796). *Courtesy of the Yale University Art Gallery*

scroll foot:
Furniture foot with spiral form when viewed from the side.

scroll-top pediment:
Pediment that first appeared at the peak of the Queen Anne period, in which the cornice molding rises from both sides of the upper case in a graceful cyma curve, leaving between their ends a space in which a finial could be placed. It was then quite common on tall casepieces throughout the Chippendale period and continued to appear in the Federal period.

sculpture stand:
A stand on which sculpture might be displayed. Display furniture of this type flourished during the Victorian era, driven by wealthy Americans who wanted to create living environments in which their aesthetic sensibilities might be nurtured and displayed.

Sculpture stand. This heavily constructed sculpture stand was clearly designed to display something of great weight. In addition, it featured a revolving top so the sculpture could be viewed all the way around. The materials are cherry, tulip poplar, pine, and birch. The maker is unknown. It is dated 1870–1890. *Courtesy of the Yale University Art Gallery*

ART FURNITURE

In 1980, *Fine Woodworking* magazine ran a photo of a handsomely executed padauk display cabinet by Garry Knox Bennett (b. 1934). That cabinet featured a bent, half-driven, nonfunctional common nail hammered into the outside of a cabinet door. Bennett's purpose was, in his words, "to make a precious thing less precious." But at least in my provincial mind, that bent nail was an affront, an affectation that all but destroyed the value of Bennett's cabinet, an opinion I extended to nearly all furniture having artistic aspirations during that period of my life.

But in the years since, I've come to realize that the "art furniture" movement—perhaps best exemplified in the work of Bennett and Wendell Castle (1932–2018)—has introduced many new and exciting ideas to the world of furniture design: bold colors, imaginative forms, and—well—whimsy (a word often scorned by my furniture-making dad). One such piece is Castle's "Walking Cabinet," a giraffe-spotted cabinet canted forward like a man in a hurry, elevated on a cluster of giraffe-spotted walking legs. I suppose the cabinet could function as a cabinet. There is a door, and I imagine things might be placed inside. But I don't think anybody would buy it with the intention of using it to store their socks and underwear. Like so much of Castle's work, it was eventually placed in a museum, in the case of the "Walking Cabinet," the Milwaukee Art Museum, where it's on view today, free of the burden of function.

And for my still-provincial mind, that's an issue. Function is the essential quality of furniture, the quality that separates it from sculpture, and that separation isn't a mere intellectual construct, one arbitrarily placing furniture on one side of a line and sculpture on the other. It is, instead, the essential grit from which a piece of furniture is built. For that reason, I find art furniture to be intriguing but rarely beguiling. Yes, my eyes are drawn to its imaginative use of my material of choice, but then they wander, searching for something in which function has been more equably married to form.

seat:

Panel on which the user of a chair places his or her bottom. It can be composed of woven splint, rush, Danish cord, or Shaker tape. It can also be a panel of wood or upholstery over wood.

seat rails:

Please see "seat rung."

seat rung:

The rung around which seating material is woven on a post-and-rung chair.

secondary woods:

Material used for mostly unseen components in a piece of furniture; for example, drawer sides and bottoms, cleats, and glue blocks.

Regional origins can sometimes be determined by the type of secondary wood. In the Northeast, cabinetmakers made use of several different species of white pine as secondary woods. In the South, yellow pine was commonly used for this application, and in those states west of the Appalachians, tulip poplar was preferred.

secretary:

Often-towering piece of American period furniture consisting of three parts: an upper section with shelves for the storage of books, a middle section with writing surface and cubbyholes (or small drawers, or both), and a bottom section with wide drawers.

Meeks Brothers secretary. During the mid-nineteenth century, the secretary form shifted from its eighteenth-century roots and began to take on characteristics of the many stylistic influences of the time. This Meeks Brothers (1836–1859) secretary retains the cylinder form that originated in the Federal period, but instead of being made of mahogany, it is made of rosewood, the preferred mid-nineteenth-century material for high-style furniture. In addition, it incorporates details from the Gothic Revival period, specifically the Gothic-style traceries of the windows and the quatrefoil moldings on the two doors. The piece is dated 1836–1850. The materials are rosewood, satinwood, poplar, walnut, and pine. *Courtesy of the Metropolitan Museum of Art*

Meeks Brothers secretary with open doors. *Courtesy of the Metropolitan Museum of Art*

secretary (*secretaire a' abbatant*):

A French-influenced drop-leaf secretary, often with a plain, boxy exterior designed to provide a neutral setting for the display of beautifully figured veneer.

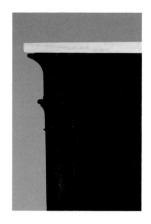

Molding and marble top of *secretaire a' abbatant. Courtesy of the Metropolitan Museum of Art*

Secretary (*secretaire*) *a' abbatant*. This secretary *ab-batant* is thought to have come from the shop of New York City maker Duncan Phyfe (1770–1854). When the drop leaf is lowered into the writing position, a simple interior is revealed, consisting of four drawers and a mirror flanked by two classical columns. The piece is dated 1840–1847. The materials are mahogany, mirrored glass, marble, ivory, white pine, and tulip poplar. *Courtesy of the Metropolitan Museum of Art*

Secretaire a' abbatant with drop leaf down. Courtesy of the
Metropolitan Museum of Art

secretary, block and shell:

Secretary conceived and executed by a member of the Goddard and Townsend families of craftsmen in Newport, Rhode Island. John Goddard is usually credited with originating the form. These towering constructions (one is almost 9½ feet tall) are among the very greatest pieces of American furniture. The lower cases are blocked with large shells carved on the drop leaf, with a second group of large carved shells atop the three door panels. In addition, there are three small shells carved on the doors of the amphitheater. Four of the existing nine-shell (often called six-shell) secretaries are now in museum collections. The last privately held example was sold in 1989 for $12.1 million dollars, then the highest price ever paid for a piece of American furniture. It was purchased in 1989 by antique dealer Harold Sack (1911–2000) for a private collector. In the words of Sack on the day the gavel came down on that sale: "Not all masterpieces hang on walls."

Newport secretary. The block-and-shell version of the Boston block front was the mainstay of Newport craftsmen in the second half of the eighteenth century. This secretary, by an unknown Newport maker, is typical of that form, with the block front continuing on the drop leaf, where it terminates in three large carved shells, the two outside convex and the one inside concave. The materials are mahogany, chestnut, white pine, tulip poplar, and cedar. The piece is dated 1760–1790. *Courtesy of the Metropolitan Museum of Art*

Amphitheater of Daniel Spencer nine-shell secretary.
Courtesy of the Yale University Art Gallery

Previous page and above: Block-and-shell secretary. This nine-shell secretary, by John Goddard's nephew Daniel Spencer (1741–1796) of Providence, Rhode Island, is related to the towering Goddard/Townsend nine-shell secretary—probably the work of John Goddard—which is among the supreme achievements of American furniture making. Like the Goddard/Townsend secretaries, the Spencer piece features six carved shells on the exterior and three more on the interior. The piece makes dramatic use of two different kinds of mahogany: a lighter, possibly Honduran or Santo Domingan species for the case itself, and a darker, possibly Cuban species for the framing of the upper case. The secretary is dated 1772–1790. *Courtesy of the Yale University Art*

secretary, block front:

A secretary originating in the Boston area, with a blocked lower case.

secretary, bombé:

Rare variation of the rococo secretary, with a lower case exhibiting the characteristic bombé swelling and an upper case typical of the secretary form. Like the other bombé forms, this originated in the Boston area.

Interior of block-front secretary shown at left. *Courtesy of the Yale University Art Gallery*

Block-front secretary. This handsome block-front secretary is the work of an unknown maker from Boston or Salem, Massachusetts. This secretary has an unusually well-developed interior, with cubbyholes and drawers even in the upper case. The piece is made of mahogany and white pine. It's dated 1770–1790. *Courtesy of the Yale University Art Gallery*

Next page: Bombé secretary. The bombé form is one of the most challenging for craftsmen to build. It's probably for that reason that there are fewer than sixty known bombé pieces, all coming from the Boston area. But the bottom section of this secretary goes one step beyond bombé: it is also a block front. It is, in fact, the only known piece to combine these two attributes. The upper case is equally impressive, a masterpiece of neo-classical design and execution, with two wide, stop-fluted pilasters supporting acanthus-leaved capitals, which themselves support a wide cornice featuring dentil and egg-and-dart moldings topped with a broken pediment also lined with dentil moldings. Legend has it that this was George Washington's desk during the siege of Boston, and it was exhibited under that description at the 1893 World's Columbian Exposition in Chicago. It is dated 1765–1790. The materials are mahogany and white pine. *Courtesy of the Metropolitan Museum of Art*

secretary, bonnet top:

Secretary with the characteristic bonnet top. Please see "bonnet top" discussion.

secretary, Federal:

Compared to the Chippendale forms that preceded it, a lighter, more feminine piece. A Federal secretary is typically veneered and possesses French feet or turned Sheraton feet or square tapered Hepplewhite-style feet. The writing surface is exposed in any of several ways. On some, the secretary is outfitted with a false top drawer front that falls to create a writing surface and to reveal a small amphitheater with drawers or cubbyholes (or both). On others, the writing surface drops to be supported on lopers. And on still others, a tambour drum or cylinder of solid wood is raised to reveal the writing surface and drawers and cubbyholes. The glass doors in the upper case typically have elaborately muntined glasswork.

Federal secretary. This cylinder secretary by an unknown Boston maker stands on four dainty Sheraton-style legs. The material is mahogany and white pine, with mahogany, birch, and maple veneers. The piece is dated 1800–1810. *Courtesy of the Art Institute of Chicago*

Federal secretary. This is not, strictly speaking, a Federal-era secretary. It's a Chippendale secretary onto which the maker—Nathan Lumbard of Massachusetts—decided to create this wonderland of Federal decoration. It is an eccentric, wholly original take on the secretary form. He begins by eschewing the *de rigueur* use of mahogany as a primary wood, instead relegating the material to mere inlay status, choosing American cherry as his primary. The thing that makes this generally Chippendale form clearly Federal is the use of elaborately detailed inlay work, rather than detail executed in solid wood. For example, instead of an actual dentil molding in the cornice, we have an inlaid strip that mimics the look of dentil molding. And instead of the raised-panel doors we see on Chippendale secretaries, we see a triple frame of light- and dark-wood banding with a strip of mahogany between the two outer frames of banding. The lower case has a serpentine front framed in bands of light and dark woods, like the frames of the doors in the upper case. Around each of the drawer escutcheons, there is a spray of inlaid vegetative work, and on the drop leaf, there is an inlaid urn surrounded by still more inlaid vegetative work. All this detail is thoughtfully conceived and flawlessly executed. In my opinion, this is a work of genius. The materials are cherry, mahogany, basswood, and pine. The piece is dated 1798–1802. *Courtesy of the Winterthur Museum*

Desk amphitheater of Federal secretary. *Courtesy of the Winterthur Museum*

Pediment of Federal secretary. According to Charles F. Montgomery in his 1966 book *American Furniture. The Federal Period*, the lacy filigree between the gooseneck moldings is a sandwich of two layers of wood, one running horizontal and one running vertical, which is just good engineering, an approach that reduces the likelihood of the impossibly delicate fretwork disintegrating. *Courtesy of the Winterthur Museum*

Next page: Renaissance Revival secretary. If this 1893 secretary were any larger, a family could move right in. There's a shingled roof and a widow's walk, and there are four heavy doors: the doors on the bottom case with a column on either side, and the doors on the top sharing a pair of flanking columns. But it is still a piece of usable furniture, with doors and drawers below, and, above, four smaller drawers arranged on both sides of a bookcase. As a decorative piece, it's so far over the top as to be fascinating. It's certainly a piece I'd love to explore. The material is oak. The maker is the Polish-born Ladislaus Zdzieblowski (1857–1929). *Courtesy of the Art Institute of Chicago*

secretary, Renaissance Revival:
     Heavy, blockish secretary tricked out in architectural detail.

secret compartment:

Hidden compartment built into casework, in which valuables can be secured. A secret compartment can be a secret drawer, a compartment covered by a false drawer bottom, a pullout pilaster, etc. Eighteenth-century furniture makers were notoriously clever at creating and siting secret compartments.

serpentine front bombé chest of drawers:

Please see "chest of drawers, serpentine front bombé."

serpentine front chest of drawers:

Please see "chest of drawers, serpentine."

serpentine stretchers:

Cyma-curved, crossing stretchers often found in William and Mary casepieces.

Serpentine stretcher. The stretchers on this William and Mary lowboy have double cyma curves. Stretchers that cross like this are called X-stretchers. The piece dates from the first quarter of the eighteenth century and was probably made in Connecticut. The primary wood is cherry. *Courtesy of the Metropolitan Museum of Art*

server:
> Please see "serving table."

serving table:
> A sideboard with few, if any, drawers.

settee:
> A chair wide enough to seat two or more.

Hunziger settee. Jakob Hunziger (1835–1898) of New York City designed and produced furniture that was often based on the twenty-one patents he received in his life. This particular settee has mesh on the seat, back, and end panels, a mesh made of fabric-covered steel for which he received a patent. The settee was likely made between 1876 and 1898. The materials are ebonized cherry and fabric-covered steel mesh. *Courtesy of the Metropolitan Museum of Art*

Four-back settee. During the Federal era, settees with multiple chair backs became fairly common. This four-back settee has some features in common with other Philadelphia chairs of the period and with drawings in Thomas Sheraton's *The Cabinet-Maker's and Upholsterer's Drawing-Book*. The material is mahogany and ash, and the date is 1800–1815. *Courtesy of the Los Angeles County Museum of Art*

Settle:

Wide, panel-back wooden bench with arms. The form dates to the thirteenth century and continued to be made throughout the colonial era of the United States, where the hardwood seat was often upholstered. The tall panel back was used to capture heat from an open fire.

settle, Arts and Crafts:

A revival of a colonial-era form without a high back, used simply as a piece of seating furniture; more of a settee than a true settle.

sewing chest:

Small chest in which sewing notions are stored.

Settle. Walnut-and-leather settles like this one appear to have been made only in the Philadelphia area. The high, leather-covered back of this example would have protected users from drafts, as well as collected heat from an open fire, in poorly heated eighteenth-century homes. The piece is dated 1710–1740. *Courtesy of the Metropolitan Museum of Art*

Below: Arts and Crafts settle. Probably a Harvey Ellis (1852–1904) design, this settle was made by Gustave Stickley's (1858–1942) Craftsman's Workshop in 1903. The decorative inlays on the back and sides are a signature of Ellis's brief time with Stickley. The materials are oak, copper, pewter, fruitwood, and leather. *Courtesy of the Los Angeles County Museum of Art*

sewing desk (cabinet):

Example of Shaker casework with many drawers, often on two sides, around which Shaker Sisters might have gathered to work on sewing projects.

sewing rocker:

An armless rocker that allowed the user's arm space for sewing or needlework.

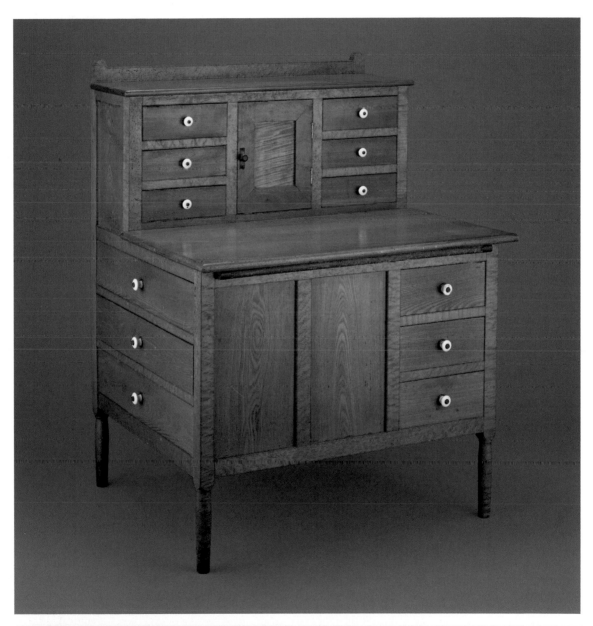

Shaker sewing desk. When Shaker work is good—as it is in this example—it often makes use of figured material. This sewing desk has a post-and-rail frame of highly figured bird's-eye maple. Then, in the upper case, there is a cherry frame around a panel of highly figured fiddleback maple. True: The miters in that frame are a little rough, but there is, nevertheless, a thoughtfulness in the arrangement of woods that raises this piece above the level of unschooled country furniture. The material is cherry, birch, ash, and maple. The piece is dated 1860–1870. *Courtesy of the Art Institute of Chicago*

sewing stand:

A Shaker form with a tripod base and one or more underslung drawers, around which Shaker sisters might gather to work on sewing projects.

sewing steps:

A two-step assembly not intended to take the weight of a human. They were, instead, built so that a Shaker sister might raise her feet to a comfortable working height while seated.

Sewing steps. Shaker sewing steps were never intended to carry human weight. Instead, they were intended as a place ment for the feet of a Shaker sister during often-long sessions of hand sewing. This set of carpeted pine sewing steps was— according to an inscription on the upper step—the property of A. Rosetta Stephens (1861–1947), a sister in the New Lebanon, New York, Shaker community. *Courtesy of the Metropolitan Museum of Art*

sewing table:

A modern variant of the Shaker sewing stand.

Shaker chair:

Any chair made in any Shaker community. The best known are those made in the chair factory at the New Lebanon, New York, Shaker community in the second half of the nineteenth century under the direction of Brother Robert Wagan (1833–1883). Because so many chairs were made in the New Lebanon chair factory, they tend not to bring the highest prices at auction, usually only several hundred dollars By contrast, a bench-made chair from the Union Village, Ohio, Shaker community brought $67,250 at the Willis Henry Shaker Auction in 2013. That chair was one of a handful known to exist with serpentine arms.

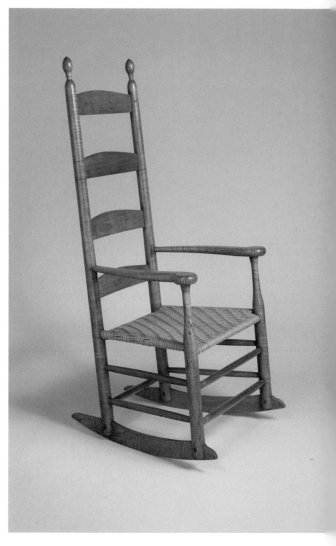

Shaker chair. This rocking chair was made in the New Lebanon, New York, Shaker community sometime in the first half of the nineteenth century—before Brother Robert Wagan had transformed New Lebanon chair making from the construction of bench-made chairs for use within the community to a manufacturing concern shipping chairs all over the United States. The material is maple and birch. *Courtesy of the Metropolitan Museum of Art*

Shaker oval boxes:

Shaker-made bentwood boxes held together with tacked, knife-cut fingers.

Shaker oval box. The American Shakers, a communal society that flourished in the mid-nineteenth century, developed a number of identifiably Shaker crafts, among them the production of Shaker oval boxes—the Tupperware of their day—like the one pictured here, which was made in one of the many Shaker communities somewhere in the United States. The material is white pine and maple. *Courtesy of the Art Institute of Chicago*

Shaker pegs:

Turned wooden pegs attached to long, wall-mounted cleats, found in most Shaker rooms. These pegs provided the Shakers with places from which they could hang their clothes and other household items—even chairs—so that floors could be easily swept. Typically, these have a dome-shaped head above a necklike half cove widening into a gracefully curved shank, although there are many variations on this theme.

Shaker tape:

Fabric tape woven by Shaker sisters, used to seat chairs. This material was being used very early in the nineteenth century. In Charles Muller and Tim Reiman's book *The Shaker Chair*, they quote an 1814 journal entry from the Watervliet Shaker community, stating that "the Elders moved the tape loom into the North Shop."

shaved spindles:

Spindles crafted not on a lathe but with a drawknife or spokeshave. On a Windsor chair, shaved spindles make up the back, while turned spindles make up the chair's undercarriage.

shaving stand:

A stand with a horizontal surface, above which is a mirror to facilitate the shaving of a man's face. In America, the form dates to the early nineteenth century.

shelf:

A board or narrow panel fixed on a wall or between cabinet sides, used to store or display books, china, or miscellanea of any kind.

shelf bracket:

Bracket of metal, wood, or plastic used to attach a shelf to a wall.

shelf clock:

Please see "mantle clock."

shelf pegs:

Small pegs, usually brass, that can be fit into holes drilled on the inside of cabinet ends. Shelves can be positioned on four pegs set at the same height.

shell:

Please see "carved shell."

shellac:

A finishing material originating in a secretion of the female lac bug. After cleaning and drying the collected secretions, the resulting material—shellac—is sold as flakes or "buttons," which are then ground and mixed with ethyl alcohol before applying. When applied using the French polishing method, it can produce wonderfully smooth and glossy surfaces, bringing out the very best in highly figured woods. The downside is that shellac is a relatively fragile finishing material capable of being damaged by water.

shield-back chair:

Hepplewhite-inspired Federal chair with a back resembling a shield in contour. The strapwork connecting the shield contour takes many different forms, including drapery swags, urns, tulips, etc.

shiplap:

Board preparation in which a half-thickness rabbet is cut on the front on one side and on the back of the other side. The boards are then installed—perhaps to make up the back of a casepiece—lapping one back rabbet over the front rabbet of the preceding board, leaving narrow gaps between board faces. They are installed without glue, using small nails. The advantage of such a construction is that

McIntire shield-back side chair. This handsome side chair is almost certainly the work of Salem, Massachusetts, maker Samuel McIntire (1757–1811). During his working life he was a successful architect and designer of interiors, as well as being a gifted carver. The chair is based on a design in George Hepplewhite's 1788 book *The Cabinet-Maker and Upholsterer's Guide*. The materials are mahogany, ebony, ash, birch, and pine. The chair is dated 1794–1799. *Courtesy of the Metropolitan Museum of Art*

expansion and contraction can take place across the width of the panel without the materiel cracking and without the creation of visible gaps.

shiplap panel:

Panel made up of shiplapped boards.

shoulder:

Please see "tenon shoulder."

show rung:

Rung on post-and-rung chair below the seat rung, so named because it shows in the finished chair. Chair makers typically hide rungs with cosmetic issues—perhaps a sapwood streak or a bit of wane—by using them as seat rungs where they will be concealed by seating material. The best rungs then are used as show rungs.

side-bead molding:

Molding profile cut on the edge of a board, having a semicircular bead set off by a quirk.

Side bead molding in cross section

sideboard (buffet):

Initially a serving table without drawers. In the Federal era, it became a large serving cabinet with doors and drawers. These waist-high pieces were placed in the dining room as a repository for the silver and dishware necessary for dining, with the top of the sideboard reserved for the serving dishes required for the meal of the moment. Some of the sideboards of the Federal era are among the finest examples of American furniture making.

Lipton Keystone Sideboard. This dramatic sideboard features Swiss pearwood and quilted maple doors and drawer fronts, as well as etched glass panels on the top. It is the work of current maker Gregg Lipton (b. 1957) of Cumberland, Maine. *Photo by Paul Avis, courtesy of Gregg Lipton*

sideboard, Arts and Crafts:

Sideboard made in the Arts and Crafts style, usually featuring oak, hand-hammered hardware, and simple—some might say blocky—lines.

sideboard, Empire:

Sideboards of the post-Federal era, noted for their exotic veneers, carving, ormolu, and gilding. Not all Empire sideboards featured all these decorative elements, but many of the finest examples did. In addition, some included pillars with Corinthian capitals, inlaid metals, mirrors, marble, etc. They are among the largest and—in the eyes of some—the gaudiest forms of the period.

sideboard, Federal:

Serving-table form created during the Federal era. Most are rooted in the Hepplewhite style with square tapering legs, while others have their origin in the designs of Thomas Sheraton (1751–1806) and feature turned, usually reeded, legs. Most Federal sideboards of either design ancestry have veneered doors and tops.

Stickley sideboard. This 1905 Gustav Stickley (1858–1942) sideboard residing now in the Indianapolis Museum of Art is typical of the work produced by his company. *Courtesy of Getty Images*

Sideboard, Empire. Charles-Honoré Lannuier (11779–1819) emigrated from France early in 1803 and quickly became one of the very best cabinetmakers in New York City and, in fact, one of Duncan Phyfe's chief rivals. This sideboard, made in the second decade of the nineteenth century, features flame-grain mahogany, animal paw feet, and four Corinthian columns. The secondary woods are tulip poplar and pine. *Courtesy of the Metropolitan Museum of Art*

Federal-era sideboard. This striking Federal-era sideboard is attributed to Thomas Seymour (1771–1848) in part because of the alternating light and dark strips of wood in the tambour, a motif of contrasting woods that is carried on throughout the piece. The sideboard is dated 1805–1810. The primary woods are mahogany, curly maple, pine, casuarina, sabicu, maple, and cherry. *Courtesy of the Metropolitan Museum of Art*

sideboard, Hepplewhite:

Most common (and often the most magnificent) of Federal-era sideboards. This variety features square-in-cross-section legs, tapering as they move down to the floor. Sometimes these legs have spade feet. More often the foot is simply identified by a band of stringing around the ankle, or perhaps contrasting wood used to veneer the feet. The finest examples are cloaked in spectacular mahogany veneer ornamented with inlay work done in contrasting woods.

side chair:

Simply a chair without arms. Buyers of dining-chair sets usually purchase two armchairs to go with two, four, or six side chairs. Please see "armchair" entry for a discussion of period differences.

Eames side chair. This chair, made of aniline-dyed plywood and tubular metal, was designed by Charles (1907–1978) and Ray (1912–1988) Eames and manufactured by Evans Products Company and Herman Miller, Inc. The chair was designed in 1946, then released as a retail product in 1950. *Courtesy of the Yale University Art Gallery*

Hepplewhite-style sideboard with *eglomise* glass. This extraordinary (some might say overcooked) example of Federal-era cabinetmaking likely originated in Baltimore or Philadelphia between 1795 and 1805. Notice the two *eglomise* panels flanking the central lunette. The materials are mahogany, satinwood, silver, copper, *verre églomisé*, tulip poplar, and pine. *Courtesy of the Metropolitan Museum of Art*

Shastey side chair. In 1873, George A. Shastey (1839–1894)
of New York founded a furniture company that would eventually employ 125 craftsmen. Like the Herter Brothers,
George A. Shastey and Company was one of the premier
interior-decorating firms of the Gilded Age. This chair, one
of a pair, was designed for the townhouse of Arabella Worsham
(1851–1924), the mistress and later second wife of Collis P.
Huntington (1821–1900), who built his fortune in the railroads.
Courtesy of the Metropolitan Museum of Art

Detail of side chair. The faces of a dog, maybe a lamb, and something else are inscribed into the inlay work shown here. According to the Metropolitan Museum website, these are drawings of "grotesque masks," but I can't quite see that. *Courtesy of the Metropolitan Museum of Art*

side chair, whimsical:

A side chair intended to invoke humor or whimsy. Rooted in the pop culture movements of the 1960s, the "whimsical era" encouraged some designers to imagine functional or non-functional furniture that would produce a smile.

Michael Gloor window chair. This imaginative side chair by current maker Michael Gloor (b. 1954) of Exeter, Rhode Island, is constructed of mahogany, African satinwood, ebony, and leather. Like the Brown/Venturi chair below, this example has an element of whimsy, but it is first and last a piece of solid shopwork assembled with care and a coherent sense of woodworking traditions. *Photo courtesy of Michael Gloor*

Left: Whimsical side chair. The designers of this chair and several others very much like it, Denise Scott Brown (b. 1931) and Robert Venturi (1925–2018), believed that this particular example evokes the work of Thomas Chippendale (1718–1779). Well, okay. Maybe in their eyes it does. Further, according the Yale University Art Gallery, the bird's-eye veneer on the outside of the chair's plywood "evokes early American furniture." Really? This piece of bent plywood? The chair was manufactured by Knoll Inc. in East Greenville, Pennsylvania, in 1987. *Courtesy of the Yale University Art Gallery*

side rails (bed):
     The long, relatively narrow boards con-
necting a bed's headboard and footboard.
Typically, these have cleats on their hidden
sides that accept the ends of the slats that
support the box spring and mattress.

side table:
     A generic term used to identify a myriad
of small tables without a specific function.

sill cupboard:
     Cupboard with upper and lower case
separated by a narrow ledge or sill on the
cupboard front.

skirt:
     Please see "apron."

skyscraper furniture:
     Bookcases and cabinets designed to look
like skyscrapers. These originated in the work
of modernist designer Paul Frankl (1886–1958).

slant-front desk:
     Please see "drop-leaf desk."

slat:
     A narrow board used under a bed to hold
the box spring or, when planed very thin, to
connect a chair's back posts. The term "slat"
can also be used more generally to identify
any relatively narrow, relatively thin length
of wood, like those composing the backs of
many country chairs.

Sill cupboard. This pine sill cupboard from the first half of the nineteenth century is the work of an unknown Shaker craftsman probably in the New Lebanon, New York, Shaker community. *Courtesy of the Metropolitan Museum of Art*

slat-back:

Chair back composed of posts rising above the seat, joined, typically, by two to five slats.

sleigh bed:

A modern version of the ancient Roman daybed or *lectus*. The top of the headboard arches back toward the wall, and the top of the footboard arches in the other direction.

sliding-dovetail joint:

Please see "dovetail, sliding."

sling chair:

Please see "campeche chair."

sling sofa:

Sofa composed of a leather sling suspended from a chromed-steel tubing frame, into which are placed three seat and three back cushions. The piece stands on six chromed-steel legs. The design is attributed to George Nelson (1908–1986).

slipper chair:

Any chair with a seat set unusually close to the floor. Modern examples are upholstered.

slipper foot:

Long, slender, and pointed variant of the spoon foot used at the termination of some Queen Anne cabriole legs.

Slipper chair. This walnut-and-tulip-poplar slipper chair was built in Philadelphia by an unknown maker between 1750 and 1770. *Courtesy of the Yale University Art Gallery*

slip seat:

A removable upholstered seat for high-style dining chairs. Traditionally, these were stuffed with horsehair for comfort, although modern slip seats use synthetic materials for that purpose.

sofa:

An upholstered bench with a back and two ends, wide enough to seat several people.

sofa table:

Tall, narrow table designed to stand behind a sofa, often used for the display of family photos or collectibles.

Slipper foot. The cabriole legs on this dainty Newport, Rhode Island, lowboy terminate in pointed slipper feet. The material is mahogany. The maker is unknown. The piece is dated 1740–1750.

Sofa. This boldly carved mahogany sofa by an unknown maker
originated in Boston circa 1820. *Courtesy of the Metropolitan
Museum of Art*

Sofa table. Both the sofa and the sofa table became essential
home furnishing for prosperous nineteenth-century Americans.
The sofa table, a high table that stood behind the sofa, was a
place on which one might place a vase of flowers or a display
of travel souvenirs. This particular example was produced in
the New York shop of John (?) and Joseph Meeks (1761–1868)
in about 1840. The material is rosewood, ash, and pine. *Courtesy
of the Art Institute of Chicago*

softwood:

Generic term used to identify wood taken from coniferous trees. American softwoods used in furniture making include white pine, yellow pine, and spruce. Softwood species are usually reserved for secondary applications; for instance, cabinet backs and cleats.

Soss hinge:

Brand name of so-called invisible hinge without pin or knuckles. Its two ends are mortised into the edges of the parts being joined.

spade foot:

Square foot that tapers downward from square shoulder, typically found on Hepplewhite case furniture and tables. A spade foot can also be created through the use of an inlaid band above the foot or simply by using a contrasting wood for the foot section.

spalted wood:

Wood exhibiting early evidence of decay, which can produce a striking pattern of dark lines across its surface.

spandrel (spandril):

Space between the top of arch housing and the arch itself.

Spanish foot:

Composed of several narrow lobes leading downward, then curling underneath themselves. They appeared primarily on chairs of the William and Mary period. This construction is sometimes called a "paintbrush foot" or "Portuguese foot."

spice cabinet (chest):

Small cabinet with many drawers, usually built to stand on a table or sideboard, but some rare examples have cabriole legs, which raise the cabinet from the floor to waist height.

Spade foot. This chair, which features spade feet on the front legs, is based on a drawing in George Hepplewhite's book the *Cabinet-Maker and Upholsterer's Guide. Courtesy of the Metropolitan Museum of Art*

Spanish foot. Although Spanish feet were much more common in the William and Mary period, the Spanish foot was favored by some makers of Queen Anne furniture and their customers. This particular example is the work of an unknown maker in the Delaware River valley in the middle of the eighteenth century. The material is walnut and yellow pine. *Courtesy of the Yale University Art Gallery*

Previous page, right: Spice cabinet. This William and Mary spice cabinet, which stands less than 29" tall, is designed to resemble a full-size piece of storage furniture. Constructed of black walnut, yellow pine, and white cedar, this little charmer is fitted with a number of small compartments in which spices would have been stored. *Courtesy of the Metropolitan Museum of Art*

spider, table:

Please see "table spider."

spindle:

A turned, shaved, or sawn strip of wood.

spindle-back armchair:

Chair with back composed of an arrangement of turned or shaved spindles.

spinning wheel:

Construction built around a large wheel that was used to spin thread from undifferentiated fiber. In the eighteenth and early nineteenth centuries, spinning was a popular activity for wealthy women, so wheels of that period were often highly decorated with elaborate turnings.

spiral turned spindle:

Spindle shaped so that it resembles a spiral. This is not, strictly speaking, a turned product. Instead, it is produced by a combination of turning and carving. After turning the spindle from which the spiral will be cut, the craftsman wraps a strip of paper or thin cardboard around the turning, in a spiraling manner. The spindle is then marked following the strip of paper, and after the pattern is removed, the spiral is created with carving gouges and rasps. Today, these can be made more quickly by using a router running on a long metal jig along the slowly turning spindle.

splat:

Central upright component of many Queen Anne and Chippendale chair backs. Some are thin panels of solid wood cut into the profile of an urn or a fiddle. Others are composed of interwoven strapwork.

splay (as in splayed legs):

Outward spread of chair legs as they descend from the seat. "Splay" is outward spread seen from the front. "Rake" is outward spread seen from the side. Windsor chair legs, for example, always manifest some degree of "splay" and some degree of "rake" as well.

Spinning wheel. Made of oak and maple, this spinning wheel is dated 1780–1800. Both the maker and city of origin for this American piece are unknown. *Courtesy of the Yale University Art Gallery*

Spiral turning. The pedestal of this mahogany-and-birch candlestand features a spiral turning. The piece originated in Salem, Massachusetts, and the maker is unknown. *Courtesy of the Metropolitan Museum of Art*

spline (short grain):

A thin and narrow length of cross-grain strips used to strengthen a joint.

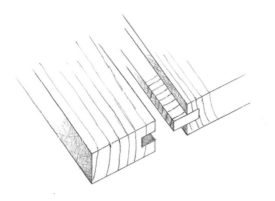

Short-grain spline in edge-to-edge butt joint

splint, ash:

Seat-weaving material harvested by pounding ash billets so that the wood separates along the annular rings. It is then split, resplit, and scraped with a knife until strips of the desired width and thickness have been produced. Unfortunately, the emerald ash borers have killed almost every ash tree in my part of the country (central Ohio), and trees must be living to be harvestable. Along with cattail rush, this was the seat-weaving material of choice for country chair makers until the advent of cheap rattan splint from Southeast Asia. Ash splint is still widely used in the craft of basket weaving.

splint back:

Name given to a chair with a woven splint back.

splint, rattan:

Seat-weaving material made by splitting the pith of the rattan palm (the same plant that gives us cane).

splint seat:

A chair seat woven from either ash splint or rattan splint. The seat-weaving process begins by establishing the warp (the rows of splint that wrap the front and back seat rungs). When the warp is completed, the weavers are woven into the warp, working from side to side in any of a variety of patterns.

split spindle:

Turning composed of one longitudinal half of a spindle. Typically, these were made by gluing together two long pieces of wood, then separating them along the glue line after turning. These were used to form the backs of banister-back chairs. They were also used to decorate some Pilgrim casepieces, such as the Hadley chests of western Massachusetts. A variant of the split turning is the quarter column used to ornament the front corners of some Chippendale casework.

sponge painting:

A nineteenth-century method for applying decorative paint by using sponges. This is seen on country and Shaker objects.

spoon foot:

Furniture foot from the Queen Anne period that resembles an unhollowed spoon bowl, sometimes used as a synonym for pad foot and club foot.

spoon rack:

A wall-hung rack for displaying fancy spoons.

Spoon rack. This 1737 spoon rack was possibly made in New Jersey. The maker is unknown. The material is tulip poplar. *Courtesy of the Yale University Art Gallery*

springwood:
Please see "early wood."

spur (as in "spurred"):
Peaked return in scrollwork.

square:
The state of perpendicularity. A board has a square cross-grain edge when that edge is 90 degrees from the face of the board.

square nails:
Please see "cut nails."

stain:
A finishing product that imparts color to a wood surface. This can have the effect of reducing the contrast between heartwood and sapwood. It can also cause a relatively inexpensive wood to take on the color of a more expensive species such as mahogany, walnut, or cherry, although it would be a mistake to think that any stain can transform white pine into mahogany. A stain is different than a dye, because the coloring particles in a stain are quite large and can collect in the grain, while dye particles are microscopic and are more likely to spread evenly across the surface. Please see also "dye."

stand:
Term that can be applied to any small table.

stave:
Fitted board, curved in cross section, used with others to form walls of a coopered work.

stay:
Please see "lid stay."

steamer trunk (sometimes called "flat tops" or "packers"):
Trunk named for the steamships on which people of the period (1880–1920) often traveled. Typically, the trunks were only 14" tall to conform to steamship luggage regulations.

step-down Windsor:
Please see "Windsor, step down."

step stool:
Stool designed to make it possible to reach items otherwise beyond reach. Some are nothing but a single step, while others may have two or three steps and a hand post to assist in balance. Some Shaker step stools are noted for their elegant simplicity.

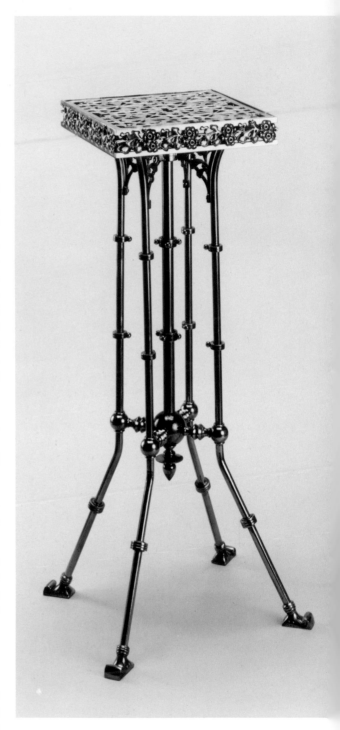

Stand. With its knobby, attenuated legs, this stand evokes the ambulatory structures of an overly large insect—you know, in my mind. The material is iron and brass. It's dated 1880–1885. *Courtesy of the Metropolitan Museum of Art*

stile:
Vertical member of a frame or door, as opposed to "rail," which identifies a horizontal member.

stippling:
Punch-made texture used as background in some leatherwork and wood carving; for example, the stippled backgrounds of the carving on Hadley chests.

stool:
Small, backless seating furniture usually supported by four often-turned legs but occasionally by three. Some working stools are quite low; for example, so that a cobbler might adjust the fit of a man's shoes. Others, designed to be used at, perhaps, a high retail counter, are quite high. Most modern examples are intended primarily to serve as ottomans.

Stippling. This close-up of the surface of a late-seventeenth-century chest reveals the repetitious punch marks of stippling between bits of carved vegetation. *Courtesy of the Metropolitan Museum of Art*

Joiner's (joint) stool. Today, most of the stools we use are intended for our feet, but in earlier centuries, when chairs were expensive, people sat on stools, such as this early-eighteenth-century example. The piece probably originated in New England. The material is maple. *Courtesy of the Metropolitan Museum of Art*

stool with cabriole legs:

Fancy stool with cabriole legs and occasionally ball-and-claw feet.

stop-fluted column:

Use of flutes that don't reach the end of the column into which they're cut.

stopped dado joint:

Please see "dado joint, stopped."

stopped mortise-and-tenon joint:

Please see "mortise-and-tenon joint, stopped."

stopped sliding dovetail joint:

Please see "dovetail joint, sliding, stopped."

straight grain:

Grain that runs approximately parallel to the edges of a board.

strap hinges:

Hinge in which at least one leaf is extended—strap-like. These are often used on dower chests, with the extended leaf reaching halfway across the lid.

strapwork:

Narrow, ribbonlike forms such as those comprising scroll-sawn and usually carved splats of Chippendale chairs.

Strap hinges. These wrought-iron strap hinges by an unknown Pennsylvania maker could have been intended for a dower chest. *Courtesy of the Yale University Art Gallery*

Strapwork. James Graham (1728–1808) of Boston is the possible maker of this handsome Chippendale form, which has a back composed of a complex pattern of strapwork. The materials are mahogany, ash, and white pine. *Courtesy of the Yale Museum Art Gallery*

Stool with cabriole legs. American stools with cabriole legs are rare. This example by an unknown maker is probably of New York origin. The stool is dated 1750–1790. The materials are mahogany and American beech. *Courtesy of the Metropolitan Museum of Art*

straw marquetry:

Style of marquetry in which patterns of straws, rather than patterns of wood, are inlaid into a surface.

stretcher:

Component connecting legs below a seat or case. This connection gives the construction additional strength. On post-and-rung chairs, all the show rungs can be classified as stretchers.

stringing:

Narrow lines of inlaid wood, usually in a contrasting color. Holly was the wood of choice for much Federal-era stringing on mahogany.

stripe figure:

A quality of some mahoganies and walnuts to present the appearance of longitudinal stripes.

striping:

Use of thin painted lines on a piece of furniture.

stub tenon:

Short tenon usually used to keep the component to which it is attached from twisting.

stump wood:

Wood processed from the stump of the tree. Typically the stump extends from the top of the buttresses down to a level that might be several feet into the ground. Although rarely used, this material features exotic grain patterns and colors, as well as inclusions. The harvesting of stumps, however, has become controversial because of the disturbance this process can cause in the forest floor, including loss of nutrients; disruptions of molds, mosses, and insects; and the encouragement of soil erosion.

sugar chest:

Large, often-freestanding wooden box with a locked lid, used to store sugar. In the first two centuries of American colonization, sugar was an expensive imported food, and sugar chests were used to hold the cones into which sugar was compressed for sale, as well as the nippers used to cut pieces from the cones.

sunburst carving:

Semicircular carved abstraction of a sun's bursting rays. This form—often used on the bottom-central drawer front and the top-central drawer front—was often found on Queen Anne and Chippendale casework. This sunray abstraction is sometimes indistinguishable from a lobed shell abstraction.

Sutherland table:

A table in which the main section of the top is quite narrow and has two hinged leaves that reach almost to the floor. Please see the photo on page 142 for an example.

swag:

Drapery or fruit garlands carved, inlaid, or painted on a surface.

swan-neck pediment:

A broken pediment in which the two arches of the pediment form graceful cyma curves resembling the neck of a swan. These arches typically end in mitered returns, carved rosettes, or carved scrolls. These can also be identified as broken-arch pediments and gooseneck pediments.

swell front:

Please see "bow front."

swivel chair:

Chair with a fixed foundation and a revolving seat.

swivel-top card table:

A card table with a top that rotates 90 degrees so that the playing-surface leaves can be supported by the table's undercarriage. This was in contrast to many other period card tables, which depended on a hinged fifth leg to support the open leaf.

tabernacle mirror:

Please see "Constitution mirror."

table:

Flat-topped construction standing on one or more legs. This construction provides a surface on which tableware can be placed, games can be played, and work can be accomplished.

Lotus table. Although not as well known today as some of his contemporaries, John Scott Bradstreet (1845–1914) was an important designer during the Arts and Crafts and Art Nouveau eras. His work was heavily influenced by the decorative arts of Japan, and that influence can be seen in this object: the *Lotus Table from the Gables, Lake Minnetonka*. The material is cypress. The table is dated circa 1903. *Courtesy of the Yale University Art Gallery*

Swivel-top card table. This swivel-top card table is attributed to the shop of New York maker Duncan Phyfe (1770–1854). The material is mahogany, white pine, tulip poplar, and rose-wood. *Courtesy of the Metropolitan Museum of Art*

table, card:

Please see "card table" entries.

table chest:

A chest small enough to be kept on a tabletop.

table desk:

Early colonial form consisting of a table with four turned legs, an apron with drawer, and large top with significant overhang all around. The defining detail is the presence of two small cubbies in the drawer: one for ink and one for a pounce pot, and possibly a third for a blotter.

table leaves:

Sections of a tabletop. Some of these are hung from the sides of the top's central panel via hinged rule joints. At other times, they are completely separate from the table and fit

Table chest. This little—less than 26" long—charmer was made somewhere in Pennsylvania between 1760 and 1800 of figured walnut. *Courtesy of the Yale University Art Gallery*

into place when the table is lengthened through the use of telescoping extensions.

table spider:

A legged iron or steel reinforcement for the underside of pedestal tables. The spider's body is mortised into the bottom of the pedestal, with the legs of the spider mortised into place along the bottom edges of the table legs. There are holes for at least one screw into each leg of the table, and one screw into the base of the pedestal. They come with three arms for tripod tables or four arms for four-legged tables.

tablet:

Any narrow, horizontal element, in particular any narrow, horizontal element ornamented with carved, inlaid, or painted detail.

tablet back:

Neo-classical chair with narrow horizontal crest rail.

table yokes:

U-shaped steel construction in which the legs of the "U" are slid into brackets on the underside of tables and leaves, with one leg bracket on the table and the other leg bracket on the leaf being placed in the table. Their purpose is to hold together sections of a dining or banquet table.

tabouret **(taboret):**

Small table of various heights and configurations. Some have square tops, some round. These tables are usually credited to Gustav Stickley (1858–1942), but other Arts and Crafts companies also offered these tables, including the Charles P. Limbert Company and Roycroft Furniture.

Tabouret. Francis Asbury Reinhol made this *tabouret* in Washington, DC, in 1898. The material is oak with dark- and light-wood inlays. *Courtesy of the Yale University Art Gallery*

Tablet. The tablet on this Herter Brothers (active 1864–1906) chair is decorated with floral inlay work. *Courtesy of the Metropolitan Museum of Art*

tailpiece, Windsor:

A narrow extension of the seat behind the back spindles of a brace-back Windsor that provides an anchor point for extra bracing spindles that rise to the crest rail.

tallboy:

Please see "chest-on-chest" and "highboy."

tall case clock (tall clock):

Generic name for tall clocks, often specifically used to denote period grandfather and grandmother clocks. (These are distinguished primarily by the waist size. If the clock's waist is narrow, the clock is likely to be identified as a "grandfather clock." If there is little or no waist, the clock is likely to be identified as a "grandmother clock.") In addition, during the Arts and Crafts era, the term was used to identify tall clocks without gender, particularly some of those by the Roycroft Furniture Shop. One monumental 8-foot-high tall case clock built by the Roycroft Furniture Shop stands in the Grove Park Inn near Asheville, North Carolina.

talon:

On an animal, the hard, keratinous extension of a claw outside its fleshy sheath. In the case of carved ball-and-claw feet, the length of exposed talon can be used as a clue to the origin of the piece to which the ball-and-claw feet are attached. Philadelphia feet tend to show little evidence of this unsheathed talon, while the ball-and-claw feet of Boston and Newport, Rhode Island, typically have much more talon exposure. In the case of the feet carved by the Goddard and Townsend families of Newport craftsmen, the exposed talon is often separated from the ball it encloses.

Edwards clock. The modern maker of this tall clock, W. Patrick Edwards (b. 1948), was able to purchase the late-seventeenth-century, original, unrestored movement in this clock at a reasonable price because it came into his shop in an undistinguished Georgian case. The maker of the movement, Daniel LeCount, was a French clockmaker who came to London in the second half of the seventeenth century and there entered the Worshipful Company of Clockmakers in 1676, prior to the construction of this movement. Before beginning work on this clock, Edwards searched for examples of period clocks containing LeCount's movements, and used one of these as his model in designing the clock you see here. The case features English yew wood oysters and olive wood, with mixed species used as secondary woods and marquetry. *Photo by David Harrison, courtesy of W. Patrick Edwards*

Edwards clock. W. Patrick Edwards (b. 1948), a San Diego–based marqueter, built this tall clock for a woman who wanted a special gift for her husband's eightieth birthday. The flower imagery on the case reflects the purchaser's love for flowers. This particular piece is the most expensive clock ever to leave Edward's shop, and when the buyer questioned its price, Edwards said: "That's the price for the marquetry; the clock is free." The movement was made by David Lindow of Gravity, Pennsylvania. The primary woods are French walnut and ferreol, a seventeenth-century South American wood rarely seen today. A mixture of species were used for the secondary woods and the marquetry. *Photo by David Harrison, courtesy of W. Patrick Edwards*

Federal-era tall clock. Jacob Diehl (1776–1858) of Reading, Pennsylvania, is the maker of this tall clock, dated 1800. The materials are mahogany, satinwood, white pine, and tulip poplar. *Courtesy of the Metropolitan Museum of Art*

CRAFTSMANSHIP

In the year 2000, I did a book for the Taunton Press, *The Custom Furniture Sourcebook*. The book's purpose was to present the work of the finest designer/craftsmen then working in North America. It was to be a book that would serve as a purchasing resource for interior designers, architects, and homeowners, as well as a font of inspiration to furniture makers.

To select the work, the Taunton Press and I assembled a jury composed of three nationally known individuals in the world of contemporary American furniture. One of those was Art Carpenter (1920–2006), a designer/craftsman I had admired for most of my life. During the days in which submissions were judged, Art and I stayed at the same Newtown, Connecticut, hotel, where we breakfasted together each day. In one of our early-morning conversations, Art made the startling—at least for me—revelation that he didn't consider himself to be a great craftsman.

My world shifted on its axis. Art Carpenter? Not a great craftsman? What did that make me?

I mean, Art's work was in the collections of the Smithsonian and the Metropolitan Museum of Art. His home state had designated him a "living treasure of California," and he'd appeared in *Life* magazine back when that was a really big deal.

But then I thought back to the examples of his work I had seen, and I began to nod my head as if I understood. His work was imaginative. It reflected a probing mind always in search of new forms, although if you look back on it today, it might not seem that way, simply because Art's work has been so influential that dozens of late-twentieth-century designer/craftsmen were incorporating Art's themes into their work. But in its day, in the middle of the twentieth century, Art's work was a revelation, a breath of fresh air in a world infested with manufactured furniture designed to accommodate the manufacturing process.

I began to think about some of the work we were reviewing for my book. I wasn't sure that there was any that would turn out to be as important as the work Art had done in his long career, but oh my, there was work of stunning technical achievement.

Over the next fifteen years, I returned to Art's comment many times, in particular at the time of his death in 2006. I knew I would never be the designer Art had been, but I had always hoped I might someday achieve technical mastery of those furniture-making skills I practiced. But the truth is, I have always known that there were people out there who were better turners than me, better cabinetmakers, better chair makers. I have always done my best, and my customers have always been pleased, but maybe I lack that drive or talent that must be at the core of those individuals who execute their work with unparalleled skill.

Was that what Art Carpenter had meant? That he lacked the drive or physical skills to achieve technical mastery? No, that idea was ridiculous. Anyone who had achieved what Art had achieved during his long working life lacked neither drive nor skill. As I thought more about his statement, I realized it had been more of an acknowledgment that there were others who possessed higher levels of technical virtuosity, and that for him, such wizardry with tools might have been a distraction from what he saw as his essential process.

At least that's what I choose to think. I'll never know for sure because our discussion was interrupted by the arrival at our table of another of my three jurors, Marc Adams, the founder and leader of the Marc Adams School of Woodworking, and the breakfast conversation took off in other directions.

tambour:

A sliding door (shutter) or desk cover made by gluing narrow strips of wood to a canvas or linen backing (or, alternatively, by wiring the strips together). The wood strips can then be finished to match the casepiece to which they are attached. When the tamboured desktop is raised, it disappears into a housing in the cabinet. Similarly, the vertical tamboured doors (shutters) often used in Federal secretaries to conceal the cubbyholes slide into housings on each side of the cabinet.

tambour desk:

A desk in which the cubbyholes and drawers can be concealed and locked between a pair of vertically aligned tambour panels, one on either side. This style of desk was popular during the Federal period.

tambour shutter:

Please see "tambour."

tansu:

Japanese all-purpose portable storage chest. These chests have a history dating to the seventeenth century in Japan, and in the

Tambour desk. Built by New Bedford, Massachusetts, maker Reuben Swift (1780–1843) when he was only twenty-five, this handsome Federal-era desk has two tambour panels bracketing a central door. The materials are walnut, flame birch, tulip poplar, maple, and pine. *Courtesy of the Metropolitan Museum of Art*

centuries since, they have evolved into a number of different forms. Some were outfitted with small drawers to serve as apothecary chests, others with long drawers to hold sword blades, and others outfitted to hold kitchen supplies and food. Traditionally, they were made of elm, chestnut, cedar, and cypress. They were often decorated with elaborate metalwork. In the late twentieth century, some American makers became interested in this form and began producing them, particularly on the West Coast.

tape back:
Name given to a chair with a back composed of strips of Shaker tape woven around the back posts and two back rails.

tape seat:
Name given to chair seat that is composed of strips of Shaker tape woven around the seat rungs.

tavern table:
Small table with four turned legs joined by stretchers. The top is square, round, or oval. Some examples have legs extending downward perpendicular to the tabletop, but the finest examples have legs that exhibit both splay and rake. Many of these tables also have leaves hinged to the top via rule joints and supported by butterfly leaf supports. Please see "rule joints" and "butterfly leaf supports."

T-bridle joint:
Please see "bridle joint, T."

Tavern table. Small tables of this type are often referred to as "tavern tables," and while it's true that many were used in this way, many others were used in homes for a variety of domestic purposes. This powerful little composition has legs exhibiting rake and splay, bold William and Mary turnings, and Spanish feet. This maple-and-oak table, which originated in New England, is dated 1735–1760. *Courtesy of the Metropolitan Museum of Art*

Trestled tavern table. This diminutive trestle table by an unknown maker might have seen use in a tavern or as an occasional table in a home. The table is dated 1700–1725. The materials are maple and pine. *Courtesy of the Metropolitan Museum of Art*

tea caddy:

Please see "tea chest."

tea chest, period (sometimes referred to as a "tea caddy"):

Box, usually of mahogany, for the storage of tea.

teardrop brasses:

Brasses used on William and Mary casework, consisting of a brass teardrop hanging from a cotter pin that passes through a small, usually engraved, brass plate. The user grasps the teardrop to pull open the drawer or door.

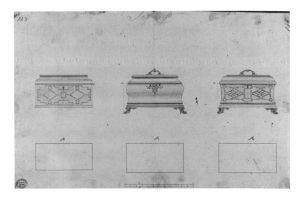

Chippendale tea-chest drawing. This preparatory drawing for Thomas Chippendale's 1754 and 1755 editions of *The Gentleman and Cabinetmaker's Director* shows a form that was a reference for many American cabinetmakers who desired to make tea chests. *Courtesy of the Metropolitan Museum of Art*

Previous page: Highboy with tear-drop brasses. This Boston William and Mary highboy from the first quarter of the eighteenth century is veneered with sheets of burl or stump wood, which gives surfaces a lively energetic appearance. The highboy stands on six boldly turned legs connected by scroll-sawn stretchers. The wood is walnut, maple, tulip poplar, hickory, and pines. The maker is unknown. *Courtesy of the Metropolitan Museum of Art*

Tear-drop brasses, hanging from two cotter pins. *Courtesy of the Metropolitan Museum of Art*

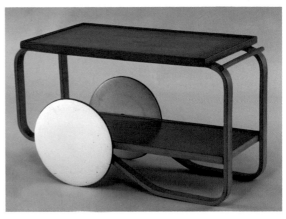

Tea trolley (cocktail cart, bar cart). A tea trolley is a Victorian-era replacement for the tea table so common in eighteenth-century America. This example is a mid-century modern version made of hard maple, birch, plywood, and tulip poplar. The design was conceived in 1941–1942 by Alvar Aalto (1898–1976). *Courtesy of the Yale University Art Gallery*

Tilt-top tea table. This handsome New York tea table is dated 1760–1780. The top is made from a cut of crotch-grain mahogany. *Courtesy of the Metropolitan Museum of Art*

tea table:
 Small, usually rimmed, period table. Some have galleries rather than rims. Queen Anne examples are typically dainty with quite slender cabriole legs. Chippendale tea tables with ball-and-claw feet often have a more masculine appearance.

tea trolley:
 A wheeled contrivance for moving a tea service from the kitchen to another room.

television stand:
 Please see "TV stand."

tenon:
 The male half of a mortise-and-tenon joint, that part that is glued into the female half, the mortise.

tent bed:
 Usually portable four-post bed topped with a tent rather than a conventional canopy.

tenon cheek:
 The broad sides of a tenon.

tenon shoulder:
 Surfaces adjacent to and perpendicular to the tenon cheeks.

tern foot:
 Foot composed of triple scroll, rarely seen in American Chippendale work, but often seen in French rococo work.

terrarium:

A bottle, a bowl, or a case with at least one glazed side in which land plants and animals can be displayed. Typically these are equipped with a metal or wood stand to raise the terrarium to a convenient viewing height. Please also see "Wardian case."

tessellated inlay:

An inlaid surface composed of many repeating shapes, such as a checkerboard.

tester:

Wood or cloth-covered wood construction acting as canopy over a bed.

tester bedstead:

A four-post bed supporting a full canopy.

tête-à-tête:

A sofa designed by the John Henry Belter company that featured two upholstered seats facing in opposite directions, separated by an S-shaped back surmounted by a heavily carved crest rail.

Thonet chair:

Named for the German Austrian Michael Thonet (1796–1871), who developed the form. Thonet chairs are noted for the extreme and graceful bends of their components.

through dado joint:

Please see "dado joint, through."

through dovetail joint:

Please see "dovetail joint, through."

through mortise-and-tenon joint:

Please see "mortise-and-tenon joint, through."

through sliding-dovetail joint:

Please see "dovetail joint, sliding, through."

thunderbox:

Appropriately named box with a hinged lid that, when raised, reveals a toilet seat and a chamber pot. These were devised in the

Tester bedstead. This delicate tester bedstead, dating to the second half of the eighteenth century, has four very slender posts, each rising from a Marlborough foot. It also features a rare fabric-covered cornice. According to the Metropolitan Museum, the bed is related to bedsteads made by the Connecticut master craftsman Eliphalet Chapin (1741–1807), and likely originated in Connecticut. The wood is birch and white pine. *Courtesy of the Metropolitan Museum of Art*

Belter *tête-à-tête.* New York maker John Henry Belter (1804–1863) used a patented process for bending laminated wood in two planes. This provided him with a shaped canvas on which he could execute his extravagant carving of naturalistic forms. This *tête-à-lête* offers users a chance for a comfortable but discreet conversation. This 1850s piece is made of rosewood, ash, pine, and walnut. *Courtesy of the Metropolitan Museum of Art*

Thonet rocking chair. In the 1830s, Michael Thonet (1796–1871) of Germany began to experiment with steam-bent wood as a furniture medium, ultimately resulting in the Thonet chairs we know today. Although they were never made in this country, they have been offered by American retailers since the 1870s. This particular example is dated circa 1876. The material is beech. *Courtesy of the Yale University Art Gallery*

nineteenth century and are still in use today as camping toilets.

tilt-top table:
Table with a top that can be tilted until it stands perpendicular to the floor. Sometimes the tilting is achieved through the use of a "birdcage," but sometimes the tilting is achieved via round spigots carved onto extensions of a thick wood block fastened to the top of the pedestal. These round spigots pass through round holes in a pair of cleats fastened to the underside of the tabletop. Please see also "birdcage top support."

tilt-top tea table:
A tea table with a top supported on a wooden "birdcage" that allows the tabletop to tilt into the vertical through the use of round spigots on the "birdcage."

Tilt-top table with the top exposed. This handsome piecrust table by an unknown eighteenth-century Philadelphia maker features a single-board top over 33" in diameter mounted on a birdcage. *Courtesy of the Metropolitan Museum of Art*

tip-table catch:
Catch designed to secure the top of a tilt-top table in its horizontal orientation.

"T" lap joint:
Please see "lap joint, 'T.'"

toilet table:
Synonym for the term "lowboy" appearing in some late-nineteenth-century sources.

tongue:
A narrow projection along the edge of a board, usually centered across the width of that edge. The tongue is intended to fit into a matching groove on an adjacent board. Please see "tongue-and-groove joint."

tongue-and-groove joint:
Joint used to supplement an edge-to-edge joint by creating a tongue on one edge and a groove on the mating edge. The tongue and the groove were traditionally fabricated with match planes. Today it is more often done with a router, a table saw, a shaper, or a molding machine.

tongue-and-groove panel:
A panel composed of boards with a tongue on one side and a groove on the other. To create the panel—often used for a cabinet back—the tongue of the second board is tapped into the groove of the first, then nailed. This is repeated across the width of the panel. Like the shiplapped panel, the advantage of the tongue-and-groove panel is that it allows expansion and contraction without the creation of visible gaps between the boards.

tool chest:
Traditionally a chest constructed by a workman to hold the tools of his trade. One of the most famous of these is a chest made by the early-nineteenth-century master craftsman Duncan Phyfe, a chest now in the possession of the New-York Historical Society. The exterior of the Phyfe chest is composed of green-painted white pine, but the interior is a glory of mahogany highlighted by ivory and brass details. The chest houses over three hundred woodworking tools.

tortoiseshell:

Shell slices—usually from the endangered hawksbill sea turtle—used to decorate woodwork: mirrors, boxes, and sometimes furniture. André Charles Boulle, in particular, made use of tortoiseshell in his marquetry. Since 1973, however, it has been illegal in this country to work with real tortoiseshell, so various synthetic materials have taken its place.

torus:

Semicircular in cross section molding appearing at the base of a column.

towel rack, freestanding:

A freestanding rack of metal or wood on which towels can be hung to dry.

toy box (chest):

A usually simple box in which a child's toys are kept.

tracery:

Latticelike construction of carved or assembled lines or bars to create geometrically pleasing arrangements. This was a feature found on the doors of some Gothic Revival furniture.

tramp art:

Art form practiced by tramps and nontramps alike, using discarded bits of wood to create useful objects.

Tracery. The back of this Meeks Brothers Gothic Revival chair from 1850 is made up of a tracery of mahogany. *Courtesy of the Metropolitan Museum of Art*

THE CHANGING ROLE OF THE DESIGNER

In the seventeenth and eighteenth centuries, the makers of American furniture were, by and large, the individuals who designed that furniture. A customer would outline a set of needs, the maker would design to fill those needs, and once the concept was approved, the craftsman set to work building what he'd designed—with the help of whatever slaves, indentured servants, or apprentices might be at his disposal.

In the nineteenth century, that began to change. Men such as Duncan Phyfe (1768–1854), himself a supremely skilled cabinet-maker, might employ a hundred craftsmen who would turn his vision into furniture. This continued throughout the century with men such as Gustave (1830–1898) and Christian Herter (1839–1883), leading a firm that designed and executed some of the most elaborate interiors of the Gilded Age. Like Duncan Phyfe, the Herter brothers both had been trained as cabinetmakers, but the enormous output of the firm required a large number of highly skilled employees.

In the twentieth century, everything changed again. The men and women who designed the iconic furniture of the age often had no background in cabinetmaking. Charles Eames (1907–1978) had trained as an architect, and his design and life partner Ray Eames (1912–1988) was trained as a painter. But together they designed some of the most iconic forms in the mid-century modern idiom—for example, the Eames chair and the Eames lounge—forms that were manufactured by others, most notably by Herman Miller, Inc.

Then a curious thing happened in the late twentieth century. Men and women who had grown up with manufactured furniture, with mid-century modern coffee tables and colonial dining room sets and faux Louis-the-whatever bedroom sets—well, some of those men and women began to take up tools and build their own furniture. And if they applied themselves diligently to the craft and if they had the talent and maybe a little luck, some of them carved out careers for themselves, becoming full-time designer/makers, much like those designer/makers in the seventeenth and eighteenth centuries.

Traveling desk. This laptop desk by an unknown maker originated in Boston during the first fifteen years of the nineteenth century. The material is mahogany, satinwood, and brass. *Courtesy of the Art Institute of Chicago*

traveling desk:
A small portable desk, often designed for laptop use. Usually a desk of this type is fitted with cubbyholes for ink, pens, and paper.

tray top:
Tea table top with raised edge to keep things from sliding off onto the floor.

treenware:
Relatively small utilitarian objects shaped from wood; for instance, spoons, forks, boxes, cups, bowls, and butter molds.

trefoil arch:
Three-lobed leaf, a motif often used in Gothic furniture.

Trefoil arch. There is a trefoil arch in the middle of the back of this Meeks Brothers chair. It lies between the large upper medallion and the smaller lower medallion. The wood of this Gothic Revival chair is mahogany. The chair is dated circa 1850. *Courtesy of the Metropolitan Museum of Art*

trestle base:
A table base consisting of a pair of feet almost as wide as the width of the tabletop they carry, from which rise two simple pillars or columns connected by one long stretcher.

trestle table:
A usually long table with its top resting on a trestle assembly.

triffid/trifid foot:
Foot terminating some Queen Anne–period cabriole legs, with three lobes emanating from the ankle, sometimes used interchangeably with the term "drake foot."

tripod base:
A pedestal standing on three legs, each of which has a centerline 120 degrees from its neighbors' centerlines.

tripod table:
A table with its top supported by a single pedestal, which is, in turn, supported by three, usually cabriole, legs.

triptych:
Three-paneled assembly originally used as a painted altarpiece, later adapted to mirrors.

Trestle table. In 1901 William Lightfoot Price (1861–1916), a Philadelphia architect, founded a utopian arts community, Rose Valley, near Moylan, Pennsylvania. Inspired by the English Arts and Crafts movement, Rose Valley was intended for the "manufacture of . . . materials and products involving artistic handicraft" according to its incorporation documents. One of the handicrafts practiced there was furniture making. This trestled library table represents the very best furniture making done at Rose Valley. Unfortunately, the furniture shop closed in 1906, two years after the creation of this table. The wood is stained white oak. *Courtesy of the Metropolitan Museum of Art*

trompe l'oeil:

The use of imagery to fool the eye; for example, the Wendell Castle (1932–2018) chair and hat rack on which there are hanging coats sculpted from wood. In the field of marquetry, this technique is used to good effect by contemporary artisan Silas Kopf (b. 1949) and others.

trousseau chest:

Please see "dower chest."

trundle bed:

Low—often collapsible—bed designed to be rolled under another, taller bed, or, more generally, any bed on rollers.

Trompe l'oeil: I tried to keep non-American woodworking out of this book—I think there are two violations—but this room is so extraordinary I had to use it despite its European origin. This masterpiece of Italian deception presents what appears to be a cluttered library filled with books, benches, and musical and scientific instruments, but when we look closer, we see it's nothing but flat walls surfaced in thousands of bits of wood in different colors, which, combined, give the appearance of a three-dimensional image. The room in which this panel appears was probably designed by Francesco di Giorgio Martini (1439–1501) and executed in the shop of Giuliano da Maiano (1432–1490). The work is dated circa 1480. The materials are walnut, beech, rosewood, and various fruitwoods. *Courtesy of the Metropolitan Museum of Art*

Trundle bed. This trundle bed was made in the New Lebanon, New York, Shaker community in the first half of the nineteenth century. As required by the Shaker Millennial Laws, the bed is painted green. The wood is pine and maple. *Courtesy of the Metropolitan Museum of Art*

trunk:

Boxlike container in which a traveler's personal goods can be stored during transit

Trunk. This diminutive trunk—6½" × 14½" × 12"—is made of pine, leather, and leatherlike paper. It's American made and is dated circa 1750. *Courtesy of the Yale University Art Gallery*

tsuba:

A detail of Greene and Greene furniture originating in a Japanese sword guard. The *tsuba* form manifests itself in several different ways in the realm of Greene and Greene furniture, from the profile of tabletops to small cutouts lined with contrasting wood.

tuck-away table:

Form originating in the William and Mary era; literally, any table that can be folded into a smaller package. The William and Mary versions sometimes looked like mini gatelegs. Later forms took on a number of conformations, all of which shared the capacity to be folded into a fraction of their opened size. Please see also "Sutherland table."

tuck-away trestle table:

A tuck-away table with a trestle base.

tulip poplar:

Wood of the *Liriodendron tulipifera* tree (also known as yellow poplar and American tulipwood) is prized by furniture makers as a premier secondary wood. It is moderately dense and easily worked and has a range of appealing colors, from black, through various greens, all the way to a creamy whitish green.

tung oil:

Oil pressed from the seeds of the tung tree in southern China, used as a wood-finishing material. Tung oil imparts a slightly golden cast to wood surfaces and, when applied in the form of a number of thinned coats, can produce a wet look that some makers prize.

turned knob:

Wooden door or drawer knob turned on a lathe, usually by the cabinetmaker.

turned spindle:

Anything turned between a lathe's centers, as opposed to faceplate turnings, which involve only the headstock center.

turnip foot:

Please see "onion foot."

turret-top card table:

An invention of the Chippendale era, named for the turret-like apron extensions at each corner.

Turret-top card table. This New York mahogany card table features four turret-like extensions on the apron, one at each corner. These identify the table as a turret top. The maker is unknown. *Courtesy of the Metropolitan Museum of Art*

Tuscan order:

The simplest of two classical orders devised by ancient Rome. Please see "classical orders."

tusk tenon:

Please see "mortise-and-tenon, through and tusked."

TV stand:

A table on which a television is placed for viewing. Initially, a TV stand was whatever table was at hand, but over the last half century, specialized tables have evolved that place the television at the proper height for viewing. Unfortunately, many of these are flimsy metal and plastic constructions, and in an era of increasingly immense TVs, these metal and plastic fabrications have proven unreliable. As a result, in the second decade of the twenty-first century, many TV owners are opting to hang their big-screen televisions on the wall.

twig-and-branch furniture:

Rustic furniture made from twigs and branches, often still retaining their bark.

twist turning:

Please see "spiral turning."

two-tiered bookstand:

In oak, produced by the Roycroft Furniture Shop to hold a special edition of the writings of Elbert Hubbard (1856–1915), the founder of the Roycroft shops, who died aboard the *Lusitania* on May 7, 1915.

tympanum:

A flat area above the upper-case drawers and below pediment moldings, such as, for instance, on the upper case of a secretary or highboy.

umbrella stand:

A small stand placed in the foyer in which wet umbrellas are placed to dry.

The tympanum on this walnut highboy from Philadelphia is decorated with an exuberant flourish of vegetative carving. *Courtesy of the Yale University Art Gallery*

underslung drawer:

Drawer sliding on an arrangement of cleats attached to the bottom of a tabletop. The American Shakers devised a number of variations of these forms, all with two drawers. The goal, I believe, was to create the largest possible working space with the least amount of labor and material.

upholstery:

Fabric-covered cushionings.

upholstery spring:

Sturdy metal springs underlying upholstery so that the cushions on a chair or sofa may yield under the weight of a user.

Carved tablet from McIntire sofa. *Courtesy of the Metropolitan Museum of Art*

upholstery tacks:

Dome-headed nail used to secure fabric to seating furniture.

upper case:

The top of two attached cases; for example, the upper case of a highboy that rises above the waist molding.

urn:

Based on a classical urn, a shape in widespread use in furniture of several periods. For example, an urn-shaped profile often appears as Queen Anne chair splats. Turned urns can surmount a Chippendale highboy as a finial. The form can also be found painted on *eglomise* glass on a Federal sideboard.

urn-shaped finial:

Lathe-turned urn at the top of a tall Chippendale casepiece. These are sometimes gilded.

urn-shaped splat:

Splat appearing on some period chair backs.

Upholstered sofa. Samuel McIntire (1757–1811) of Salem, Massachusetts, is thought be the maker of this handsome Federal sofa, which features McIntire-style carving on a crest tablet. The material is mahogany, pine, and birch. The piece is dated 1800–1810. *Courtesy of the Metropolitan Museum of Art*

Urn-shaped splat. This neo-classical chair by an unknown
New York maker has a painted urn-shaped splat. The materials
are cherry, ash, and white pine. The chair is dated circa 1800.
Courtesy of the Yale University Art Gallery

urn stand:

Simply a table designed for support and display of an urn.

vanity:

A type of dressing table. This nomenclature was favored by Arts and Crafts designers and manufacturers, whereas "dressing table" and "lowboy" were used during earlier periods to denote very similar forms.

vanity chair:

Small, armless chair designed specifically for use with a vanity.

varnish:

A clear finish that can be formulated to produce very durable satin, semigloss, or glossy surfaces. Originally a simple mixture of a natural resin, such as pine sap, with a solvent; today's varnishes, however, often involve the use of synthetic resins.

veneer:

Thin sheets of wood—usually selected for their decorative appeal—glued to a thicker substrate.

vernacular furniture:

Furniture built for those who were not wealthy or lived outside the nation's urban centers.

verre églomisé:

Glass that has been gilded with gold or other metals. Often the gilding is done in a pictorial fashion.

vessel:

A turned vase-like container.

volute:

Carved or inlaid scroll such as is found on an Ionic capital.

wainscot chair:

A heavy Pilgrim-era chair with turned front legs, a board seat, and a large board back, usually decorated with low-relief carving. The best-known example was made by Thomas Dennis (1638–1706) of Ipswich, Massachusetts, in the late seventeenth century.

Vernacular furniture. This moderately handsome but crudely made corner cupboard is an example of "vernacular" furniture; that is, furniture not seen as "high style." It was likely made outside an urban area by a craftsman lacking the skill set and the woodworking education to make the high-style Federal and Empire furniture then in vogue. The wood is white pine. The piece was constructed by an unknown New England maker between 1810 and 1840. *Courtesy of the Yale University Art Gallery*

Verre églomisé. The tablet at the top of this mirror features a rural scene of a cabin and an antlered buck done in *verre églomisé. Courtesy of the Metropolitan Museum of Art*

Wainscot chair. This simple wainscot chair was made in Chester County, Pennsylvania, in the mid-eighteenth century. Unlike earlier New England examples, the frame-and-panel back sports no carving. The wood is walnut. *Courtesy of the Metropolitan Museum of Art*

waist:
Casework midsection.

waist molding:
Molding used as demarcation between the upper and lower cases of a highboy or a chest-on-chest.

wall clock:
Please see "Massachusetts wall clock."

wall pocket:
Small wall-hung form originating in colonial America, made of ceramic, metal, or wood. Wall pockets were intended for short-term storage of just about any kind of paperwork.

wall trunk:
Trunk designed so that the lid can be raised when the trunk is positioned against a wall.

walnut:
Woods from the *Juglans* genus, prized for its dark-brown color and workability. Although walnut species are grown around the world, it is the American black walnut that is most prized by furniture makers. When kiln-dried, the heartwood becomes a creamy dark brown, but sometimes when it's air-dried, the wood takes on a deep purple-brown hue. Many years ago my dad, Jim Pierce, also a furniture maker, took down some walnut trees from the Lake Erie shore, had them sawn up, and air-dried the lumber over a period of several years, and the color of that wood was such a pronounced purple it looked like some kind of tropical wood. The sapwood of the black walnut is a creamy white.

wane:
The natural edge of a board with or without the bark. Material exhibiting this characteristic is seen in some country furniture. Current Kentucky maker Warren May (b. 1946) sometimes incorporates wancy boards into his "Kentucky" furniture, and the noted twentieth-century maker George Nakashima (1905–1990) made widespread use of it.

Wardian case:
A nineteenth-century glazed case in which plants were kept alive while isolated from the outside air. The original Wardian case was conceived by Dr. Nathaniel Ward (1791–1868) and presented to the public in his 1842 book *On the Growth of Plants in a Closely Glazed Case*. In the latter half of the nineteenth century, these boxes became popular on both sides of the Atlantic, giving rise to vivariums, terrariums, and aquariums, many of which were equipped with quite elaborate custom-made stands.

wardrobe:
A catchall term that includes "armoire," "chifforobe," and "kas" and denotes a large moveable cupboard for storing clothes.

wardrobe trunk:
The largest and grandest of the traveler's trunks. These are designed to be stood on end. When the lid is opened, a complex interior is revealed. One side of that interior might be given to clothing on hangers, while the other side probably featured a rack of drawers. In

Previous page: Herter Brothers wardrobe. Perhaps in response to what some saw as John Henry Belter's curvilinear excess, the Herter Brothers, Gustave (1830–1898) and Christian (1839–1883), sometimes worked in the Anglo-Japanese style of the 1870s. That influence can be seen in this 1875–1883 wardrobe. The forms are plain, rectilinear, and lacking—as the English designer Charles Eastlake (1836–1906) recommended—"extravagant contour and unnecessary curves." This delightfully spare and clean cherry wardrobe exemplifies the approach laid out in Eastlake's book *Hints on Household Taste*, which was published in this country in 1872. *Courtesy of the Metropolitan Museum of Art*

Marquetry detail of Herter wardrobe. *Courtesy of the Metropolitan Museum of Art*

Washstand. This Shaker washstand from the New Lebanon, New York, community dates to circa 1825. The material is pine. *Courtesy of the Metropolitan Museum of Art*

addition, these trunks sometimes included small suitcases, mirrors, and makeup cases; in other words, a lady's dressing room in a box.

warp:
　Twisting distortion of wood caused by changes in moisture content.

washstand (basin stand):
　Table or cupboard holding a large basin and a pitcher of water for washing one's hands and face.

water bench:
　An American creation designed for the back porch so that farmhands could wash up before a meal. A water bench would have been equipped with one or more basins and a water source, usually a pitcher or a hand-powered water pump.

wax:
　A class of materials with a long history as wood finishes. The most important of these is carnauba wax. Carnauba wax is, in fact, the preferred finishing material for smoking pipes. Waxes can be applied directly to bare wood and will polish to a glossy luster. Unfortunately, its luster fades over time, and it offers little protection to the wood underneath. I use wax only as a topping over more-conventional finishes, in this way combining the tactile appeal of wax with the durability of a varnish or lacquer.

weaver's stool (chair):
　A piece of seating furniture with an elevated seat for a person working at a loom.

western furniture:
　Furniture rooted in western US motifs. In the shop of John Gallis, of Cody, Wyoming, those roots are expressed in the form of debarked but unsawn timber, live edges, and a chunky sturdiness that probably originates in the furnishings of nineteenth-century ranches.

wheelchair:
　A wheeled chair for the conveyance of the infirm.

Wheelchair. This early American wheelchair featured tiny white oak wheels, maple posts, and rungs and slats, as well as ash arms. The chair dates to the second half of the eighteenth century. *Courtesy of the Yale University Art Gallery*

white oak:

Please see "oak, white."

white pine:

Wood of *Pinus strobus*, used as a secondary wood in the American Northeast. It's a good choice for Windsor chair seats because it is easily worked and takes paint well, and it has traditionally been used as a secondary wood in casework. The color is creamy white with darker grain lines.

whorl foot:

Scrolled foot.

wicker furniture:

Furniture made by weaving components in basketlike fashion, usually from willow osiers and parts of the rattan palm. Wicker furniture has a long history in the United States, having originated in the colonial era, but it had occupied only a small segment of the furniture market until the mid-1850s, when Cyrus Wakefield (1811–1873), a Massachusetts grocer, began manufacturing rattan wicker furniture on a large scale.

Wicker chair. This American wicker chair by an unknown maker is dated circa 1890. The material is uncited on the Yale University Art Gallery website. *Courtesy of the Yale University Art Gallery*

window:

A usually glazed construction that allows light and air to enter a building.

window seat:

A backless sofa or bench intended to be placed in front of a window.

window stool:

An upholstered bench without ends, intended to be placed in front of a window.

Phyfe window seat. Window seats were a popular nine-teenth-century form. This example, attributed to the shop of Duncan Phyfe (1770–1854), features a pair of cyma-curved legs with scrolls on the top and bottom. The piece is dated 1837. The woods are mahogany, ash, and pine. *Courtesy of the Metropolitan Museum of Art*

LOOKING AT A MASTERPIECE

Nearly all of the furniture that appears on these pages is first rate, among the best of the period and the best of the type each represents, but there are a half-dozen pieces that stand head and shoulders above the rest, pieces of profoundly sublime beauty. I'm thinking here of the John Townsend chest of drawers on page 373, the Queen Anne lowboy on page 9, and the John Henry Belter *tête-à-tête* on page 319, but most of all I'm thinking of the Stephen Badlam chest-on-chest shown in the photos accompanying this sidebar.

Take a moment and let your eyes wander across this piece.

First you see its massive scale. This piece is deliberately monumental, perhaps as an homage to the man who commissioned it, Elias Hasket Derby (1739–1799), the wealthy Salem, Massachusetts, merchant. The bracket feet are made massive by the canted front corners of the lower case, and the very architectural cornice is oversized, with a greater vertical dimension than other cornices on other similarly grand pieces by other makers. In addition, the chest-on-chest is not simply designed to appear immense; it is in actual fact an immense piece of furniture, measuring 8½ feet in height and over 4 feet in width, making it taller and wider than almost any other known period chest-on-chest.

Once you've appreciated the scale, send your eyes back over the piece and take in the detail.

There is carving, but it's not sprayed

Carving on canted corner of Badlam chest-on-chest. *Courtesy of the Yale University Art Gallery*

willy-nilly across the facade; it is, instead, confined to the borders, creating with its detail a kind of framing device. It is thoughtfully conceived carving, carving that enhances the chest-on-chest's basic structure. The Skillin brothers, who designed and executed (at the very least) the pediment carving, crowned that pediment with the figures of three women in neo-classical costuming: the one on the left

Detail of bracket feet on Badlam chest-on-chest. *Courtesy of the Yale University Art Gallery*

Back of female figure representing Virtue on Badlam chest-on-chest. *Courtesy of the Yale University Art Gallery*

personifying Peace, the one on the right personifying Plenty, and the standing figure in the middle personifying Virtue. Each is equipped with symbolically appropriate accoutrements. Classical references such as these have long been out of fashion, but in the eighteenth century, they were as widely admired as a high-def television is today.

Notice the Ionic columns flanking the upper case, the gentle serpentining of the lower case, the ruffle of acanthus leaves that rises up from the bracket feet onto the base molding, and the tablet just below the pediment, with its carved acanthus leaves and drapery swags. Every detail has been carefully weighed and balanced against every other aspect of this enormous but graceful piece to create a nearly perfect expression of restrained American rococo design and execution.

Front of female figure representing Peace on Badlam chest-on-chest. *Courtesy of the Yale University Art Gallery*

Previous page: Badlam chest-on-chest. This is one of the supreme examples of American furniture making, combining the cabinetmaking skills of Stephen Badlam (1751–1815) and the carving skills of John (1746–1800) and Simeon (1757–1806) Skillins. The man who commissioned the work, the merchant Elias Hasket Derby (1739–1799), took the unusual step of separately contracting Badlam and the Skillin brothers, instead of following the traditional practice of allowing the cabinet-maker to hire his own carvers. The materials are mahogany, white pine, chestnut, and red pine. The piece is dated 1791. It was made in Dorchester Lower Mills and in Boston, Massachusetts. *Courtesy of the Yale University Art Gallery*

Windsor chair:

A chair with a sculpted wood seat, turned legs, and, usually, shaved back spindles. The form originated in England in the early eighteenth century, then came to America, where it became very popular during the colonial era.

Windsor chair, bow back:

Windsor chair with a back composed of shaved spindles mortised into a bow that rises from the seat on one side to become the crest rail, then descends to the seat on the other. The arms of bow-back armchairs are mortised into the bow with their front ends supported by short turned spindles.

Painting of man sitting before fire in Windsor chair. By the time Eastman Johnson (1824–1906) painted this domestic scene in 1876, the Windsor form had become ubiquitous in American households. The bow-back baluster-legged armchair in which the gentleman sits while warming his hands by the fire could, at that time, be found in homes all across the eastern half of the United States. *Courtesy of the Metropolitan Museum of Art*

Bow-back Windsor. From its introduction in the colonies circa 1730, the Windsor chair form spread rapidly across the American landscape. In fact, according to Charles Santore, the author of *The Windsor Style in America*, by the 1760s it was possible for a furniture maker to build only Windsors. This specialization on one form made it possible for chair makers to increase the speed of construction, thereby lowering the price enough so that almost anyone could afford a Windsor. And another innovation—the bamboo turnings seen on this chair—made it possible to lower the price even further, because these legs could be turned out by semiskilled craftsmen. This chair originated in Philadelphia, from which Windsors were being shipped in such numbers that Windsors became popularly known as Philadelphia chairs. This chair is dated 1796–1806. The materials are maple, oak, poplar, and hickory. *Courtesy of the Metropolitan Museum of Art*

Windsor chair, comb back:
Windsor chair in which the shaved back spindles pierce the back piece and rise to a crest rail. The chair is so named because that section above the arm rail resembles a lady's comb.

Windsor chair, continuous arm:
Windsor chair with a back that flows without interruption into a pair of arms, each end of which is supported through the use of a turned spindle.

Comb-back Windsor: The unknown maker of this eighteenth-century Philadelphia chair didn't follow standard
practice. Instead of using a variety of woods—pine or poplar
for the seat, maple for the legs, and oak or hickory for the
shaved spindles—he constructed this chair entirely of walnut.
Courtesy of the Art Institute of Chicago

Continuous-arm Windsor. This continuous-arm Windsor is attributed to Jebediah Browning (1767–?) of either Connecticut or Rhode Island. The material is oak, maple, poplar, and pine. The chair is dated 1790–1810. *Courtesy of the Yale University Art Gallery*

Windsor chair, fan back:
Similar to a comb back, a Windsor with a crest rail. The difference is the spreading of back spindles as they rise to the crest of a fan back.

Windsor chair, high chair:
A child's high chair built in the Windsor style.

Windsor chair, low back:
Windsor in which the spindles terminate in the arm rail, which is typically thickened in the back by the addition of another layer of wood radiussed on top for comfort. These chairs are sometimes called club chairs or captain's chairs.

Windsor chair, rod back:
Windsor with a squared-off back and bamboo spindles. It's sometimes referred to as a "square back."

Fan-back Windsor. According to his Wikipedia article, Wallace Nutting (1861–1941) was a photographer specializing in pastoral landscapes and scenes of domestic colonial life. But for those of us in the furniture world, Nutting will always be the first—and perhaps greatest—cataloger of American colonial furniture. His immense book, *Furniture Treasury*, first published in 1928, contains exactly 5,000 black-and-white images of 5,000 pieces of colonial-era home furnishings. The photos are often poorly lit, published without much focus or clarity. But there are 5,000 of them, many of which represented pieces that have since disappeared from history. So *Furniture Treasury* is a treasure, an amazing resource for those of us who love period furniture. But Nutting was more than a photographer and a cataloger of furniture. He was also an entrepreneur who never missed a chance to make a buck. This fan-back Windsor represents one of Nutting's entrepreneurial efforts. In 1917 he launched a furniture reproduction business, and this skillfully wrought chair is one of the Nutting reproductions. The materials are maple, hickory, and tulip poplar. The chair is dated 1917–1922. *Courtesy of the Yale University Art Gallery*

Right: Windsor high chair. Executed in the style of a comb-back Windsor, this chair was built to bring a small child up to table height. The chair is built of oak, sycamore, and hickory. It is dated 1755–1775. *Courtesy of the Yale University Art Gallery*

Low-back Windsor chair. The work of an unknown Rhode
Island maker, this low-back Windsor is made of oak and maple.
The chair is dated 1755–1775. *Courtesy of the Yale University
Art Gallery*

Rod-back Windsor. This child-sized rod-back Windsor is
composed of oak, tulip poplar, and birch. The chair is dated
1800–1810. *Courtesy of the Yale University Art Gallery*

Windsor chair, sack back:

Like the comb back, a Windsor in which the back spindles pierce the arm rail and rise to the crest rail. The difference between the two styles is that the crest rail of the sack back is a bow that rises up from the arm rail on one side and descends to the arm rail on the other, whereas the comb back has a wide crest rail that does not descend toward the arm rail on either side.

Windsor, square back:

Please see "Windsor, rod back."

Windsor chair, writing arm:

A chair having a small panel (paddle) of wood used as a writing surface, added to the arm of any style of Windsor. Some of these panels had underslung drawers so that paper and other writing materials could be housed there. These were nearly always added to the chair's right arm, but a few lefties are known to exist.

Windsor settee:

A settee made as a Windsor, with a solid seat and turned legs and stretchers, as well as a back fashioned from shaved spindles. Some of these were built to accommodate only two people. Others reach a length of 7 feet.

Windsor settee, bow back, armchair:

A Windsor settee with a crest rail that rises from the seat on one side, then descends to the seat on the other end. The arms are

Windsor chair, sack back. By an unknown late-eighteenth-century maker, this sack back is constructed of oak, pine, and birch. *Courtesy of the Yale University Art Gallery*

Writing-arm Windsor. According to Charles Santore, the author of *The Windsor Style in America*, the writing-arm Windsor likely originated in Connecticut, and 60–70 percent of all the known writing-arm Windsors can be traced to that state, and of those, approximately half can be traced to the shop of Ebenezer Tracy (1744–1803) of Lisbon, Connecticut. This particular writing-arm Windsor by an unknown maker is dated 1760–1790. The woods are maple and pine. *Courtesy of the Metropolitan Museum of Art*

Fan-back Windsor settee. This fan-back Windsor settee is different than most in that it is made of butternut. It was made in the last quarter of the nineteenth century, probably by a Rhode Island maker. *Courtesy of the Metropolitan Museum of Art*

mortised into the crest rail, and each is then supported by several short spindles.

Windsor settee, comb back:
Windsor settee with a high comb rising above the chair.

Windsor settee, fan back:
A settee in which the back spindles spread slightly as they reach for the crest rail.

Windsor settee, low back:
A low-back Windsor with two or more scooped-out saddle seats.

Windsor settee, hoop back:
Windsor settee with a back composed of a single crest rail that arches up from either the arms or the seat.

Windsor settee, square back:
Like a square-back or rod-back Windsor chair, a settee composed of bamboo turnings with a squared-off back.

Bow-back settee. This hickory, pine, and maple bow-back settee with arms originated in Wayne County, Maine, circa 1810. *Courtesy of the Yale University Art Gallery*

Windsor table. This may look like a stool, but its 24" height and extra-wide top (24½") make it a table. The material is tulip poplar, maple, and ash. *Courtesy of the Metropolitan Museum of Art*

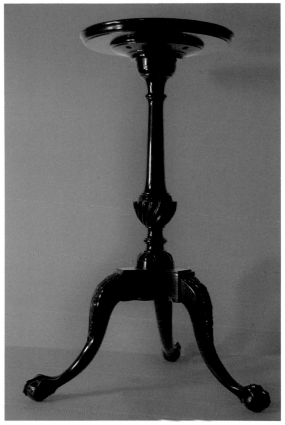

Wine stand. During the mid-twentieth century, when most furniture that most people bought was manufactured, many designers turned to furniture of the colonial era for inspiration. This small stand looks very much like an eighteenth-century candlestand, with its cabriole legs terminating in ball-and-claw feet, as well as its turned and carved pedestal. The stand was manufactured by the Kittinger Furniture Company in Buffalo, New York, circa 1945. The material is mahogany. *Courtesy of the Yale University Art Gallery*

Windsor, step-down:
Windsor named for the stepped appearance of the crest rail in profile.

Windsor table:
A table constructed like a Windsor chair, with turned legs and stretchers and a solid top.

wine stand:
A small stand big enough for a bottle of wine and several glasses.

wing chair:
A fully upholstered period chair with an upholstered "wing" at each side of the user's head. These wings were intended to protect the user from drafts.

winged bureau:
Chest of drawers with a wide central flight of drawers bordered by flights of short drawers on either end.

wishbone chair:
A chair designed by Arthur Espenet Carpenter (1920–2006) of California. The four posts of the chair are divided into two pairs, each of which resembles a wishbone.

wood box (wood bin):
Large box used to store firewood.

wood finishes:
Please see "finishes."

wood, furniture making:
Structural material found in the roots and stems of trees, long used for furniture making. While almost any species of wood can be used in the construction of furniture, current American makers are focusing on American hardwoods and softwoods, as well as some tropical species, not on an endangered-species list. Please see also "cherry," "hickory," "mahogany," "maple" "red oak," "tulip poplar," "walnut," "white oak," "white pine," and "yellow pine."

wooden implements:
Tools and other utilitarian objects fashioned largely from wood; for example, the hayfork, the wooden scoop, the yoke, and the beetle.

Boston wing chair. This Boston easy chair by an unknown maker is one of the earliest examples of a fully upholstered American chair. Dating to 1715–1730 with William and Mary turnings in the undercarriage, it is a precursor to the many Queen Anne easy chairs to follow. The wood is soft maple, oak, and black tupelo. *Courtesy of the Metropolitan Museum of Art*

wood oyster:

Please see "oystering."

wood pins:

Please see "pegs."

wood screw:

Sharply pointed metal fastener for wood components. These screws have a deep helical ridge (or thread) that seats itself in the wood as the screw is turned. Wood screws come with flat, pan, or oval heads, equipped with emplacements for Phillips, slotted, or torx drivers.

Wooton desk:

Designed by Indianapolis entrepreneur William Wooton (1835–1907), a large desk done in the Renaissance Revival style with a multitude of storage places. The best-known Wooton desks were massive vertical cabinets with winged sides that could be closed and locked at the end of a workday. They were the forerunners of today's desktop computers as organizing devices for businesses involving significant amounts of information. They were made in a variety of formats, all riding on heavy-duty castors. The interiors were often broken into forty or more cubbyholes, several dozen horizontal or vertical file spaces, and a dozen or more drawers. Theoretically, a user could, while sitting in one position, access up to 110 compartments. The desks were so appealing that John D. Rockefeller purchased an "Extra Grade" Wooton desk for use in his office. Unfortunately, these office wonders were manufactured for only ten years, from 1874 to 1884.

work bag:

Fabric bag hanging underneath a Federal-era ladies' work table. The bag was used to store ladies' sewing projects.

workbench:

Often-large, sturdy table made of thick pieces of wood or sheet steel, usually equipped with one or more vises.

work counter:

Essentially a work table with ranks of drawers. The Shakers were noted for the utilitarian beauty of many of their—often-painted—work counters.

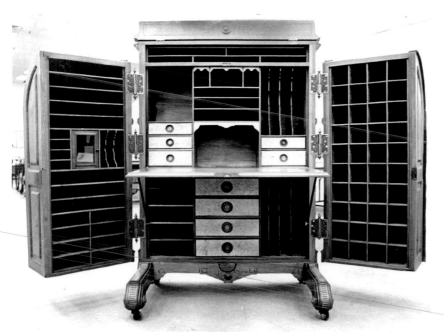

Wooton desk. William Wooton (1835–1907), an Indianapolis businessman and Quaker, was granted a patent for the Wooton desk in 1874, and his company, the Wooton Desk Company, manufactured these Victorian marvels until 1884. The materials in this example are walnut, cherry, tulip poplar, and other woods. *Courtesy of Getty Images*

Shaker work counter. This work counter was made circa 1825 by a New Lebanon, New York, Shaker craftsman. It is constructed of pine, applewood, and pearwood. *Courtesy of the Metropolitan Museum of Art*

work table (period):

Small lady's work table. Some are square. Some have canted corners. Some have astragal[8] ends. Often these tables were equipped with a fabric bag hanging underneath. The bag was a Federal-period development that provided a place for a lady to store her sewing projects.

---

8 Astragal: When viewed from above, the top of this table has two ends that consist of a semicircle with filets where the arcs terminate, reminiscent of the form in cross section that an astragal molding plane cuts.

Astragal-end work table. This is an example of an "astragal-end" work table, a term that refers to the profile of the top when viewed from above. It stands on four slender, Sheraton-style legs, terminating in castors. The silk bag, which was used to hold a lady's sewing work, is patterned after one in Thomas Sheraton's *The Cabinet-Maker and Upholsterer's Drawing-Book*, published in 1794. The table, by an unknown New York maker, is dated 1805–1815. The materials are mahogany, rosewood, Spanish cedar, white pine, and poplar. *Courtesy of the Metropolitan Museum of Art*

Work table. This work table is interesting because of its date of construction—1890–1920—in other words, a hundred years after a Sheraton piece would have been considered high style. I know little about the turn-of-the-century market for reproduction Federal furniture. My impression is that the market then for such work was very weak. Could it have been made for that market? Or was it made to deceive? It appears to be excellent work, and a piece of such quality might have been passed off as a genuine late-eighteenth-century antique. Plus, there are those lovely legs, so slender that if you pushed the case, the springiness in the legs would cause the case to wobble. The material is listed as *Swietenia* (the genus that includes all the genuine mahoganies), with tulip poplar as the secondary wood. *Courtesy of Winterthur Museum*

work table (Shaker):
> Any of a variety of large, sturdy tables used in Shaker kitchens and workshops.

writing-arm Windsor chair:
> Please see "Windsor chair, writing arm."

writing box:
> Very similar to the travel desk, with a lid on which writing can be done, and cubbyholes to hold paper, ink, and pens.

Work table with lyre pedestal. This Empire work table with the lyre pedestal is one of the most elegant Boston pieces of that era. The chalk inscription "Churchill" presumably refers to Lemuel Churchill (active circa 1805–1828), a Boston cabinetmaker of the period. According to the Metropolitan Museum of Art, a second possibility is Thomas Whitman (active circa 1809–1827). The materials are mahogany, ebony, tulip poplar, brass, and ivory. The work table is dated 1810–1815. *Courtesy of the Metropolitan Museum of Art*

Shaker work table. This colossal work table (over 8 feet in length), built at the Pleasant Hill, Kentucky, Shaker community by Leander Gettys (1832–?), was likely the scene of food preparation for the Shakers living in the Centre Family Dwelling there. *Photo by Al Parrish, courtesy of Popular Woodworking Books*

Writing box. This example was made in the Shaker community of Watervliet, New York, by an unknown Shaker, probably in the first half of the nineteenth century. The material is chestnut. *Courtesy of the Art Institute of Chicago*

Left: Empire work table. This Empire work table is skillfully wrought, but there is no way to ignore the menace in those powerful acanthus-draped legs. The table is the work of an unknown New York maker between 1820 and 1840. The materials are mahogany, tulip poplar, and white pine. *Courtesy of the Yale University Art Gallery*

writing desk:

Federal-era desk often having tambour-concealed cubbyholes and drawers above the writing surface.

writing table:

A usually small table with one or two drawers and a fixed flat top or—in some cases—a writing-surface top that can be tilted up for the convenience of the user.

X-stretcher:

Found on some William and Mary tables and some Windsors as well, in which the stretchers cross in an X shape.

yellow pine:

Moderately dense, immensely strong, yellow pine—*Pinus echinata*—from the American South, often used by furniture makers as a secondary wood. In most lumberyards in the eastern half of the United States, construction lumber in narrower sizes (2 × 4s, 2 × 6s) is usually a whitewood called SPF (spruce/pine/fir), but the wider sizes (2 × 10s and 2 × 12s) are most often southern yellow pine. This can be important because construction-grade yellow pine can be resawn, shop-dried, and used as a secondary wood in furniture. In fact,

Lady's writing table. This superb example of Federal-era casework is based on a drawing in Thomas Sheraton's *The Cabinet-Maker's and Upholsterer's Drawing-Book* (1794). The lively but highly controlled surfaces are mahogany banded in satinwood on the lower case and mitered sheets of satinwood framing glass-painted mythological figures on the upper case. The materials are mahogany, satinwood, cedar, and glass. The maker appears to be an S. E. Waite, whose name is written on the top drawer of the lower case, along with the date 1812. *Courtesy of Winterthur Museum*

I've used it as a primary wood when I wanted those orange-brown stripes. The problem with that application is that the creamy wood between the stripes can be quite soft, vulnerable to denting and scratching. The presence of yellow pine used as secondary wood in antique furniture usually means a southern US origin.

yoke:
Raised saddlelike area on the crest of some Queen Anne chairs.

yoke, table:
Please see "table yoke."

yoke back:
A crest rail with a drooping central section found on some country chairs, usually paired with a fiddle-shaped splat. It's most often found on chairs of New York and Connecticut origin.

Zoar chair:
Chair made in Zoar Village, Ohio, between 1817 and 1900.

Federal-era writing desk. Standing just over 5 feet tall, this is much smaller than earlier secretaries. The materials are satinwood, mahogany, tulip poplar, and pine. The desk is dated 1790–1810. *Courtesy of the Los Angeles County Museum of Art*

Lipton Gazelle Writing Table. The gazelle-like legs of this writing table by current maker Gregg Lipton (b. 1957) of Cumberland, Maine, support a beautifully veneered top. The materials are Chilean tineo, ebonized cherry, and ebony. *Photo by Paul Avis, courtesy of Gregg Lipton*

Zoar chair. In 1817, two hundred disaffected Germans fleeing religious persecution founded a settlement in northeastern Ohio—Zoar—where they remained for eighty years. This chair—clearly Germanic in origin—was constructed by an unknown maker in that village. The following ink inscription appears on the back of the chair: "This is an original Zoar chair / Pattern: 1825. / Hilda D. Morhart, / Zoar, Ohio." A second inscription, in pencil, also appears on the back: "Josehp Bunehuter (?)." The material is chestnut and oak. *Courtesy of the Art Institute of Art*

PART 3

A FEW NOTABLE AMERICAN FURNITURE DESIGNERS/CRAFTSMEN

Regrettably, many gifted American furniture designers/makers neglected to sign or label their work, and as a result the names of those men are lost to history. The following list includes a sampling of noteworthy American furniture makers who did sign or label their work. It also includes a few to whom important work was attributed by scholars, and a few whose contribution to the art and craft of furniture making was not achieved at the drawing board or in shop but was, instead, a result of their accomplishments in the manufacture of good-quality—and affordable—American furniture for the middle class. In addition, I added the names of some men who have been identified as among the earliest American practitioners of the furniture maker's craft. These last are not necessarily men whose contributions to American furniture making would be described as innovative. Instead, they are men I've come to admire simply because they found ways to produce fine furniture on the American frontier as early as 1630, in conditions that we can only imagine.

Affleck, Thomas (1740–1795, Philadelphia)

Scottish-born craftsman who immigrated to America in 1763 at the invitation of the governor of Pennsylvania, John Penn (1729–1795). After his arrival in this country, Affleck made a number of high-style mahogany pieces for the governor's mansion, in addition to furniture for other notable Pennsylvania families. Throughout his career, his design work was based on his personal copy of Thomas Chippendale's 1754 book *The Gentleman and Cabinetmaker's Director*. Among Affleck's finest work was a chest-on-chest made for William Logan, crowned with a swan-neck pediment enclosing a sculpture of a phoenix rising from the ashes, and a bold and very masculine rococo highboy made for Levi Hollingsworth with a delightfully abstracted cartouche (both can be seen in Albert Sack's *The New Fine Points of Furniture: Early American*). Affleck is considered by many to be greatest furniture maker in Philadelphia during the Chippendale period.

Affleck chair. Thomas Affleck (1740–1795) of Philadelphia is thought to have been the maker of this handsome mahogany side chair. The chair is dated 1765–1780. *Courtesy of the Yale University Art Gallery*

Aitken, John (1770–1814, Philadelphia)

Scottish-born John Aitken, best known for his long association with George Washington, for whom he supplied two dozen side chairs, two Federal sideboards, and one Federal secretary, which were used at Washington's residence, Mt. Vernon.

Allison, Michael (1773–1855, New York)

Along with Duncan Phyfe, one of the leading furniture makers in New York during the first half of the nineteenth century. Early in Allison's career, he worked primarily in the Hepplewhite style, later switching to work modeled on Sheraton's designs. One of the most exquisite pieces attributed to Allison is a neo-classical mahogany card table with a lyre pedestal, surfaced with highly organized low-relief acanthus carving, which is echoed on the upper surface of the four sweeping legs.

Allison table. Notice the unusual support mechanism for the leaves of this Michael Allison (1773–1855) drop-leaf table. The materials are mahogany, pine, and ash. The table is dated 1817. *Courtesy of the Metropolitan Museum of Art*

Badlam, Stephen (1751–1815, Dorchester, Massachusetts)

One of the most accomplished late-eighteenth- and early-nineteenth-century American furniture makers. Trained as a surveyor and cabinetmaker, Badlam was commissioned as a second lieutenant in 1775 during the opening days of the Revolutionary War. He rose quickly to the rank of major in the artillery. However, an intractable fever resulted in his resignation from his commission. In 1777, he and his wife, Mary, settled in Dorchester, where he established a cabinetmaking shop. His business was immediately successful, sufficiently so that—at one point—he was selling excess work through the furniture warehouse of Thomas Seymour of Boston. The most important commission of his career came from Elias Hasket Derby, a merchant in Salem, Massachusetts, and reputedly one of the richest men in the country. This commission—a Chippendale-style chest-on-chest—was a wedding present to Derby's daughter, Anstis Derby.

Badlam chest-on-chest. One of the crowning achievements of American furniture making, this chest-on-chest was built in the shop of Stephen Badlam (1751–1815) for Elias Hasket Derby (1739–1799). Please see the sidebar on page 337 for more information about this piece. *Courtesy of the Yale University Art Gallery*

Belter, John Henry (1804–1863, New York)

German-born furniture maker best known for his exuberant rococo designs. He opened a shop in New York in 1833, which quickly developed a reputation for furniture of the highest quality. Then in 1854, he established a five-story furniture factory on 76th Street. In 1861, he took as partners three brothers—John, William, and Frederick Springmeyer—which resulted in a new name for the business: Springmeyer Bros. Nevertheless, despite these new partners, the business went bankrupt in 1867. Belter is less known for the work produced by his hands than he is for the work produced in his factory using four ingenious devices and processes, all of which were patented between 1847 and 1860. The factory's output included chairs, sofas, tables, and beds, all done in—often-laminated—rosewood, which featured pierced and elaborately carved fruits, flowers, scrolls, and leaves executed in high relief. In the words of Rita Rief, writer for the *New York Times*, Belter was "the cabinetmaker who produced the finest and most innovative work in mid-nineteenth-century America."

Belter "slipper" chair. John Henry Belter (1804–1863) was
known for the flurries of carved vegetation he spread over
crest rails and along legs and stretchers—wherever there was
wood to which carving might be applied. This slipper chair is
an exuberant expression of the Rococo Revival as imagined
by Belter. *Courtesy of the Metropolitan Museum of Art*

Carpenter, Art (1920–2006, Bolinas, California)

One of the leading figures in twentieth-century American furniture making. A self-taught woodworker, Carpenter achieved fame for his sleekly designed mid-century modern furniture, much of it based on bandsaw work. He is probably best known for his Wishbone Chair with a Woven Seat. His work is in the permanent collection of the Smithsonian Institution and the Museum of Modern Art in New York. He received the Furniture Society's Award of Distinction in 2001.

Castle, Wendell (1932–2018, Scottsville, New York)

One of a handful of furniture makers who successfully melded furniture making and sculpture. In fact, Castle is often described as the founder of the "art furniture" movement in America. (This kind of furniture was assigned the word "artiture" by Art Carpenter, the designer/craftsman in the previous entry.) Castle's work can be found in nearly every notable art museum in the United States. After leaving Kansas with a bachelor's degree in industrial design and a master's in sculpture (both from the University of Kansas), Castle went to New York in 1961 to seek his fortune as a sculptor. But he didn't find success until he entered a chair in a competition at the American Craft Museum, a move that led to a teaching position at the Rhode Island School of Design. There he developed his signature style: stack laminations sculpted into organic forms that—coincidentally—could be used as furniture.

Wendell Castle music stand. This 1966 photo shows a young Wendell Castle (1932–2018) oiling one of his music stands. Castle eventually became one of the leaders of the "art furniture" movement in this country. *Photo by Nina Leen,* the Life Picture Collection, *courtesy of Getty Images*

Chapin, Eliphalet (1741–1807, Connecticut)

The most noteworthy of a group of furniture makers working in Connecticut late in the eighteenth century. Born in Massachusetts into a family of furniture makers, Chapin moved to Philadelphia in 1767 to add to his woodworking education. In 1771, he moved to East Windsor, Connecticut, where he practiced his trade until 1798. Like the work of so many of the Connecticut makers around him, Chapin took an eccentric approach to his work in the Chippendale style. Chapin's work is lighter and cleaner than the Philadelphia work he left behind, without the proliferating surface carving that typified so much Philadelphia casework of the day. It's a kind of "rococo light."

Chapin highboy. This highboy made by Eliphalet Chapin (1741–1807) has the massive stance of the Philadelphia highboys of the era, but unlike the work of the urban makers, Chapin preferred a cleaner surface, one less ornamented by carved detail. Also unlike those urban makers, Chapin chose a native wood, cherry, for this piece. The secondary wood is white pine. The piece is dated 1780–1790. *Courtesy of the Yale University Art Gallery*

Cogswell, John (1738–1819, Boston)

The leader in the Boston bombé furniture movement. Although he married into an important Boston family (the Goodings), Cogswell struggled financially for much of his working life as a result of the Seven Years' War (1756–1763) and the depression that followed it. To make ends meet, he took work in government—constable, surveyor of boards, surveyor of shingles, surveyor of mahogany. He rented out his "back house," and he was licensed as an "innholder." Fortunately, he was able to patch together enough of a financial life to carry him and his family until he was able to establish himself as a maker of fine furniture. And by 1782, he was sufficiently established to earn a commission from one of the wealthiest men in America, Elias Hasket Derby. That commission was for a bombé chest-on-chest that bears his signature. In all, there are thirteen bombé pieces associated with the shop of John Cogswell, including several with serpentine fronts. (The bombé form is a European import, perhaps resulting from a bombé piece imported from England or France, but the form was reinforced on the American shore by the presence of bombé images in Thomas Chippendale's 1754 book *The Gentleman and Cabinetmaker's Director*.)

Connelly, Henry (1770–1826, Philadelphia)

One of the leading Philadelphia furniture makers in the opening decades of the nineteenth century. He was known for his often-delicate Sheraton-style furniture. Connelly was working at a time when a shop might employ several highly skilled craftsmen, and some of the work that has been attributed to him—even some labeled work—is now being seen as the work of others in his shop, in particular Robert McGuffin (1779–1863).

Cogswell bombé serpentine-front chest of drawers. John Cogswell (1738–1819) was the most prolific maker of American bombé work in the Chippendale era. This bombé chest of drawers is one of the most impressive pieces in that genre of furniture making. The material is mahogany and white pine. The piece is dated in the second half of the eighteenth century. *Courtesy of the Art Institute of Chicago*

Connelly dolphin table. Henry Connelly is the probable maker of this table, an attribution the Metropolitan Museum makes based on similarities to documented Connelly work. Notice the pair of upside-down dolphins supporting this side of the table. The materials are mahogany, maple, and pine. The table is dated 1815. *Courtesy of the Metropolitan Museum of Art*

Dennis, Thomas (1638–1706, Ipswich, Massachusetts)

Maker of the renowned Ipswich Wainscot Chair, which is one of the greatest pieces of surviving Pilgrim furniture. The chair's enormous scroll-sawn frame-and-panel back is decorated with lively carved arabesques with a figure on each side, as well as a trio of urn-shaped finials. The chair is currently housed in the Peabody Essex Museum in Salem, Massachusetts.

Disbrowe, Nicholas (1613–1683, Hartford, Connecticut)

Among the earliest-known American cabinet-makers. According to author John Gloag, Disbrowe was working in Hartford, Connecticut, between 1639 and 1683, primarily engaged in the making of chests. According to *The Grove Encyclopedia of the Decorative Arts*, his signature on a Connecticut Hadley chest is now thought to be fraudulent.

Dennis chest. Attribution of seventeenth-century American work is a pretty slippery business. The work isn't labeled and very rarely signed. Bills of sale no longer exist—if they ever did. So, in most instances, an attribution is given as a "probable" or "possible" or an "either/or." According to the Metropolitan Museum of Art, this three-panel chest is attributed to Thomas Dennis (1638–1706) or his Ipswich, Massachusetts, contemporary William Searle (?–1667). But since it is dated 1685–1700, I think we can assume that it is, in fact, likely the work of Thomas Dennis. The material is red oak, white oak, hard maple, and white pine. *Courtesy of the Metropolitan Museum of Art*

Dunlap, John (1746–1792, New Hampshire)

Most prominent member of a family of New Hampshire cabinetmakers. Unlike the furniture being made in the nation's urban centers, which valued imported mahogany above all other species, the furniture being made in New Hampshire often employed native American hardwoods (in particular, cherry and curly maple), and also unlike urban furniture, New Hampshire work was slower to embrace the new genre of Federal furniture.

At a time when the Seymours of Boston were making exquisitely delicate Federal work, John Dunlap (as well as many of his New Hampshire peers) was still working in the Chippendale style, although his Chippendale work was quite different than that produced in the cities a generation earlier. His squared-off cornices often brandished palmetto growth, basket weave panels, and scallops wrapped around corners. It was an eccentric but wholly original take on the Chippendale style.

Dunlap highboy. This chest-on-chest is one of the landmarks of American cabinet making by an extremely talented but eccentric practitioner of the Chippendale style. Squared-off pediments and squared-off scrolls of this type were made only by members of the Dunlap family, a group of New Hampshire makers led by John Dunlap. This piece is dated 1773–1777, shortly before Dunlap began his service in the Revolutionary War. The materials are maple and pine. *Courtesy of Winterthur Museum*

Eames, Charles (1907–1978, Los Angeles); Eames, Ray (1916–1988, Los Angeles)

Husband-and-wife team of furniture designers. Charles and Ray each had successful solo careers prior to their 1941 marriage—Charles as an architect, Ray as a painter—but it was the work on which they collaborated after their marriage for which they are known. They were a formidable team of furniture designers working within the mid-century modern idiom, making full use of material that, formerly, had seen only peripheral use in furniture making: plywood, metal, plastic. They are perhaps best known for the Eames lounge and ottoman and the Eames chair.

Eames lounge. According to the website of the Yale University Art Gallery, this pairing of chair and footstool "became the preeminent male status symbol in interior furnishings following its market appearance in the late 1950s." The chair was designed by Charles (1907–1978) and Ray (1912–1988) Eames and manufactured by Herman Miller, Inc. The material is molded plywood, rosewood, and cast aluminum. *Courtesy of the Yale University Art Gallery*

Frothingham, Benjamin (1734–1809, Charlestown, Massachusetts)

Among the most accomplished furniture makers in eighteenth-century Massachusetts, who dutifully labeled his work, making it possible for historians to create a highly informed portrait of his working life. He was the son of a joiner, also named Benjamin, who likely provided his son with basic woodworking skills. Frothingham's furniture-making career began in 1756, when he opened his own shop, where he worked until he was interrupted by his service in the Revolutionary War during which he rose to the rank of major. Frothingham's surviving work included highboys, lowboys, secretaries, dining tables, card tables, chests of drawers, etc., all designed and executed with supreme skill.

Goddard, John (1723/24–1785, Newport, Rhode Island)

Arguably one of the eight or ten greatest furniture designer/makers America has ever produced. After his birth in Dartmouth, Massachusetts, his father, Daniel Goddard, moved the family to Newport, Rhode Island, to join the Quaker community there. At age thirteen, John began an eight-year apprenticeship with Job Townsend, and he later married Townsend's daughter, Hannah, thereby uniting two dynastic families of American furniture making. Although Goddard was not the inventor of the block front, it was Goddard and his Newport contemporary and relative-by-marriage John Townsend who raised the block front—specifically their Newport block-and-shell variation—to its greatest heights. While other furniture makers of the day might have produced a half-dozen masterpieces over their career, John Goddard produced dozens, a record of achievement unmatched in American furniture making. Today his works brings higher auction prices than that of any other American maker. A secretary he made for Nicholas Brown (1729–1791) fetched $12.1 million. A tea table realized $7.5 million, and a pair of chairs brought $3.28 million.

John Goddard card table. This John Goddard (1724–1785) card table is a masterpiece of Newport, Rhode Island, design and execution, with its boldly curved cabriole legs, its powerful open-taloned feet, and its bandsawn apron. The wood is mahogany. The table is dated after 1760. *Courtesy of the Metropolitan Museum of Art*

Hitchcock, Lambert (1795–1852, Riverton, Connecticut)

Furniture designer who ignited the lust for "fancy chairs" in America. Hitchcock was not a great craftsman, but he was a man who ushered in the era of good-quality, mass-produced furniture, specifically the painted chairs that have become known generally as Hitchcock chairs.

Hitchcock side chair. Hitchcock chairs, manufactured in Hitchcocksville, Connecticut, under the direction of Lambert Hitchcock (1795–1852), became an American brand that still resonates today. The materials of this particular example are beech, maple, white pine, oak, and tulip poplar. The chair is dated 1825–1832. *Courtesy of the Yale University Art Gallery*

Krenov, James (1920–2009, Fort Bragg, California)

Maker of flawlessly executed bench-made furniture. Born in Siberia, Krenov and his parents lived in Shanghai, in a small Alaskan village, and finally in Seattle, where the family settled during his teenage years. After World War II, Krenov and his mother went to Europe, where he met his future wife, Britta. After their marriage, James and Britta traveled still more, exploring France and Italy and spending summers in Sweden. It was in Sweden that he began his formal study of furniture at the Malmsten School, where he stayed two years before setting up his own shop. He soon built a reputation for cleanly designed furniture executed with meticulous attention to detail, and in 1976 he wrote his first book on woodworking, *A Cabinetmaker's Notebook*, a volume that led to four more. After lecturing and teaching at a number of US locations, he became one of the founders of the renowned College of the Redwoods, where he taught for many years.

Lannuier, Charles-Honoré (1779–1819, New York)

Contemporary of and rival to Duncan Phyfe. He emigrated from France to New York in 1803 and immediately set up shop. The work of his shop is typified by flawless design and crisp, clean execution in the neo-classical and Empire styles. Among his clients were some of the richest and best-known Americans of his day, among them the Stuyvesants and the Rensselaers.

Charles-Honoré Lannuier card table. This magnificent table is one of a pair purchased by the father-in-law of Stephen Van Rensselaer IV (1789–1868). The invoice in which the pair of tables appears still exists, and it shows a price of $250 for these two card tables. Today, of course, that would be an astonishing bargain, but in the year of their construction—1817—that sum would have paid nine months' wages for a working man. The materials are mahogany, white pine, and tulip poplar. *Courtesy of the Metropolitan Museum of Art*

Maloof, Sam (1916–2009, Alta Loma, California)

Creator of the renowned—and often-imitated—Maloof rocker. After serving in World War II, Maloof married Alfreda Louise Ward, and the couple settled in Ontario, California. There, from necessity, because they couldn't afford to buy furniture, he began to build pieces in their garage. Commissions soon followed, and in 1953 he and his wife moved to a home in Alta Loma, to which he added rooms and studio space. The Maloof rocker is the epitome of Maloof's approach to furniture making: start with native hardwoods—chiefly walnut—glue up rough-sawn components, then sculpt those components until the finished piece is revealed.

Sam Maloof rocker. American designer/craftsman Sam Maloof (1916–2009) stands with one of his iconic sculpted rocking chairs at the Beverly Hills City Hall Gallery. The chair is titled "Beverly's Rocking Chair." *Photo by Anacleto Rapping, courtesy of Getty Images*

Mason, Ralph (1599–1678/79, Boston)

With Henry Messinger (?–1681), founded the Mason-Messinger shop in Boston in the 1630s. Several early chests have been attributed to this partnership, including a wonderful, very early, chest of drawers in the Museum of Fine Arts in Boston. This precursor to the more evolved chests of the William and Mary and Queen Anne periods has four full-width drawers and two small drawers at the top. Each drawer front is a frame-and-panel construction defined by a pair of molding enclosures. The chest is decorated with twenty-four split ebony turnings. The top has a thin, molded edge supported by seven corbels between which run lines of a mock-dentil molding.

McIntire, Samuel (1757–1811, Salem, Massachusetts)

Architect, builder, carver, and furniture maker whose career bridged the Chippendale and Federal periods. McIntire benefited from a long relationship with the Salem merchant Elias Hasket Derby, who is thought to have been America's first millionaire. McIntire built or restored a number of homes for members of the Derby family and did the carving for a number of pieces purchased by Derby, including a truly monumental chest-on-chest built by William Lemon and decorated with some of the finest carving ever to grace a piece of American furniture. In addition, in 2011 a chair carved by McIntire and sold to Derby achieved the highest-ever price for a piece of Federal furniture: $662,500.

McIntire side chair. Because of its Salem, Massachusetts, origin and its superbly executed carving, this Hepplewhite-style shield-back chair is attributed to the Salem architect and carver Samuel McIntire (1757–1811). The material is mahogany, ash, birch, and white pine. The chair is dated 1794–1799. *Courtesy of the Metropolitan Museum of Art*

Nakashima, George (1905–1990, New Hope, Pennsylvania)

Furniture maker noted for building with thick, live-edged slabs. His largest commission was an order from Nelson Rockefeller for two hundred pieces to furnish Rockefeller's Pocantico Hills, New York, home. Nakashima's work is represented in many prestigious collections around the world.

Nakashima "Conoid" chair. George Nakashima (1905–1990) is one of the more important figures in twentieth-century American furniture making. The material of the "Conoid" chair is walnut and hickory. The particular design was introduced in 1962. *Courtesy of the Yale University Art Gallery*

Phyfe, Duncan (1768–1854, New York)

Like John Goddard and John Townsend, one of the eight or ten greatest furniture makers America has ever produced. Phyfe and his family emigrated from Scotland in 1784 to Albany, New York, where he served a seven-year cabinetmaking apprenticeship. Then, in 1791, he moved to New York, where he was inducted into the General Society of Mechanics and Tradesmen. In 1792, he opened his own cabinet shop, where he found immediate success. His carefully conceived and flawlessly executed neo-classical compositions soon became the dominant stylistic force in the shops of New York cabinetmakers, and in 1808 he became one of the first American makers to work in the Empire style. His work is distinguished by his use of Santo Domingo mahogany, his carefully organized proportions, and his immaculately conceived and articulated detail. He set a standard for neo-classical furniture, the influence of which is still felt today. In fact, the Winterthur Museum in Winterthur, Delaware, has one room devoted solely to furniture from the shop of Duncan Phyfe.

Pembroke table. This form—a tabletop with a hinged leaf on either side—dates to the middle of the eighteenth century, but the shop of Duncan Phyfe (1768–1854), the probable origin of this table, added a four-spindle pedestal and four sweeping legs terminating in brass castors—all executed with the razor-sharp crispness typical of Phyfe's shop. The materials are mahogany, white pine, and cherry. The table is dated 1810–1820. *Courtesy of the Metropolitan Museum of Art*

Seymour, John (1738–1818, Boston)

One of the most important American furniture makers of the Federal era. The Seymour family immigrated to the United States from England in 1784, when John's son Thomas was thirteen. Originally they settled among a group of other English immigrants in Maine, but in 1793, John Seymour moved his family to Boston, looking for better business opportunities. But in the 1790s, things were pretty bleak in Boston. A tax valuation in 1800 identified the Seymour family as "poor—one room." The problem was that the exquisite work John Seymour and his son Thomas were doing was simply too expensive for the local customer base. Eventually, however, despite John's refusal to advertise, to instead let the work speak for itself, the shop became more and more successful. And by the middle of the first decade of the nineteenth century, there was demand for the Seymour brand. Unfortunately, after his wife died in 1815, his financial circumstances required John Seymour to enter the Boston Almshouse, where he died in 1818.

Seymour, Thomas (1771–1847, Boston)

Son and partner of John Seymour. Thomas and his father moved from Axminster, England, to Portland, Maine, and finally to Boston, where they settled and established a cabinet-making business. In the opening years of the nineteenth century, Thomas began to design his own furniture, introducing new techniques and new materials to the Seymour repertoire, and in 1804, Thomas opened his own shop, the Boston Furniture Warehouse, where he employed other craftsmen, including—probably—his father. Thomas Jefferson's 1807 embargo on shipping goods to and from England created hardship for the Boston Furniture Warehouse, hardship that was later exacerbated by the War of 1812 and the bitter anti-British sentiment that conflict fostered. Thomas's business losses and the financial demands of a family with seven children caused him to close his shop in 1817 and take employment as a foreman in the shop of a younger cabinetmaker. In 1824, he left cabinetmaking for good, and, like his father, he died in obscurity.

Townsend, Edmund (1736–1811, Newport, Rhode Island)

Brother to Job Townsend, yet another gifted member of the Townsend family. His only known labeled piece is a Goddard/Townsend kneehole bureau of the highest quality. It's a piece that antique dealer and author Albert Sack (1915–2011) identified as "one of the supreme achievements of New England artisans in the Chippendale era."

Townsend, Job, Jr. (1726–1778, Newport, Rhode Island)

Son of Job Townsend Sr., a cabinetmaker. Although he was the maker of several superb pieces of period furniture (among them a secretary that sold for $8 million), his greatest contribution to the craft might have been as the man who trained a young John Goddard.

Townsend, John (1733–1809, Newport, Rhode Island)

Like Duncan Phyfe and John Goddard, one of the most gifted furniture makers in American history. The son of prominent Newport, Rhode Island, cabinetmaker Christopher Townsend, John married Phila Feke in 1767, who bore him five children. Unlike so many of his contemporaries, Townsend signed enough furniture to give modern scholars a look at the way his work evolved over his career. In all, thirty-five surviving pieces by John Townsend are either signed or labeled. His first signed piece is a 1756 dining table done at age twenty-four, and already his sure and steady hand as a designer and craftsman are on display. Although Townsend didn't invent the blocked front (that distinction goes to Boston makers fifteen years earlier), according to Morrison H. Heckscher of the Metropolitan Museum of Art, Townsend did introduce the much-admired Newport block-and-shell variation in about 1765.

John Townsend chest of drawers. John Townsend (1732–1809) signed or labeled eight casepieces, a group that includes this chest of drawers from early in his career in 1765, which features the robustly carved block-and-shell front for which the Goddard/Townsend families of Newport are justifiably famous. The materials are mahogany, tulip poplar, pine, and chestnut. *Courtesy of the Metropolitan Museum of Art*

Wagan, Brother Robert M. (1833–1883, New Lebanon, New York)

Name of designer / shop manager / CEO of the Shaker chair factory at New Lebanon, New York. There is no evidence that Brother Wagan was himself a great craftsman, but in the history of American furniture making, he stands out as champion of craftsmanship as it was expressed in Shaker chair-making shops.

Wright, Frank Lloyd (1867–1959, Primarily Chicago)

Known for designing furniture to suit the interiors of the homes he designed.

Frank Lloyd Wright (1867–1959) side chair. Wright worked from 1916 to 1922 designing the Imperial Hotel in Tokyo, as well as its furnishings. This chair was part of those furnishings. The material is oak. *Courtesy of the Yale University Art Gallery*

BIBLIOGRAPHY

A word about my bibliography: During the last decade of my thirty-two-year career as a high-school English teacher, I was pretty stiff necked on the subject of internet sources for student research papers, limiting students to those internet sources with impeccable pedigrees, such as the *Encyclopedia Britannica*. However in the ten years since my retirement from the English classroom, my views have changed. I now realize that there are many legitimate sources on the internet, among them Wikipedia, which began simply as a noble but chaotically expressed idea but has since become what I believe to be the largest repository of human knowledge ever assembled. I don't mean that I take everything I find there as gospel, but it is an invaluable source for corroborating information I find elsewhere. (The truth is that—even in those few subjects in which I can claim some slight expertise—I rarely find errors in Wikipedia entries.) Dictionary.com was similarly useful, as was Britannica.com, Chipstone.org, and ColonialSociety.org. In addition, a number of highly respected institutions have websites containing impeccably researched information. I'm thinking here about sites maintained by organizations such as the Metropolitan Museum of Art, PBS, the Museum of Fine Arts in Boston, Yale University, and the Peabody Essex Museum. All these came into play during my research for this book.

Alexander, John. *Make a Chair from a Tree: An Introduction to Working Green Wood.* Newtown, CT: Taunton, 1978.

Allen, Douglas R., and Jerry V. Grant. *Shaker Furniture Makers.* Hanover, NH: University Press of New England, 1989.

Aronson, Joseph. *The Encyclopedia of Furniture.* New York: Crown, 1965.

"Arthur Espenet Carpenter." *Craft in America.* PBS. www.craftinamerica.org.

Art Institute of Chicago. Many entries. www.artic.com.edu/.

"Artiture." *Urban Dictionary.* www.urbandictionary.com.

Associated Press. "Card Table, a $25 Garage Sale Bargain, Is Sold for $541,500." *New York Times*, January 19, 1998.

Auslander, Leona. *Taste and Power: Furnishing Modern France.* Berkeley: University of California Press, 1998.

Barlow, Ronald S. *The Antique Tool Collector's Guide to Value.* Gas City, IN: L-W Book Sales, 2004.

Bartolucci, Marisa, and Dung Ngo. *American Contemporary Furniture.* New York: Universe, 2000.

"Benjamin Frothingham." Colonial Society of Massachusetts. www.colonialsociety.com.

"Bogus Brewster Chairs, The." Henry Ford Museum. www.thehenryford.org/explore/blog/the-bogus-brewster-chair.

Bolton, Angie. "Woot Woot for the Wooten: The King of Desks." www.HISTORICINDIANAPOLIS.com.

Butler, Joseph T. *Field Guide to American Antique Furniture.* New York: Henry Holt, 1985.

Campbell, Gordon, ed. *The Grove Encyclopedia of Decorative Arts* Vol. 1. Oxford: Oxford University Press, 2006.

"Campeachy Chair." Thomas Jefferson Foundation. www.explorer.monticello.org.

Carr, Dennie, Nancy Goynes Evans, and Patricia E. Kane. *Art and Industry: Rhode Island Furniture, 1650–1830.* New Haven, CT: Yale University Art Gallery, 2006.

Charles P. Limbert and Company. *Limbert Arts and Crafts Furniture.* New York: Dover, 1992.

Chippendale, Thomas. *The Gentleman and Cabinetmaker's Director.* New York: Dover, 1966. (Reprint)

Cornelius, Charles Over. *Furniture Masterpieces of Duncan Phyfe.* New York: Dover, 1970.

Crow, Michael. *Mid-century Modern Furniture.* Cincinnati: Popular Woodworking Books, 2015.

Day, David, and Albert Jackson. *Good Wood Finishes.* Cincinnati: Betterway Books, 1995.

Day, David, and Albert Jackson. *Good Wood Handbook.* Cincinnati: Betterway Books, 1995.

Day, David, and Albert Jackson. *Good Wood Joints.* Cincinnati: Betterway Books, 1995.

"Description of Papers Regarding the Life of John Gaines II and Thomas Gaines I." Winterthur Library. www.winterthur.org.

Dictionary.com. Various entries. www.dictionary.com.

Dubrow, Eileen, and Richard Dubrow. *American Furniture of the Nineteenth Century.* Atglen, PA: Schiffer, 1983.

"Duncan Phyfe: Past Results." Christie's Auction House (undated).

Edwards, W. Patrick. "Daniel LeCount Project." www.wpatrickedwards.blogspot.com/2012/10/daniel-lecount-project.html.

Emmet, Ric. *America's Art Deco Furniture.* Coral Gables FL: Art Deco Pros, 2015.

Encyclopedia Britannica. Various entries. www.britannica.com.

Fairbanks, Jonathan L., and Robert F. Trent. "New England Begins: The Seventeenth Century." *Magazine Antiques*, May 1982.

Fales, Dean A., Jr. "Boston Japanned Furniture." Colonial Society of Massachusetts. www.colonialsociety.org.

"Federal Carved Mahogany and Brass-Inlaid Accordion-Action Dining Table Attributed to Henry Connelly, Philadelphia, circa 1810." Sotheby's.com (undated).

Fine Americana: Vol. II. New York: Sotheby Parke Bennett, 1980.

Fitzgerald, Oscar P. *Three Centuries of American Furniture.* New York: Gramercy, 1982.

Flexner, Bob. "The Great Brewster Chair and How It Was Created." *Woodshop News*, July 16, 2017.

Flynt, Suzanne L., and Philip Zea. *Hadley Chests.* Deerfield, MA: Pocumtuck Valley Memorial Association, 1992.

"Freemasonry: Secret Organization." *Ency-clopedia Britannica.* www.britannica.com.

Gloag, John. *A Short Dictionary of Furniture.* New York: Bonanza Books, 1965.

Greene, Jeffrey P. *American Furniture of the Eighteenth Century.* Newtown, CT: The Taunton Press, 1996.

Greenfield Tool Company. *Illustrated Catalogue and Invoice Price List of Joiners' Bench Planes, Moulding Tools, Handles, Plane Irons, &c., Manufactured by the Greenfield Tool Company, Greenfield, Mass.* Fitzwilliam, NH: Kenneth Roberts, 1978 (originally published in 1872).

Guernsey, Anne. "The Fancy Chair Craze of the 1800s: Lambert Hitchcock and the Story of the Hitchcock Chair." Connecticut History. www.connecticuthistory.org.

Hamler, A. J. *Civil War Woodworking.* Fresno, CA: Linden, 2009.

Hayley, Anne Rogers, and Robert Mussey. "John Cogswell and Boston Bombé Furniture: Thirty-Five Years of Politics and Design." Chipstone. www.chipstone.org.

Heckscher, Morrison H. "John Townsend (1733–1809)." Metropolitan Museum of Art. www.metmuseum.org.

Hoadley, R. Bruce. *Identifying Wood: Accurate Results with Simple Tools.* Newtown, CT: Taunton, 1990.

Horner, William Macpherson. *Horner's Blue Book: Philadelphia Furniture.* Washington, DC: Highland House, 1977.

Indianapolis Museum of Art. Many entries. www.imamuseum. org

Johnson, Bruce E. *Grove Park Inn: Arts and Crafts Furniture.* Cincinnati: Popular Woodworking Books, 2009.

Kassay, John. *The Book of Shaker Furniture.* Amherst: University of Massachusetts Press, 1980.

Kenney, Peter. "Duncan Phyfe (1770–1854) and Charles-Honoré Lannuier (1779–1819)." Metropolitan Museum of Art. www.metmuseum.org.

Kovel, Ralph, and Terry Kovel. "Box Gives a Sweet History Lesson: Antiques; Handsome Chest held a Once Valuable Product—Sugar." *Baltimore Sun,* September 15, 1996.

Krenov, James. *The Art of Cabinetmaking.* New York: Sterling, 1977.

Metropolitan Museum of Art. Many entries. www.metmuseum. org.

Miller, Bruce W., and Jim Widess. *The Caner's Handbook.* Asheville, NC: Lark Books, 1991.

Montgomery, Charles F. *American Furniture: The Federal Period.* New York: Viking, 1966.

Morris, Charles. *Universal Dictionary of the English Language.* New York: Peter Fenelon Collier, 1899.

Muller, Charles R., and Timothy D. Rieman. *The Shaker Chair.* Boston: University of Massachusetts Press, 1992.

Mussey, Robert D., and Clark Pearce. "Classical Excellence in Boston: The Furniture of Isaac Vose, 1789–1825." Colonial Society of Massachusetts. www.colonialsociety.com.

"Nail Cabinet." *Fine Woodworking,* October 24, 2012. www. finewoodworking.com.

Naeve, Milo M. *Identifying American Furniture.* New York and London: W. W. Norton, 1998.

Noll, Terrie. *The Joint Book: The Complete Guide to Wood Joinery.* London: Chartwell Books, 2006.

Obbard, John W. *Early American Furniture: A Guide to Who, When, and Where.* Paducah, KY: Collector Books, 2006.

The Oxford English Dictionary. Many entries. Glasgow and New York: Vivian Ridler, 1971.

Paterwic, Stephen J. *The A to Z of the Shakers.* Toronto: Scarecrow, 2009.

Pirc, Andrea, and Richard Vlosky. "A Brief Overview of the U.S. Furniture Industry." Louisiana Forest Products Development Center Working Paper 89.

Pierce, Kerry. *Chairmaking Simplified.* Cincinnati: Popular Woodworking Books, 2008.

Pierce, Kerry. "Fidelity in Period Molding Profiles." *Journal of the Society of American Period Furniture Makers,* 2007.

Pierce, Kerry. *Hand Planes in the Modern Shop.* Atglen, PA: Schiffer, 2010.

Pierce, Kerry. *Pleasant Hill Shaker Furniture.* Cincinnati: Popular Woodworking Books, 2007.

Pierce, Kerry. *Storage and Shelving the Shaker Way.* Cincinnati: Popular Woodworking Books, 2009.

Pollack, Emil, and Martyl Pollack. *A Guide to the Makers of American Wooden Planes.* 4th ed. Mendham, NJ: Astragal, 2001.

Quimby, Ian M. G., ed. *American Furniture and Its Makers.* Chicago: University of Chicago Press, 1979.

"Ralph Mason and Henry Messinger Shops." Museum of Fine Arts: Boston. www.mfa.org.

Rief, Rita. "Antiques: Furniture with Million Dollar Legs." *New York Times,* February 8, 1987.

Rief, Rita. "Antiques: A Museum Focuses on Belter's Furniture." *New York Times,* March 8, 1981.

Rief, Rita. "Eighteenth-Century Desk Sold for $12.1 Million." *New York Times,* June 4, 1989.

The Roycrofters. *Roycroft Furniture Catalog, 1906.* New York: Dover, 1994.

Sack, Albert. *Fine Points of Furniture: Early American.* New York: Crown, 1950.

Sack, Albert. *The New Fine Points of Furniture.* New York: Crown, 1993.

Salaman, R. A. *Dictionary of Woodworking Tools.* Newton, CT: Taunton, 1990.

The Sandusky Tool Company, Catalog No. 25. Mendham, NJ: Astragal.

Santore, Charles. *The Windsor Style in America.* 2 vols. Edited by Thomas M. Voss. Philadelphia: Courage Books, 1981.

"The Seymour Story: Luxury and Innovation: Masterworks by John and Thomas Seymour." Peabody Essex Museum. www.luxury.pem.org/story.

Silk, Sarah. "John Scott Bradstreet: The Minneapolis Crafthouse and the Decorative Arts Revival in the American Northwest." *Nineteenth-Century Art Worldwide* 4, no. 1 (2005). www. nineteenthc-artworldwide.org.

Steinbaum, Bernice. *The Rocker.* New York: Rizzoli, 1992.

"Stephen Badlam, 1751–1815." Dorchester Atheneum. www. dorchesteratheneum.org.

Stickley, Gustav. *The 1912 and 1915 Gustav Stickley Craftsman Furniture Catalog.* Philadelphia: Athenaeum, 1991.

St. John, Richard W. "Friedrich Wenzel." Texas State Historical Association. www.tshaonline.org.

Strogoff, Erin. "Connecticut Valley Style: Eliphalet Chapin Inspires a Tradition of Craft." Connecticut History. www. connecticuthistory.org.

Taylor, Vic. *The Woodworker's Dictionary.* Pownal, VT: Storey Communications, 1990.

Vandal, Norman. *Queen Anne Furniture: History, Design, and Construction.* Newtown, CT: Taunton, 1995.

Vincent, Gilbert T. "The Bombé Furniture of Boston." Colonial Society of Massachusetts. www.colonialsociety.org.

Webster's New World Dictionary and Thesaurus. Many entries. Cleveland, OH: Wiley, 2002.

Whelan, John. *The Wooden Plane: Its History, Form, and Functions.* Mendham, NJ: Astragal, 1993.

Whitehill, Walter Muir, ed. *Boston Furniture of the Eighteenth Century.* Charlottesville: University Press of Virginia, 1974.

Wikipedia. Many entries. www.wikipedia.com.

The Wood Database. Many entries. www.wood-database.com.

Yale University Art Gallery. Many entries. https://artgallery. yale.edu/.

Zimmerman, Paul D. "New York Card Tables, 1800–1825." Chipstone. www.chipstone.org.